Wisdomkeepers *of* Stonehenge

"Astonishing yet highly convincing theory on the function of the megalithic monuments of Britain by one of the world's most unique historical writers. Graham Phillips explains how our Neolithic and Bronze Age ancestors possessed an acute knowledge of medicine and healing practices, using the stone circles to enhance the cultivation of plant life. A must-read for everyone interested in the lost technologies of our ancient past."

ANDREW COLLINS, SCIENCE AND HISTORY WRITER AND AUTHOR OF *DENISOVAN ORIGINS*, *THE CYGNUS KEY*, AND *GÖBEKLI TEPE*

"Imagine if Egypt's Great Pyramid stood alone in the desert without any remaining evidence of the civilization that built it. This is the enigma of the magnificent stone circles of the British Isles. These ancient wonders are found from the extreme north on Scotland's Orkney Islands to Stonehenge in the south. Graham Phillips's deep research for his compelling *Wisdomkeepers of Stonehenge* pulls together all the pieces of one of humanity's most fascinating archaeological puzzles."

RAND FLEM-ATH, COAUTHOR OF *THE MURDER OF MOSES* AND *ATLANTIS BENEATH THE ICE*

"Graham Phillips has always been noted for his meticulous historical research, depth of vision, and ability to follow the threads of a mystery throughout history."

NEW DAWN MAGAZINE

Wisdomkeepers *of* Stonehenge

The Living Libraries and Healers of Megalithic Culture

······················

Graham Phillips

Bear & Company
Rochester, Vermont

Bear & Company
One Park Street
Rochester, Vermont 05767
www.BearandCompanyBooks.com

Bear & Company is a division of Inner Traditions International

Cataloging-in-Publication Data for this title is available from the Library of Congress

ISBN 978-1-59143-297-5 (print)
ISBN 978-1-59143-298-2 (ebook)

Printed and bound in the United States by McNaughton & Gunn, Inc.

10   9   8   7   6   5   4   3   2   1

Text design and layout by Virginia Scott Bowman
This book was typeset in Garamond Premier Pro with Nocturne Serif used as the
display typeface.
Photography by Deborah Cartwright

To send correspondence to the author of this book, mail a first-class letter to the
author c/o Inner Traditions • Bear & Company, One Park Street, Rochester, VT
05767, and we will forward the communication, or contact the author directly at
www.grahamphillips.net.

In loving memory of my mother, Joyce

Contents

Acknowledgments

THE AUTHOR WOULD LIKE TO THANK the following people for their invaluable help: Deborah Cartwright for the wonderful photography; Yvan Cartwright for his fantastic IT support; Jodi Russell for extra research material; my researchers Maia Wille and Orion Wille; Sally Evans, Dave Moore, and Claire Silverman in helping with translations; and Jon Graham, Mindy Branstetter, Patricia Rydle, Kelly Bowen, and all the rest of the team at Inner Traditions.

1

An Enigma in Stone

STONEHENGE IS ONE OF THE MOST FAMOUS monuments in the world. Although it stands in isolated countryside in south-central England, miles from any major town, it is one of Britain's most popular tourist sites, attracting more than a million visitors every year. It is also one of the most ancient. Around five thousand years old, it predates the Great Pyramids of Egypt by over four centuries. In fact, it predates even recorded history and the use of metal implements, making it both a prehistoric and a Stone Age construction. And above all, it is one of the most *mysterious* monuments in the world. Those who created it spent years toiling away with little more than animal horns, shaped rocks, dry bones, and their bare hands for tools. The time and effort thought necessary to have built Stonehenge is staggering. Archaeologists have estimated that the cutting, hauling, and erection of the stones for just the main part of the circle would have taken almost forty million work-hours and over ten thousand people toiling full time on the project for years on end, when the entire population of south-central England was only around thirty thousand.[1] Stonehenge must have been of immense importance to those who made it, yet its purpose remains a mystery. Why did the ancient people of Britain go to such extraordinary lengths to construct this enigma in stone?

Remarkably Stonehenge was only one of thousands of stone circles erected throughout the British Isles—together with countless solitary standing stones, stone rows, huge earthen mounds, embankments, ditches, avenues, and other earthworks—that continued to be built and maintained for a period spanning over three millennia, between around 3100 BCE and the arrival of the Romans in Britain during the first century CE, and even longer in Ireland. Through this entire era the basic design of these various monuments remained consistent. This vast array of ancient constructions is just as enigmatic as Stonehenge itself. How was it possible for scattered settlements of people—who left no evidence of the infrastructure of civilization, such as buildings, roads, and cities, nor any indication of overall leadership, taskmasters, or central government—to continue to create these monuments in unison for so long? If we hope to understand Stonehenge, it is essential to solve the enigma of this unique, enduring society. The mystery of Stonehenge cannot be solved if seen in isolation. We need to appreciate this baffling network of ancient monuments in its entirety. To start with, who built them?

It's common knowledge that the Great Wall was built by the Chinese, the Coliseum was built by the Romans, and Machu Picchu was built by the Incas. But who built Stonehenge? Ask even those who visit the site today, and most probably don't know, the reason being that the culture that created Stonehenge, and the myriad other monuments from Britain of the period, doesn't actually have a name. Technically speaking, the first of them were Neolithic—meaning Late Stone Age— people. But so were much of the rest of the world's population at the time. We know what many ancient cultures were called because they still survive, left written records, or their remote descendants preserve their knowledge. But no such evidence exists from the ancient British Isles. However, the stone-circle builders are often referred to as the Megalithic culture because of the monuments they left behind. The name comes from the word *megalith,* meaning "large stone," specifically artificial standing stones such as those at Stonehenge. Although this is not an archaeological term for the culture, not one you will find in the official Stonehenge guidebook, it is certainly a convenient name and one we'll be using in this book. It should also be noted that a capital letter *M* is used when referring to the people who erected the monuments, as opposed to the lowercase *m* used when referring to the monuments themselves. Accordingly, the Megalithic people (or culture) were the main inhabitants of the British Isles around 3100 BCE, when the first stone circles were built and were those still using them when the practice ceased. The megalithic monuments, on the other hand, were the enigmatic constructions they left behind, be they made from stone, earth, or anything else. With that clarified, let's briefly consider the most renowned megalithic monument, Stonehenge itself, and appreciate just what an amazing accomplishment it was for the Megalithic people who built it. (We shall return to examine it in more detail as our investigation proceeds.)

Stonehenge once consisted of an arrangement of well over a hundred stones, up to more than 20 feet high and weighing as much as 50 tons each. They were quarried from rocky outcrops, cut to the desired shapes, hauled to where they were erected, and then heaved into position. Its outer circle was composed of thirty standing stones, each some 13 feet high, 7 feet wide, 3.5 feet thick, and weighing around 25 tons, spaced just over 3 feet apart. On top of them were placed thirty further 6-ton blocks—10 feet long, 3 feet wide, and 2.5 feet thick— called lintels, forming a continuous ring of rectangular arches 108 feet in diameter. (The tops of the lintels stood well over 15 feet above the ground.) This outer ring is known as the Sarsen Circle, named after the sarsen stone, a type of hard sandstone from which it was made. Immediately inside the Sarsen Circle was a simpler stone circle of about thirty smaller stones, averaging about 6 feet high, 3.5 feet wide, and 2.5 feet thick, and weighing an average of around 4 tons each. Known as the Bluestone Ring—as it was constructed from a particular type of dolerite rock commonly called bluestone due to its slightly bluish tinge—it was about 80 feet in diameter. The central arrangement of monoliths—standing stones—at Stonehenge was actually created in an open oval form. Called the Bluestone Horseshoe because of this shape, it was made from around twenty bluestones about the same size as those forming the Bluestone Ring and was some 35 feet across at its widest point. Between the oval and the circle of bluestones, there stood five massive arrangements of megaliths called trilithons. Each trilithon was formed from a pair of enormous upright sarsen monoliths, over 20 feet high and weighing up to 50 tons each, with a third sarsen stone, weighing around 8 tons, placed across the tops of them as a lintel to form a rectangular arch. As these trilithons were arranged in the same shape as the inner bluestones, this structure is known as the Trilithon Horseshoe and measured about 45 feet across. Close to the center of Stonehenge there lies a large rectangular stone. Weighing around 6 tons, this 6-foot-long megalith now lies flat on the ground; it has been called the Altar Stone, although the name is misleading, as archaeologists believe that it originally stood upright as a single monolith. The scale of these stones is even more impressive when we realize that the height of the standing stones just given is not their full size: to keep the stones erect, about a third of each monolith needed to be buried below the ground. So the trilithon uprights, for instance, were well over 30 feet long.

Time has taken its toll on Stonehenge. Of the outer ring, sixteen of the upright monoliths still stand, but only six of its lintel stones still form arches. All the same, this is enough to give us an impression of the original Sarsen Circle. Three of the trilithons also survive intact, plus one of the standing stones each from the other two. Of the bluestones, only seven remain standing from the ring and five from the horseshoe, while others lie littered around, together with a few of the larger, fallen sarsen stones. One of the once proud uprights from the trilithons, for example, lies broken in two across the Altar Stone. For more than four thousand years, the relentless British weather has eroded Stonehenge. The stones are no longer the smooth, neatly shaped megaliths they once were but have been pitted and worn by wind, rain, and ice.

But natural erosion is only part of the story of Stonehenge's gradual deterioration. Some its megaliths were long ago broken apart and taken away for building material, which can still be found in nearby

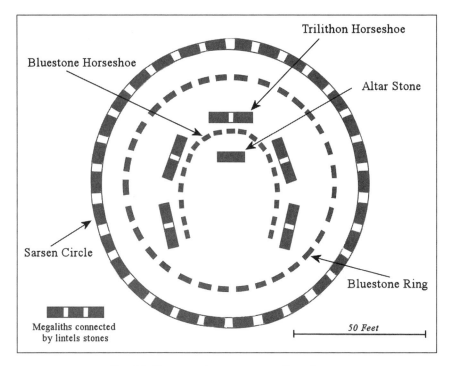

Fig. 1.1. The central monument at Stonehenge.

barns, cottages, and boundary walls. Perhaps the greatest damage to the ancient monoliths has been at the hands of tourists, who until recent years hacked off pieces of stone to take home as souvenirs. Some of the surviving bluestones have suffered particularly, having been chipped down to a fraction of their original size. In fact, it's something of a miracle that anything has survived at all. Today Stonehenge is protected from such vandalism by English Heritage, a charitable trust that manages ancient sites and buildings. Now the stone circle is fenced off to keep visitors at a distance to prevent further damage. So be prepared: a visit to Stonehenge may be something of a disappointment. You won't be able to touch the mighty monoliths or wander among the ancient weathered stones. But you can get close enough to appreciate the astonishing achievement.

This remarkable arrangement of megaliths, however, was only the heart of a huge complex of ancient constructions surrounding

Stonehenge, including a circular embankment and ditch, 360 feet in diameter, encompassing the stone circle, a parallel pair of ditches and banks leading 2 miles to a smaller stone circle, and an artificial mound over 20 feet high and 65 feet across. One of the most amazing things about the Stonehenge arrangement of monuments is that it was built by people using nothing more than flint axes, bone shovels, and antlers for picks. Imagine how long and hard a multitude of workers would have needed to toil in order to cut and shape even the smallest of the megaliths from solid bedrock with such simple tools. Imagine also the backbreaking effort needed to haul the sarsen stones from where experts have determined they were quarried, 25 miles to the north of Stonehenge, without the help of draft animals, such as oxen or horses, by a people with no knowledge of the wheel. It is even more astonishing when we realize that the bluestones were somehow transported from quarries over 130 miles away (see chapter 7). And that's just part of the story. In some way that is not fully understood, to create the Sarsen Stone Circle the builders hauled and planted the stones into upright positions, and without cranes or machines they managed to position the 6-ton blocks on top of the 13-foot-high standing stones. And remember, the trilithons were even bigger. As an engineering project, Stonehenge was, in relative terms, for its time a much grander exercise than the Apollo program, the International Space Station, or the Large Hadron Collider. It was obviously a crucial undertaking, but what exactly was it?

Before the advent of modern archaeology, a common belief was that Stonehenge was an elaborate tomb. Throughout history, powerful individuals have built some astonishing tombs: the vast burial complex of the first Chinese emperor with its terracotta army, the Great Pyramid of the Egyptian pharaoh Khufu, and the Greek mausoleum of King Mausolus, to name but three. Although human remains have been found in and around Stonehenge, there is no evidence that the stone circle itself was ever used specifically for interment at the time it was built. In 2013 archeologists did identify around sixty burials at

Stonehenge, but these seem to have dated from long before the monument we see today was built. Besides which, unlike the colossal ancient tombs erected during the lifetime of the eventual occupant, Stonehenge was created in stages over many generations.

In more recent years evidence has emerged that Stonehenge acted as an ancient astronomical observatory. When viewed from the center of the circle, various stones seem to have been placed deliberately to align with the sun and particularly bright stars at the same time each year. It is thought that such observations would allow the Stonehenge builders to determine the exact time to sow, reap, and tend to crops and also to reckon the precise time of the year to perform important ceremonies.[2] The monoliths of Stonehenge certainly did align with various heavenly bodies at particular times of the year, but why make Stonehenge so big and elaborate, requiring so much effort and drain on precious resources? Although some form of ancient astronomical thinking certainly seems to have been involved in the construction of Stonehenge, there has to have been far more to its purpose than simply to act as a giant calendar. After all, you could do the same thing by simply using wooden poles.

In searching for clues as to Stonehenge's original purpose, it would help if we had some written records. Unfortunately the peoples of Britain had no form of writing until after the Romans arrived in 55 BCE, when Julius Caesar made an attempt to conquer the country. He didn't get far, and the following year gave up entirely and returned to continental Europe to attend to more pressing matters. Between then and the eventual conquest of Britain by Emperor Claudius in 43 CE, there was a considerable influx of goods and ideas from the Roman Empire, and foreign visitors have left us a few records of life in parts of the country at the time. The Britons themselves even began to include Latin inscriptions on items such as coins and grave markers, but most of what is known concerning the British Isles before this period comes down to archaeology. There is, however, folklore surrounding Stonehenge and other megalithic monuments that might hold some interesting clues.

In the twelfth century the Welsh cleric Geoffrey of Monmouth related in his work *The History of the Kings of Britain* that Stonehenge was at that time called the Giant's Dance, as it was believed that the stones were originally erected by giants in Ireland and later magically transported to England by Merlin the magician.[3] What's interesting about this legend is that it recounts that the stones were once moved from elsewhere, far away, and indeed some of them really do appear to have been brought to Stonehenge from a great distance. The bluestones that make up the inner ring and horseshoe are of a particular type of dolerite known as plagioclase feldspar, found in the Preseli Hills of South Wales. Recently archaeology professor Timothy Darvill of Bournemouth University identified the site where the stones were quarried to have been around Carn Menyn in the Welsh county of Pembrokeshire, over 130 miles west of Stonehenge.[4] It has been suggested that they originally formed a stone circle in that region and were later transported to Stonehenge (see chapter 7). Just why these stones would be so important when equally good building materials could be found much closer to home has remained a mystery. However, although it's doubtful that Merlin (if he indeed existed) had anything to do with it, as the Arthurian story is set a couple of millennia after the completion of Stonehenge, around the year 500 CE, and Stonehenge's construction is unlikely to have involved magic, the hauling of dozens of 4-ton stones over such a huge distance could be considered an almost miraculous achievement for the time.

Many ancient sites have legends and folklore attached to them that have been helpful in rediscovering age-old historical secrets. Near the town of Mold in North Wales, for instance, there stands an earthen mound that for centuries was said to be haunted by a figure in golden armor. When the site was eventually excavated, it was found to contain a four-thousand-year-old skeleton wearing a ceremonial chest-and-shoulder adornment made from solid gold. The figure in the "golden armor" had lain there at peace for millennia, yet knowledge of his or her burial seems to have been passed down over the centuries to eventually be remembered in the form of a ghost story.[5] Another example is the Cheesewring, an unusual rock formation on Bodmin Moor in Cornwall in southwest England. Folklore related that travelers who became lost on the moors were guided to safety by an immortal Druid, an ancient Celtic priest, who dwelt in the vicinity, who would also offer them sustenance from a golden cup.[6] When a nearby burial mound called Rillaton Barrow was eventually excavated, the remains of a high-status individual, thought to have been a Bronze Age priest, were discovered, along with grave goods including a pure gold cup, probably used for ceremonial purposes. The mound had remained undisturbed for over 3,500 years, so once again it seems that folk memory of the person buried there with a gold goblet was transmitted from generation to generation, by word of mouth, until it transformed into the legend of the helpful Druid.

It is possible that the legend of the Stonehenge stones being moved from far away may reflect the same kind of transmutation of historical memory into what at first appears to be a fanciful fairy tale. But the Merlin tradition is not the only such folk memory associated with Stonehenge. About 200 feet outside the main circle there is a solitary 15-foot-tall megalith known as the Heel Stone. Legend tells how it got to be there. A friar—a wandering monk—once tried to exorcise the devil, who dwelt at Stonehenge. He failed, and in retaliation the devil hurled one of the circle's huge stones at the fleeing friar, narrowly missing him but grazing him on the heel. That, it is said, is how the Heel Stone got to be where it is and how it got its name.[7] In reality, the monolith marks the spot over which the sun rises on the summer solstice (the longest day of the year), around June 21, as seen from the center of the stone circle, presumably marking an important ceremonial occasion. Significantly, in the ancient British language, and preserved in Breton, which is still spoken in part of northern France, the word for the sun is *heol,* which sounds remarkably like "heel."[8] In all probability, the stone was originally referred to the heol stone (the sun stone), and years later those who no longer spoke the earlier language mistook the old word for "sun" as the word *heel,* and the legend subsequently developed to explain the unusual name.

I draw attention to such folklore because, as we shall see, legends, traditions, and mythology can be important tools when investigating ancient historical mysteries. That doesn't mean to say that all such folktales reveal some underlying truth, but they are certainly worth considering, especially when investigating anything from a period from when there exist no written records. The first recourse, however, is archaeology and the various modern scientific techniques, which can be employed in helping to unravel the secrets of the megalithic creations. How, for instance, do we know how old Stonehenge actually is? Well, for centuries, nobody did.

As mentioned, there is the legend that Merlin was responsible for the creation of Stonehenge. Whether or not he was based on a historical figure is immaterial so far as this perceived dating is concerned: the Arthurian tales placed Merlin's life around the year 500 CE, which would apparently make Stonehenge around 1,500 years old, give or take a few decades. And until the 1600s this is how old the monument was generally thought to be. The first relatively modern attempt to date Stonehenge was made in the late seventeenth century by the English antiquarian John Aubrey. (An antiquarian was a person who studied and collected antiquities and ancient artifacts—a kind of early archaeologist.) In 1666 Aubrey made an important survey of Stonehenge as it was during his time, concluding that it was probably built by the Druids, the priesthood of the Celts, who were native to the British Isles before the Roman invasion of the mid-first century.[9] The Celts—of whom we will be learning more in later chapters—first arrived in Britain from continental Europe around 700 BCE, and the Druids were suppressed by the Romans soon after their invasion in the first century CE. So if Aubrey was right, Stonehenge could predate the supposed Arthurian era by around a thousand years. Inspired by Aubrey, in the early 1700s another antiquarian, William Stukeley, popularized the notion that Stonehenge and the other stone circles were Druid temples.[10] Stukeley was a leading Freemason, and his ideas inspired the founding of Masonic-style orders of latter-day "druids" who reinvented what they believed to be ancient Celtic ceremonies at various megalithic sites. In fact, some modern Druids still exist today and continue to perform ceremonies at Stonehenge, particularly at the summer solstice. As we shall see, the original Druids may well have performed ceremonies at Stonehenge and other stone circles, but modern archaeology has determined that the circles were built long before the Celts ever arrived in Britain (see chapter 10).

One of the most significant modern methods of determining the age of ancient remains is radiocarbon dating, and this procedure has been used to date Stonehenge. All living things, fauna or flora, absorb a type of carbon called carbon-14. Once an organism dies, the intake ceases. Thereafter, the carbon-14 decays, or transforms, into a different type of carbon; hence it decreases over time. By scientifically measuring the amount of carbon-14 still present in an organic sample, archaeologists can determine approximately how long ago the organism died. The problem is, of course, stones are not organic remains. It's true that many rocks incorporate fossils that were once living things, but fossils are so old that they have been petrified—literally turned to stone—by geological processes and cannot be radiocarbon dated. As its name suggests, Stonehenge is a monument made of stone. So how has it been radiocarbon dated? The answer lies with organic remains found *beneath* the stones. The bottoms of the pits that were dug to hold the stones were lined with broken animal bones, probably to stop the stones from sinking farther into the earth, and bone is organic, so it can be radiocarbon dated. Of course, the results will relate to when the animals died, but it's a reasonable assumption that this was roughly the same time the stones were erected. The same technique can be used to date earthworks, mounds, and pits that were dug and later filled in, using organic remains in the soil.

Then there's geophysics: scientific equipment, such as ground-penetrating radar, is now used to produce computer-generated images of what lies buried before any invasive excavation is necessary. Using geophysics, it is possible to determine where holes were dug and later refilled, even in the remote past. (Soil strata get all jumbled up when holes are dug, and geophysics reveals where the ground has been disturbed.) Such procedures show where wooden posts for such features as buildings had been set, the location of graves, and where stones had once been erected before later being moved. Still, some features could be gleaned even before these modern methods came into use. During the seventeenth century, Aubrey noticed that a ring of depressions in the ground completely encircled the main monument at Stonehenge, and these features were named after him: the Aubrey Holes. Modern geophysics has determined that there were fifty-six Aubrey Holes, each between 3 and 4 feet wide and dug to a depth of around 3 feet, which, because of crushed rubble excavated from the bottom of the holes, obviously caused by something heavy, are thought to have been pits dug to hold monoliths. Based on the principle that about a third of a monolith needed to be implanted in the ground in order to keep it standing, it is estimated that the Aubrey Holes delineate a now vanished stone circle consisting of fifty-six stones, approximately 6 feet high, 3.5 feet wide, and 2.5 feet thick. As the size and number are approximately those of the bluestones now within the Sarsen Circle, it is generally thought that the ring of Aubrey Holes marks an original stone circle created with the bluestones brought from the Preseli Hills. It seems that they were later moved to create the Bluestone Ring and Bluestone Horseshoe in the final stage of the monument's construction. Based on all this, archaeologists have determined that Stonehenge was originally a circle of bluestones about 280 feet in diameter, dating from around 3000 BCE. Later, around 2500 BCE, the much bigger sarsen stones, with their lintel arches, were erected in the center of this circle, and the bluestones were moved to eventually form the new ring and horseshoe in the middle of the complex.

When all the data were collated, the original Stonehenge was dated to be an astonishing five thousand years old. However, it would have been very different from the monument we see today: a large circle of 6-foot-tall, freestanding monoliths, about 13 feet apart. Remarkably, we

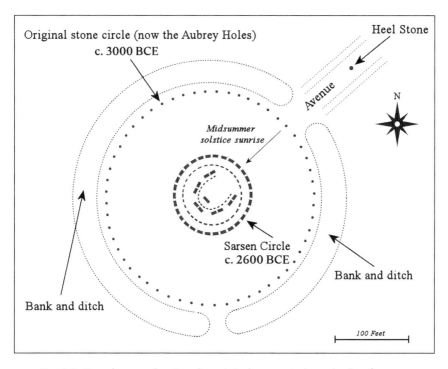

Fig. 1.2. Stonehenge, showing the original stone circle and other features.

now know that Stonehenge predates the Celts by as much as 2,500 years, the first written records from the British Isles by 3,000 years, and the legendary age of Merlin by 3,500 years, and that it existed 5,000 years before the present. So as you can imagine, solving the mysteries surrounding Stonehenge is going to be easier said than done.

Around the same time that the first bluestone circle was erected at Stonehenge, hundreds of other similar, though usually smaller, stone circles were being constructed all over the British Isles. But unlike Stonehenge, the stones they were fashioned from were usually cut from nearby outcrops of whatever rock was available. Just why the original Stonehenge stones were seemingly transplanted from so far away, and just how that might have been done, is something we shall return to later (see chapter 7). For the moment we should just be aware that the unadorned circles of standing stones, rather than the grander constructions like Stonehenge, which survives today, represent only the initial phase of stone circle building from the Megalithic era. Although Stonehenge might be the most famous megalithic monument, originally it was not the largest or most imposing; neither was it the first.

There are estimated to have been as many as 5,000 stone circles in the British Isles, of which around 1,300 still survive, both partial and almost complete.[11] The first stone circles were erected around 3100 BCE, some hundred years before the bluestone circle at Stonehenge, and similar stone circles continued to be built right through the Megalithic era. However, most were smaller than Stonehenge. They average a diameter of about 45 feet and would originally have been composed of between twelve and twenty stones, sometimes with a further single monolith, now referred to as a king stone, standing outside the main circle and aligned to the midsummer sunrise or midwinter sunset as seen from the center of the ring. The Stonehenge Heel Stone is such an example. The height and shape of the stones for these circles varied, depending on the type of rock locally available, most being between 3 and 6 feet high, though some were as tall as 15 feet. These stone circles may have been of different sizes, thought to reflect the extent of the regional population and the type of rock in the area, but they were all built around the same basic principle: a circle of standing stones with monoliths aligned to various heavenly bodies, many also having a so-called king stone. In fact, some scholars have suggested that most stone circles originally had such king stones that have been removed over the centuries, taken out to clear an area for farming, broken up for building material, or dragged away by religious zealots who considered them cursed. All in all, the stone-circle-building obsession continued unabated throughout the British Isles for over three thousand years. Not only were new circles built, but existing ones also were repaired, and judging by the excavation and radiocarbon dating of ancient animal bones that were thought to be evidence of ritual feasting at such sites, they were continuously in use throughout the entire period.

But what is so extraordinary about the Megalithic culture? There are many examples of ancient civilizations building uniform monuments for centuries: the mosques of Islam, the churches of Christian Europe, the mighty temples of ancient Egypt, the colossal shrines of classical Greece, and the stepped pyramids of Mexico, to name just a few. But these monuments were built by cultures that emerged from empires and civilizations with central leadership to initiate such projects, sophisticated infrastructure for communications to organize vast numbers of workers, and armies to implement law and order and to oversee such monumental tasks. But the Megalithic culture of the British Isles appears to have had none of these. It was very different from the civilizations of Christendom, Islam, Rome, Greece, or the Mayans. In fact, the Megalithic culture cannot really be considered a civilization at all—not in the strictest sense of the word. It had no communications network, no central authority, no armed forces, and no cities; it didn't even have large communities living and working in sizable, permanent buildings. There is no archaeological evidence of any of this in Britain until the arrival of the Romans many centuries after the last stone circles were erected. Although certain individuals appear to have enjoyed higher status than others in Megalithic society, as evidenced by their more elaborate burials, there is no indication that the culture ever had an overall king or central government of any kind. The Megalithic people lived in isolated communities, unconnected by roads, and used no horses or other animals as a form of transport. Each community kept pretty much to itself. Yet although these people lived in scattered settlements over an area of around 121,000 square miles (about the size of New Mexico), the same stone-circle-building tradition continued unabated for centuries. The Megalithic culture—and a culture it must have been, as it collectively created the same kind of monuments—was in fact an enduring, monument-building society without cities or civilization: something virtually unique in world history.

What makes the Megalithic culture all the more remarkable is that the continuation of the stone circle tradition is only part of the story. Around 2600 BCE the next phase of megalithic construction began when the largest stone circles, in the most densely inhabited areas, were spectacularly transformed. They were replaced with much larger stones, often made from a type of rock locally unavailable and required being quarried and transported from miles away (although not as far as the Stonehenge bluestones). These radical innovations were surrounded by so-called henge earthworks, after which Stonehenge gets its name: a circular bank and ditch, with the ditch often dug on the inside of the bank, the opposite way round for it to have been used for defense. The largest of these new stone circles was at Avebury, 17 miles north of Stonehenge. With a diameter of over 1,000 feet, it dwarfs Stonehenge. It originally consisted of around a hundred stones, ranging from 9 to 20 feet high, with some even larger than those at Stonehenge, weighing as much as 40 tons. It was surrounded by a ditch about 30 feet deep and 60 feet wide and an embankment 20 feet high and 40 feet thick.[12] About two hundred years later new features were added to these huge stone circles: known as "avenues," they consist of a pair of long parallel embankments, leading sometimes miles from the henge monuments to further stone circles. The avenue at Stonehenge, for example, leads 2 miles to a site called the West Amesbury Henge (see chapter 7). Then, around 2000 BCE, artificial hills started to be built close to the biggest of these circles, the largest being Silbury Hill near Avebury. Composed mainly of chalk and clay excavated from the surrounding area, the mound stands about 130 feet high and covers about 5 acres. The purpose of these mounds is a complete mystery, as excavations have revealed no signs of burials or any hidden chambers within. These huge stone circles, with their surrounding earthworks, are referred to as complexes, of which there were dozens created throughout the British Isles. Stonehenge was one such complex, but others, like Avebury, were very much bigger. However, Stonehenge was the only stone circle to have rectangular arches formed by lintel stones, which is why it is the most famous. This, along with its being in the most densely populated area of Britain at the time, implies that Stonehenge

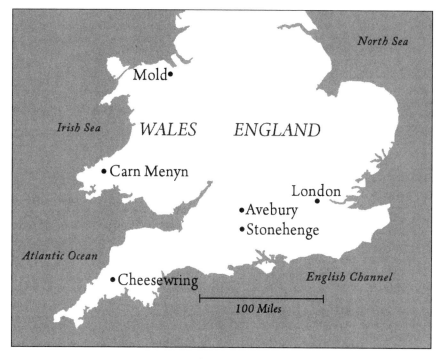

Fig. 1.3. Sites discussed in this chapter.

ultimately became the heart or hub of this remarkable network of prehistoric creations.

As we have seen, archaeology has shown that the Megalithic people lived in separate communities with no usual infrastructure of civilization, taskmasters, or central leadership. They didn't even have any form of writing to record and transmit their beliefs. So perhaps the most astonishing thing about these monuments, other than the incredible amount of work, time, and resources needed to build them, is that once the stone-circle-building practice had been established throughout the country, identical periodic modifications and developments happened at precisely the same time right across the British Isles. Archaeologists are mystified as to how the kind of multitribal structure that excavations reveal existed during this entire period and how the tribes could possibly have been consistently united and driven to create and sustain such gigantic projects. Yet for century after century the stone circle obsession continued unabated. The most tempting solution to the mystery of Stonehenge is that it—and the many other stone circles—was built for some religious purpose alone. But if this were true, then going by the fact that these monuments were built to a similar design and underwent synchronous development, it means that the same organized religion survived for millennia without any kind of central authority. Many cultures have built massive structures for purely religious purposes: the great cathedrals of Christendom, the mighty temples of Egypt, and the colossal shrines of ancient Greece, for example. But these cultures emerged from empires and civilizations with all the trappings that such integrated societies enjoy. Some long-lived religions have endured in fragmented societies, such as the pyramid-building cultures of Central America, Islam throughout the Middle East and Asia, and Christianity in Europe. But all were originally established by a powerful civilization, such as the ancient Mayan Empire in Mexico, the seventh-to-eighth-century Arabian caliphates of the Middle East, and the Romans, who molded the various Christian sects into the organized Catholic Church in the fourth century CE. But as we have seen, no evidence of such a civilization existed anywhere in the British Isles before or during the Megalithic era. There were almost certainly religious aspects to Megalithic society, but it seems highly improbable that some kind of single religion can account for the same stone-circle-building tradition existing among isolated tribal societies, spread over such a large area, and for so long.

So how and where did the tradition begin, and why did it spread so far and wide and last for so long? And why were stone circles built at all? The only way to crack the mystery of Stonehenge is by examining the culture that built these remarkable monuments in its entirety and by gaining an overall perspective of this extraordinary network of prehistoric constructions. In an attempt to solve the enigma we will be piecing together the very latest archaeological discoveries and drawing on crucial historical source material completely overlooked until now. By collating the evidence emerging from recent excavations and other archaeological evidence, together with writings of the Romans, who recorded the beliefs of those living in Britain during *their* time, and also by examining surviving mythology, legend, and folklore, we will try to finally solve the mystery of Stonehenge once and for all. But to start with let's examine what the world was like when the Megalithic culture began and what came before.

2

The Birth of Civilization

UNTIL AROUND 5,300 YEARS AGO there were no civilizations with cities, urban development, national infrastructure, and central leadership anywhere in the world. At least none that archaeologists have discovered to the satisfaction of the mainstream academic community. The world was still in the Stone Age, the period when tools and weapons were made from simple materials such as wood, bone, and stone. Modern humans are thought to have evolved around two hundred thousand years ago, and they inherited the use of such implements, along with fire, from their evolutionary predecessors. These early humans were *Homo sapiens,* just as we are today. Take one as a baby and bring her up in the modern world and she could do anything we can do. However, it took millennia of trial and error, along with the remarkable human imagination, to invent and develop the skills and innovations that ultimately led to civilization. It was at the same time as civilizations began to appear around the globe that the Megalithic culture first emerged in the British Isles, but let's start by taking a brief look at the various accomplishments and lifestyles of people around the world before this time.[1]

Animal hides may have been used as simple clothing from very early on in human history, but it took the invention of the bone sewing needle around 50,000 years ago for more elaborate garments and footwear to develop. The first threads would have been made from animal parts—sinew, tendons, or thin leather—or twine, formed from the fibrous strands of plants, such as reeds, cacti, and certain trees. By 40,000 years ago humans were well into art, making stone and bone carvings and painting on rock and cave walls. They probably decorated their skin, hair, and garments too. These prehistoric paints were made from various ground minerals and charcoal, mixed with fat. And 25,000 years ago we had begun using clay to make pots for cooking or vessels for storage by baking it hard.[2] Yet despite such advances, for their first 190,000 years, *Homo sapiens* lived in small tribal or family groups and were for the most part nomadic, moving from place to place in search of fresh pastures or following herds. They were so-called hunter-gatherers, obtaining their food by foraging, stalking animals, and moving with the seasons. In certain lush or fertile areas, some did live in permanent settlements, fishing or obtaining food locally, but these settlements remained small. During this period, known as the Paleolithic era, or the Old Stone Age, dwellings would have been simple wooden frameworks (in some cases frames made from the bones of large animals such as mammoths) covered with hides or vegetation such as branches, straw, or reeds, and sealed with mud. Some people would have lived in caves, and in frozen areas, others might have lived in huts made from ice or snow, like the Inuit igloo.[3] Then around 12,000 years ago, people began to settle, and that was due to the invention of farming.

The widespread initiative of deliberately growing plants and domesticating animals seems to have begun shortly after the last Ice Age, around 10,000 BCE. This was the birth of the Neolithic era, or New Stone Age, when crops such as cereals were cultivated and various animals, such as sheep and goats, were reared for food, wool, and milk. It's not known where this significant innovation first occurred, but it was to change everything: it meant the establishment of larger and more permanent settlements. Humans were able to live together in much greater numbers, work collectively to develop initiatives, share ideas, and have a certain amount of leisure time to contemplate and invent. Life was no longer merely a perpetual toil to survive. The Neolithic period saw many groundbreaking inventions, such as the raft, which boosted migrations, while the development of better bows and arrows, rather than just spears, for hunting increased the food supply and led to a rise in populations; also, from around ten thousand years ago, the invention of the spindle meant that animal hair, such as sheep and goat wool, could be more effectively drawn out to make yarn. Wool was plucked either by hand or by using combs made from bone, while plant fibers were woven employing crude wooden frames, and cloth began to be made. No longer did people need to wear only animal skins to keep warm.[4]

It was just over five thousand years ago that the next crucial advance occurred: civilizations suddenly emerged separately in Egypt, India, and Mesopotamia. And it was all down to the invention of bronze. People in various locations had known about metals for centuries, probably as a by-product of firing ceramics. When the temperature of clay reaches 350 degrees Celsius (662 degrees Fahrenheit), chemically bonded water begins to dry off, and at 500 degrees Celsius (932 degrees Fahrenheit), it is fully dehydrated to form permanently changed, hard, solid pottery. In their natural state metals are contained in silicate rocks known as ores. To extract them, you need to heat the rocks to the specific temperatures at which the metals melt. They can then pour out of the rock, which remains solid: silicon, the main constituent of stone, doesn't melt until it reaches around 1,400 degrees Celsius (2,552 degrees Fahrenheit), whereas many metals melt at lower temperatures. Early in their history, modern humans had the knowledge to create fire by sparking hard rocks or by friction with sticks. It was a turning point for our ancestors, providing a source of warmth, light, and protection, and a way of preparing food that would otherwise have been inedible. Right from the start people would have noticed that mud surrounding a fire would bake hard, and by twenty-five thousand years ago, they had begun to deliberately shape mud and then bake it to make solid earthenware pots. Sustained temperatures of over 500 degrees Celsius were needed to create permanent, more durable ceramics, and this could have been achieved in the so-called firing pits common throughout the world by around twelve thousand years ago. These were simple trenches into which the molded clay items were placed, then surrounded with combustible material such as peat, straw, and wood, which was kept burning for many days. Such pits were ringed by an arrangement of stones to contain the fire, and when these stones were made from metal-bearing rock, our ancestors could not have helped but notice that certain metals would melt out, to be left as a residue of small, shiny, solid chunks when the firing was done.[5]

The first metal to be discovered in this way was probably tin, as it melts at the relatively low temperature of around 232 degrees Celsius (450 degrees Fahrenheit). However, no one seems to have done much with it, as only a few isolated examples of simple tin artifacts, such as awls (small, pointed spikes for piercing leather), are known from before around 5,300 years ago. Metals such as gold, silver, and copper melt around 1,000 degrees Celsius (1,832 degrees Fahrenheit), and it was not until the invention of the kiln, basically a brick or stone oven heated from below, for the more efficient firing of clay, that the control of such temperatures was achieved. No one knows precisely where and when these kilns were first invented, but they became widely used in various parts of the world by around 5,500 years ago. There are a few isolated examples of gold, silver, and copper artifacts, such as simple jewelry, found earlier than this time, but the large-scale, deliberate making of items from these metals could not occur before the invention of the kiln. But it was the chance realization that melting copper and tin together formed a much harder and altogether more useful metal—the alloy bronze—around 5,300 years ago that kick-started what we would now call civilization. (Tin must be smelted separately and then added to molten copper to produce bronze.) Although there are a few instances of pieces of bronze being made earlier, elsewhere in the world, it was its industrial production in the ancient Near East that began the Bronze Age. It started in Mesopotamia, a fertile region around the Tigris and Euphrates Rivers system, centered on what is now Iraq, and shortly after in Egypt, and then in northwest India.[6]

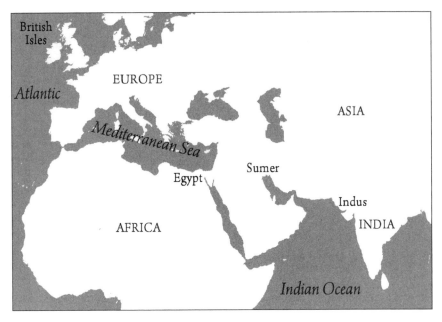

Fig. 2.1. The first civilizations.

The invention of bronze meant that useful, sturdy metal tools could be fashioned, and *that* dramatically changed everything. The metal plow replaced the stone ard (plough) for tilling the land, which led, in turn, to the use of beasts of burden. The invention of the harness meant that domesticated creatures could be used as draft animals to pull sledges or drag loads on wooden frames, which soon led, in turn, to the invention of the wheel and consequently carts. A variety of animals were domesticated for various tasks, including oxen, horses, goats, yaks, and donkeys. (Dogs had already been domesticated as hunting companions, even before Neolithic times.) A whole variety of bronze implements made agriculture immensely more efficient. Farmers no longer needed to laboriously cut cereal crops with crude flint blades but could now cut faster and easier with metal sickles. Bronze axe heads replaced stone ones, bronze spades replaced bone shovels, and knives were now made of metal rather than flint. All these innovations meant faster and vastly greater food production and accordingly a further surge in population. And with this came large urban settlements and cities.[7]

The use of animals as a form of transport led to the building of roads, which were paved in cities but were cleared, flattened, and maintained dirt tracks in the countryside. The building of roads and the use of animals as a form of transport brought about kingdoms and empires. Bronze also meant the invention of the sword, metal arrowheads, and spear tips, and so appeared the world's first armies. Warriors could travel faster and more effectively along the newly created road networks, taking with them food and supplies carried in horse-drawn carts. This meant that tribal leaders could extend and maintain their influence over large areas. Trade and communications were also made easier by the development of boats, no longer dugout canoes or simple rafts, but vessels made from wooden planks, impossible before the invention of metal fasteners, such as the nail. The nail meant that timber frameworks could be made very much larger than those tied with rope, so buildings became bigger and more impressive. Simple bricks, made from mud dried in the sun, had been in use in certain parts of the world from early Neolithic times, but harder ceramic, or fired, bricks were developed with the first cities just over five thousand years ago. And this led to the creation of elaborate temples, palaces, and public buildings and highly effective city walls. Although rope, as well as string, had been used since the beginning of Neolithic times, it was made by twisting and braiding strands of plant fiber by hand, limiting its production. With the birth of civilization came the development of special tools for making rope, and the large-scale manufacture of rope made it possible to build remarkable structures, where the effort of hundreds or thousands of workers could be synchronized to haul heavy objects such as stones.[8]

A civilization, in the anthropological definition, is a complex society characterized by urban centers or cities, an intricate social hierarchy, peacekeeping forces or armies, an elaborate communication structure, typified by roads, and writing or some symbolic transmission of information. The birth of such urbanized civilizations seems to have begun in the land of Sumer around 5,300 years ago, in what is now southern

Iraq. The Tigris and Euphrates Rivers made the area particularly fertile and allowed the growth of an abundance of grain and various crops. It was probably there that bronze was first made in any meaningful amount, and within a century or so civilization was established there, with all its trappings. Metal molding saw the development of all manner of new tools, made for a whole variety of purposes: for example, finer needles for sewing, devices for the weaving of superior clothing, chisels for carving elaborate ornamentation and statues for temples, palaces, and tombs, and the stylus for forming designs in clay. The development of the metal stylus, a small tool for intricate marking and shaping, led to the invention of writing by imprinting soft clay with symbols denoting objects, items, complex ideas, and verbal sounds. The birth of writing meant that communications were vastly superior. Orders, proclamations, and ideas could be disseminated on clay tablets, easily made and transported, and monuments could be inscribed with records of religious observances, national accomplishments, and the exploits of leaders and the ruling class. Sumer was the first place on Earth to emerge from prehistory into "history"—the era from which written, historical records survive.[9]

Citizens of Sumer's cities, such as its capital of Urak in the modern Iraqi province of Al Muthanna, enjoyed many accoutrements previously undreamed of. Early pots had been made by coiling and rolling clay into long threads and pinching them together to form vessels, but the invention of the potter's wheel, turned by hand or foot, made pottery making faster and more efficient, enabling the industrial production of ceramic ware. So as well as having large and comfortable homes and officials to keep law and order in the streets outside, city dwellers not only had decent furniture, thanks to the advances in carpentry using metal tools, they also had the kind of domestic crockery—pots, plates, cups, and storage vessels—we take for granted today. And they had metal cutlery too. Knives and spoons meant they no longer needed to eat with their hands[10] (although, strangely, no one seems to have gotten around to inventing the simple table fork for another four thousand years). And your status in society could be expressed through various ornamentations unheard of elsewhere in the world. Adornments made from shells, bones, and stones were commonly worn throughout the Neolithic period and earlier, but metalworking took personal decorations to another level entirely. Along with the manufacture of bronze, gold and silver were also smelted to produce sophisticated ornaments, such as bracelets, necklaces, and rings, together with household items such as platters, drinking vessels, and statuettes. Also, the cutting, shaping, and polishing of precious stones developed on a more commercial scale, meaning that many people could wear at least some kind of jewelry.

Sumer consisted of a number of cities about 250 acres in size, each with populations of approximately ten thousand people. Urak itself was much bigger, almost 1,000 acres in size with more than fifty thousand inhabitants. These cities were linked not only by waterways but also by an extensive network of roads, while the fields surrounding them were fed by an ingenious system of artificial irrigation channels. Each city had temples for the priesthood, palaces for the local rulers, and public buildings for centralized administration. Workers were divided into specialized groups, such as carpenters, masons, and artisans, and slave laborers were captured from the surrounding hill country. The overall leaders seem to have been a succession of priestly rulers—both men and women—advised by a council of elders.[11] Modern archaeology has determined that early Sumer was not the kind of misogynistic society it was once thought to have been. It had a pantheon of deities, but the chief among them seem to have been a male and a female of equal status: Nin, the supreme goddess, and En, the supreme god. Whoever ruled was thought to govern with the power of the deity that represented his or her gender. Just how the leader was chosen is unknown, but it may have been by some form of election, much the way the Catholic Church now chooses a new pope. It was not until around four centuries after the start of Sumerian civilization that a dynastic era of male kings emerged and the god En became known as Enlil, the chief divinity, while Nin was demoted to his consort, Ninlil.[12] It is possible that it was from Sumer that the biblical tale of the Garden of Eden originated. Genesis 2:14 refers to Eden being fed by the Tigris and Euphrates Rivers, and in Sumerian mythology Nin and En, like Adam and Eve, are said to have once dwelt as immortals in a heavenly paradise at the beginning of time.

It was about 150 years after the nation of Sumer became established that another civilization began. Around a thousand miles to the west, the land of Egypt had already grown prosperous due to the life-giving Nile River and its spreading rivulet system in the delta region, and the Egyptians traded with the Sumerians. By around 3150 BCE they had learned from their trading partners how to manufacture bronze. The Sumerian system of a centralized government, a cultural elite, law codes, social stratification, and standing armies was also adopted, and the nation of ancient Egypt was born. The Bronze Age Egyptians seem to have skipped the sexual equality era and gone straight into a male-oriented dynastic society with its kings, or pharaohs, ruling with absolute power. This second civilization was founded on the city of Memphis, about 20 miles south of modern Cairo; this first Egyptian capital had around thirty thousand inhabitants, and the towns under its control were linked by the Nile and its vast array of rivulets. By around 3100 BCE, ancient Egypt had gained nearly all the benefits of civilization enjoyed by the Sumerians. Although they lived over 1,000 miles apart, Egypt probably copied much of its early technology, such as the making of bronze and building techniques, from Sumer, but Egypt developed along separate cultural lines: it had different gods, temple designs, and other architecture, and it innovated its own writing in the form of hieroglyphics. The controlled making of bronze, which seems to have begun in Sumer, found its way not only to Egypt but also to the peoples of the Indus Valley, in what is now Pakistan, over 1,500 miles to the east. Whether these people discovered the process independently is still open to debate. Either way, around 3000 BCE the Indus Valley civilization had emerged, centered on the city of Harappa, in the modern Sindh province. It was about 400 acres in size and had a population of some twenty-five thousand people.[13]

As time passed, other civilizations arose. To put all this into a global context and time frame, the approximate dates of the births of the best-known ancient civilizations are as follows:

3300 BCE	Sumer, southern Iraq
3100 BCE	Ancient Egypt
3000 BCE	Harappa, Pakistan and northwest India
2600 BCE	The Minoans of Crete and the Aegean Islands
2300 BCE	The Akkadian Empire, based on the city of Akkad, central Iraq
2000 BCE	The Xia dynasty of China
2000 BCE	The First Assyrian Empire, based on the city of Assur, northern Iraq
1800 BCE	The first Babylonian Empire, centered on the city of Babylon, central Iraq
1600 BCE	The Mycenaean civilization of Greece
1600 BCE	The Hittites, Turkey
1500 BCE	The Olmecs of Mexico, the oldest known civilization in the Americas
1500 BCE	The Phoenician civilization, centered on Lebanon
1500 BCE	The Vedic Age in India
1000 BCE	The ancient kingdom of Israel
800 BCE	The founding of Carthage, Tunisia
750 BCE	The Mayan civilization of Mexico
550 BCE	The first Persian Empire, centered on Iran
500 BCE	Classical Greece
500 BCE	Birth of the Roman Republic, centered on Italy
300 BCE	The Tiwanaku civilization of Bolivia
27 BCE	Augustus becomes the first Roman emperor. The Roman Empire covers much of Western Europe, the eastern Mediterranean, and North Africa.

The term "ancient civilizations" refers to those dating from the period before the Common Era: in other words, BCE—over two thousand years ago. So you may be wondering why some other famous civilizations aren't on this list, such as the Peruvian Incas, the Mexican Aztecs, and the people who created the Nazca Lines and giant pictographs on the desert floor in southern Peru. The Incan civilization only began around six hundred years ago, as did the Aztec, and the Nazca culture was at its height in the first century CE. The magnificent temple complex of Angkor Wat in Cambodia is often cited as an astonishing accomplishment from ancient times, but the truth is it was only built around the year 1200 CE. The Anasazi ruins of North America, such as those at Chaco Canyon and Mesa Verde, date between 600 and 1300 CE; the Kafun period of Japanese civilization began around 250 CE, the rise of Islamic empires beginning in Arabia did not start until around fourteen hundred years ago, and the giant stone statues on Easter Island were first carved around 1100 CE.

These are only approximate dates, and there is much discussion among historians and archaeologists concerning them. Nevertheless, this gives us an idea of just when the Megalithic period of the British Isles fits in. It seems to have begun right at the very beginning of civilization, at the same time as the Sumerian civilization was forming. But unlike those of Sumer, the people of the British Isles had none of the trappings of civilization; they didn't even have bronze until its secrets were brought to the islands around 2000 BCE, well over a millennium after the first stone circles were built (see chapter 9). Bronze wasn't absolutely necessary for city-building civilizations to get started and to endure. Pre-Columbian civilizations in the Americas did outstandingly well, and erected some extraordinary buildings to rival those of the Old World, without ever discovering such hard metals. They made exquisite items out of gold and silver and created various soft alloys but never seem to have produced bronze even though they had both copper and tin. In some ways they didn't need it, as they had a plentiful supply of obsidian, a volcanically formed glassy material that is much sharper

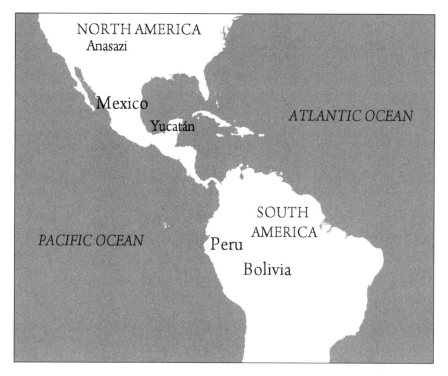

Fig. 2.2. Locations of pre-Columbian civilizations in the Americas.

and more versatile than flint and was generally used for cutting tools, arrowheads, knives, and a whole variety of purposes in other Stone Age societies. Obsidian played the role that bronze did elsewhere in the world to kick-start civilization.[14] But before we examine just how the first Megalithic people lived and exactly what kind of society they had, we should take time to examine some other "civilizations" that do not appear on our list: those mysterious "lost civilizations" that may never have existed at all.

Over the years some authors have suggested that, as the Megalithic culture began before most of the world's civilizations had even gotten going, it may have been started by people from some forgotten empire, such as Atlantis. The oldest written reference to Atlantis is by the Greek philosopher Plato around 360 BCE. In his work *Critias,* he recounts the alleged visit by the Athenian statesman Solon to Egypt in about

600 BCE.[15] There, Solon was apparently told the story of the mighty island state of Atlantis, which had existed somewhere in the Atlantic Ocean, after which it was seemingly named. Ultimately, the nation angered the gods, and the entire island sank into the sea. This is all said to have occurred nine thousand years before Solon's time. The Egyptians, Plato claims, described the inhabited plain of Atlantis as being 2,000 by 3,000 *stades* in size, 230 by 345 modern miles, with an additional, larger mountainous area to the north. Its overall size seems to be somewhat ambiguous, but it was probably imagined to be about 800 miles long and 250 miles wide at its broadest point: around the size of mainland Britain. We are not told precisely where it was, but it was seemingly somewhere just outside the Strait of Gibraltar, as a submerged bank of mud was said to still impair shipping where the island sank, which at the time would only have been coastal shipping, so presumably somewhere off what is now either Spain, Portugal, or Morocco. Atlantis, as portrayed by Plato, had the kind of civilization comparable to his contemporary Greece, with huge temples, palaces, and stately buildings. It had a similar army and navy too, as the Atlanteans are said to have conquered the coast of North Africa as far as Egypt, and the north coast of the Mediterranean as far as Italy. Eventually, the Athenians of Greece managed to defeat them and liberated the occupied territories. In Plato's work *Timaeus,* he tells us that soon afterward, "There occurred violent earthquakes and floods; and in a single day and night . . . the island of Atlantis disappeared into the depths of the sea."[16]

Historians generally agree that Plato either made up the mysterious island as a philosophical allegory or that the idea was simply myth. Plato relates how the Atlanteans besieged ancient Athens sometime around 9600 BCE, whereas archaeology has revealed that the birth of Athens as a fortified citadel only dates from around 1400 BCE, during the Mycenaean period, and even this settlement was far less elaborate than the classical city of Athens that existed during Plato's time. Moreover, modern sonar mapping of the Atlantic seabed has revealed no evidence that any such island ever existed anywhere near where Atlantis was said to have been. But although most present-day scholars regard the supposed age and location of Atlantis as fiction, some believe that a genuine civilization may have served as its inspiration.

The Minoans were a Bronze Age civilization on the island of Crete and other islands in the Aegean Sea (in the northeastern Mediterranean between Greece and Turkey). Beginning around 2600 BCE they were a seafaring power, and they came to dominate what are now the Greek Islands before the rise of the Mycenaeans on the Greek mainland. By 1600 BCE the Minoan capital at Knossos was every bit as sophisticated as any Egyptian city of the time; perhaps more so, in that it had the world's first known fully integrated plumbing system. And it supported a population estimated to have been around one hundred thousand people. The Minoans certainly had better and faster ships than anyone else in that part of the world and virtually controlled trade throughout the eastern Mediterranean. Then around 3,500 years ago, a massive volcanic eruption on the Isle of Thera (now Santorini), some 70 miles north of Crete, not only completely destroyed the Minoan city of Akrotiri on that island, but the resultant tsunami also swept away the harbor of Knossos, the Mediterranean's greatest port. Minoan Crete may not actually be the Atlantis envisaged by Plato, but it might have started the legend of the sophisticated island state destroyed by the sea.[17]

Then there's the lost continent of Mu. The idea began with the French-American archaeologist Augustus Le Plongeon, who studied the Mayan ruins in Yucatán, Mexico, in the 1870s. His translation of Mayan writings led him to believe that these ancient cities were older even than those of Egypt. In fact, he proposed that the ruins of the Yucatán Peninsula were all that remained of the Mu civilization that had once flourished on a long-ago sunken continent that had existed in the western Atlantic and that its ideas and the remnants of its culture had spread to both Mexico and Egypt. The fact that both cultures built pyramids, although quite different in design, made Le Plongeon's theory popular for a while, until other scholars threw serious doubt on his supposed translations. Nevertheless, the notion of the lost continent was revived by the British engineer James Churchward in a series of books published during the 1930s. Churchward claimed that while he was a soldier in India he met a Hindu priest who showed him a set of ancient clay tablets chronicling the history of Mu, which had not been in the Atlantic, as Le Plongeon proposed, but in the Pacific. Supposedly translating the tablets, Churchward revealed that the sunken continent had been the home of an advanced civilization that had existed from around fifty thousand years ago, and like Atlantis, it sank beneath the waves after a series of earthquakes and volcanic eruptions some twelve thousand years ago. It had a population of sixty-four million, along with colonies elsewhere, including Mexico, Egypt, *and* India.[18] Needless to say, as Churchward failed to produce the clay tablets as proof, his claims never received scholarly support. Just like the Atlantic, the floor of the Pacific Ocean has now been thoroughly mapped and charted by ship sonar and from data collected by satellites, and there is no indication that any such continent ever existed. In fact, the idea that the Mayan civilization preceded the ancient Egyptians by any period at all, let alone thousands of years, has been completely invalidated by modern techniques, such as radiocarbon dating, thermoluminescence (scientific dating of pottery), and dendrochronology (tree-ring dating). The impressive Mayan pyramids and palaces weren't built until over two thousand years *after* the Great Pyramids of Egypt. The lost continent of Mu and its very name seem to have been born in the fertile imagination of Augustus Le Plongeon and later reinvented by the even more imaginative James Churchward.

Lemuria is the Atlantis of the Indian Ocean. The name originated with the English zoologist Philip Sclater in the 1860s, after he noted the similarities of fossils in Madagascar, off the coast of eastern Africa, and fossils in western India showing that exactly the same kind of plants and animals had lived at the same time in the remote past in both these locations, now separated by 3,000 miles of ocean. The explanation, he proposed, was that the two areas were once joined by a huge landmass that long ago sank beneath the sea. He called this supposed

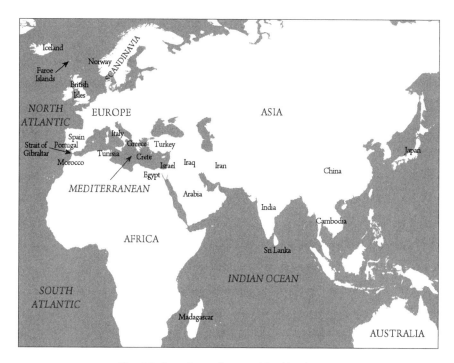

Fig. 2.3. Locations discussed in this chapter.

lost continent Lemuria, after the lemurs, the primates of Madagascar. However, the scientific explanation for the fossil evidence was eventually formulated by the mid-twentieth century with the discovery of plate tectonics: Madagascar and India were once joined together but drifted apart, starting around eighty-eight million years ago. In simple terms, solid parts of Earth's crust slowly floated apart on the molten magma below. As far as science is concerned, there is no need for there to have been a lost continent to explain the fossil similarities.[19]

Various old works from India, written in both the Tamil and Sanskrit languages, contain accounts of lands being lost beneath the sea. The earliest surviving manuscripts are around twelve hundred years old, but refer to events that purportedly occurred many centuries before. These may be purely mythological or perhaps concern actual areas that suffered from devastating tsunamis, such as the one caused by the Indian Ocean earthquake of December 26, 2004, when waves up to 100 feet high inundated coastal communities in fourteen countries, including Sri Lanka and India, and over 250,000 people lost their lives. In the mid-twentieth century, authors among the Tamil people of southern India and Sri Lanka, citing such texts, began to propose that an entire landmass, once ruled by their ancestors, had been lost to the sea. Called Kumari Kandam, it was said to have been the cradle of a civilization that had existed to the South of India. In the 1960s a number of Western authors were inspired by speculations concerning this lost land, resurrecting the name Lemuria for the supposed sunken continent of the Indian Ocean.[20] Nevertheless, modern scientific surveys have revealed no geological formations under the Indian or Pacific Oceans that correspond to the imagined Kumari Kandam or Lemuria.

Ancient Greek mythology spoke of a land called Hyperborea that lay somewhere in the far north. It was said to be a land populated by giants where the sun never set. The facts that the indigenous people of Scandinavia would have been generally taller than the Greeks and that about a third of Scandinavia lies above the Arctic Circle, where the midsummer sun does shine for twenty-four hours a day, has led some researchers to speculate that Hyperborea was a real land somewhere to the north of Britain. The Ancient Greeks certainly knew of the British Isles. The earliest known recorded visit to these islands was by the Greek geographer Pytheas of Massalia in about 325 BCE. During his voyage he not only circumnavigated and landed in Britain but also sailed farther north to describe icebergs and a place where the sun stayed above the horizon at the height of summer: a land he called Thule, possibly the coast of Norway. Later classical writers also refer to Thule, describing it as being northwest of Britain, beyond what seem to be the Faroe Islands, just possibly making it Iceland.[21] Some modern authors have suggested that Thule and Hyperborea were lost civilizations, thousands of years old, somewhere in the Arctic, although there is nothing in Greek or Roman writings to suggest that they regarded these places as some kind of northern Atlantis. They don't speak of a city-building civilization, or even a particularly ancient people, merely a rather primitive culture contemporary with their own. Needless to say, anthropologists remain highly skeptical about any kind of ancient city-dwelling civilization becoming established in the sort of climate that exists above the Arctic Circle. Certainly no evidence of such has ever been found.

So with a perspective on ancient civilizations, both real and imagined, we now have a context into which to place the beginnings of the Megalithic culture—in the British Isles at the very dawn of civilization elsewhere in the world. But what came before? Could there have been an earlier, genuine culture from which the Megalithic people sprang?

3

Prelude

The Emerging Cultures of the Late Stone Age

MYTHICAL CIVILIZATIONS ASIDE, there have been a number of surprising archaeological discoveries to suggest that civilizations were close to getting started in various parts of the world well before those of Sumer, Egypt, and the Indus Valley, but for various reasons they petered out, stagnated, or disappeared entirely. On the Mediterranean island of Gozo, a part of Malta, is Ġgantija (Giants' Tower), a temple complex dating from around 3600 BCE. The plan incorporates five large, roughly circular chambers built around a central area and a passage leading to an inner sanctum. Its rough-cut stone walls, once plastered in parts, rise to a height of almost 20 feet, and the complex covers about 10,000 square feet, much of it thought to have been covered by timber roofing. The walls are interspersed with carefully shaped, oblong standing monoliths, weighing many tons, together with smaller, similarly shaped stones, joined with lintels set into the walls to create rectangular recesses. The temple contains various features, such as carvings and what seem to be stone altars. Archaeologists have determined that the complex was in use and expanded for over approximately one thousand years, until it was abandoned. There are a number of similar but smaller such structures on the island dating from the building of

Ġgantija until around 2500 BCE.[1] Although this mysterious Neolithic Maltese culture, known as the Temple People, began some three centuries before the rise of Sumer, it never built cities or developed the other trappings of civilization in the anthropological sense. It seems to have died out when newcomers brought the Bronze Age to the island in the mid-2000s BCE.

Sechin Bajo is an archaeological site in Peru, just over 200 miles northwest of Lima. It is one of a number of ancient ruins in the area, but whereas most date from after 1500 BCE, the period of the so-called Casma/Sechin culture, part of Sechin Bajo is the site of a much earlier ceremonial terrace. It consists of a platform, some 52 feet square and just over 6 feet high, built from rocks overlaid with clay bricks. Although it has been dated to around 3500 BCE and is one of the oldest artificial structures in the Americas, there is no evidence that those who made it ever created any kind of civilization or erected complex dwellings. In fact, it seems that the original Sechin Bajo people, although they made simple bricks, had not even mastered the skill of making pottery. The mysterious platform seems to have been a one-off construction, made by a people who either died out or went into decline for centuries before reemerging as the Casma/Sechin culture.[2]

Monte d'Accoddi, on the Italian island of Sardinia, is an ancient artificial mound: a kind of truncated earthen pyramid faced with stones. Its base is almost 90 feet long and wide, rising to about 18 feet in height, where there is a flat platform 40 feet long and 24 feet wide, reached by an earthen ramp or causeway. As it contains no entrances or chambers within, it is thought to have been an open-air temple rather than a tomb. It has been dated to as early as 4000 BCE, but like the Sechin Bajo terrace in Peru, it seems to have been a one-off accomplishment, and whoever built it never got around to creating any further structures that are known. Later, around 3200 BCE, a Neolithic people known as the Ozieri culture inhabited the island and built a settlement around the mound and began to use it for their own ceremonial purposes.[3]

These three archaic anomalies date from the first half of the fourth millennium BCE, but there are two even older and more astonishing ancient constructions in what is now Turkey. Çatalhöyük is the ruins of a Neolithic settlement some 28 miles southeast of the modern Turkish town of Konya, and it was occupied from around 7500 to 6000 BCE. Covering some 32 acres, it consisted of a honeycomb arrangement of rectangular, mud-brick buildings, built closely against one another with no paths or passageways between. They are all thought to have been domestic dwellings accessed through holes in the ceiling, reached by wooden ladders or steps, effectively making the joined rooftops the town's streets. At its height, around 7000 BCE, Çatalhöyük is thought to have had a population of up to ten thousand people. Most houses contained two main rooms with smaller chambers for storage, and walls were plastered to a smooth finish and painted with murals, mainly depicting human figures and animals.[4] Numerous clay figurines have been found, mostly depicting animals, along with many of seated women, suggesting a religion based around a supreme goddess. Çatalhöyük is by far the largest Neolithic settlement found anywhere in the world, and it can certainly be described as a city—by far the world's oldest yet discovered—but was it a civilization?

Archaeologists believe that the entire settlement was composed of domestic dwellings, as there are no obvious public buildings, such as temples, palaces, or civic meeting places. Neither did the community appear to have any ruling elite or religious hierarchy, as no houses were particularly larger than others or built to a grander design. Çatalhöyük seems to have been an isolated, one-off settlement, without having extended its influence to the surrounding area or attempting to found any kind of kingdom or state. Hand-corded pottery remained simple, and Stone Age tools were no different from those used by many other Neolithic people elsewhere in the world. There was no smelting of any metals, invention of weaving, or production of fabrics. People wore animal skins, knives and cutting tools relied on obsidian or flint, and hunting appears to have been restricted to the use of the simple spear. Crops such as wheat, barley, and peas were cultivated, and various animals, such as sheep and cattle, were domesticated, but there is no evidence for the use of draft animals or beasts of burden.[5] The inhabitants of Çatalhöyük may have lived more comfortably and resided together in greater numbers than their Neolithic contemporaries, but they were still a Stone Age community with none of the trappings of a civilization.

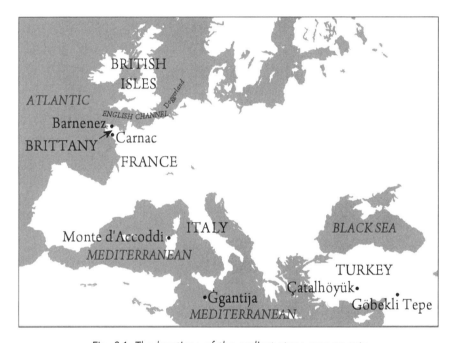

Fig. 3.1. The locations of the earliest stone monuments
of Europe and Turkey.

What seems to be the world's oldest known temple compound is also in Turkey and dates from even earlier than Çatalhöyük. Around 400 miles east of Çatalhöyük, Göbekli Tepe is a complex of ancient structures created on a hilltop, 7 miles northeast of the modern city of Şanlıurfa. It is composed of twenty separate circular constructions, about 30 to 60 feet in diameter, consisting of enclosure walls, interspersed with between ten and twelve *T*-shaped stone pillars some 10 feet tall, with two much larger *T*-shaped standing stones, about 20 feet tall and weighing up to 20 tons, in the center of each circle; the entire area of the complex covers more than 20 acres. The pillars are carved with both abstract symbols and depictions of various animals, such as birds, snakes, lizards, lions, and foxes. Radiocarbon dating suggests that it began to be erected as early as 9000 BCE, making it the oldest artificially constructed religious site so far found anywhere on Earth.[6] Yet despite its remarkable size and complexity for having been built eleven thousand years ago, there is no evidence of any accompanying cities or sophisticated settlements. Göbekli Tepe seems to have been a place of pilgrimage for people from about a 100-mile radius who lived no differently from many other early Neolithic people around the world. It was a temple complex worthy of a true civilization, though its builders never got around to developing one. Its use, expansion, and renewal continued for around two thousand years until it was abruptly abandoned around 7000 BCE.

So before the birth of civilization, there were these few isolated examples of enigmatic cultures emerging during the Late Stone Age:

9000–7000 BCE	Göbekli Tepe, Turkey
7500–6000 BCE	Çatalhöyük, Turkey
4000–3200 BCE	Monte d'Accoddi, Sardinia
3600–2500 BCE	Ġgantija, Malta
3500 BCE	Sechin Bajo, Peru

But these were single temples or complexes that seemed to have served people who lived in the immediate area, then declined into obscurity; none of their builders created anything remotely similar to the Megalithic monuments of Britain, which can be numbered in the thousands and were spread over 130,000 square miles. It is fairly safe to say that the Megalithic culture of the British Isles has no connection to any of them. There, the first stone circles began to be erected around 3100 BCE. Give or take a century, this is about the same time as the first civilizations of Sumer, Ancient Egypt, and the Indus Valley began.

In other words, the Megalithic culture started at the very dawn of civilization. However, there seems no direct link between the Megalithic culture of the British Isles and these earliest of civilizations. They were Bronze Age societies with skills and inventions completely absent in the contemporary British Isles, which remained in the Stone Age until around 2000 BCE, and even then the use of bronze did not become widespread until around eight hundred years later (see chapter 9). Yet the Megalithic culture lasted an extraordinarily long time. Sumer and Harappa fell centuries before the Megalithic culture stopped building its monuments; Egyptian civilization fell twice and rose again; while the Minoans, Akkadians, Mycenaeans, and many more emerged from and vanished back into the mists of time as the Megalithic people continued unabated for over three thousand years. And their culture existed well before those of the Greeks, Romans, or Mayans. So how exactly did the Megalithic culture of the British Isles begin?

I have been referring to the British Isles. Before continuing, it's probably a good idea to clarify just what I mean by the name. In standard geographical terms, the name British Isles refers to the territories of both Great Britain and the Republic of Ireland and the many smaller islands that surround them. Unfortunately, the name could be construed to imply political claims by the British on the territory of the Irish. Various alternatives have been proposed, such as the Anglo-Celtic Isles and the Atlantic Archipelago, although they have not found their way into common usage. Interestingly in documents drafted between the United Kingdom and Irish governments, the term "these islands" is used. For those who are not from these parts, the United Kingdom refers to England, Wales, Scotland, and Northern Ireland, all separate countries but united politically in a similar way to the United States. Southern Ireland is a completely independent republic, officially called Ireland or Éire. The status of the northern part of Ireland is a sensitive issue, and the Republic of Ireland is a self-governing nation separate from Britain as a political entity, so I would just like to make it clear that I only use the term "British Isles" for convenience, as many of my readers will be in countries where this is a familiar term, and imply no political meaning. I am simply employing the name as it is commonly used in topographical terminology.

It also might be a good idea just to jump forward a few centuries from the end of the Megalithic era to explain just how the British Isles, or "these islands," got to be politically the way they are. By around 700 BCE all of this territory was occupied by the Celts, a people of which we will be learning much later in the book. Then, in the first century CE, the Romans invaded. They called the islands collectively Britanniae, and the part that they conquered, what is now England and Wales, Britannia. They never conquered the northern region, which they called Caledonia, and built a defensive structure across the north of Britannia called Hadrian's Wall. Ireland (both North and South) they called Hibernia. So both Ireland and Caledonia, which we now call Scotland, remained Celtic realms. During the 400s, the Roman Empire in Western Europe collapsed, the legions left Britannia, and Britain broke up into a number of separate Romano-Celtic kingdoms. By the 900s the east of Britain was conquered by the Anglo-Saxons from northern Germany, who created their own kingdom of Angle-land, now called England, leaving the west as a separate Romano-Celtic country now called Wales (which still has its own language). In 1066 England was conquered by the Normans of northern France, who went on to conquer Wales by the late 1200s. From then on both England and Wales were ruled as the single kingdom of Britain, which went on to take over Celtic Ireland during the 1500s and 1600s. Scotland remained an independent Celtic country until it joined with England and Wales as a single kingdom called Great Britain in the 1700s. Ultimately, the primarily Catholic southern part of Ireland gained its complete independence from Britain in 1937, although the largely Protestant north opted to remain part of the United Kingdom of Great Britain and Northern Ireland, usually referred to simply as the United Kingdom or the UK. For convenience, I shall refer to the island that is now composed of England, Scotland, and Wales as Britain and the island that is now composed of Northern Ireland and the Republic of Ireland as Ireland, and both these main islands and the many smaller islands belonging to these various countries as the British Isles.

Returning to the Megalithic culture of the British Isles, something similar also existed in northern France. This culture, centered primarily in what is now the region of Brittany, is also often referred to as "megalithic," leading to the notion that the two were linked. But were they? The ancient stone monuments of Brittany consist mainly of stone rows and individual standing stones; although there are a few small stone ovals, there are no stone circles or henge complexes anything like those found throughout the British Isles. By far the largest such monument in Brittany is Carnac, which consists of over three thousand standing stones, ranging from 2 to 13 feet high, arranged in more than thirty rows, some stretching for three-quarters of a mile. Although there are examples of small stone rows in the British Isles, there is nothing remotely like Carnac.[7] Carnac actually dates from around 3300 BCE, some two hundred years earlier than the first megalithic monuments on the other side of the English Channel. So is it possible that the Megalithic tradition of the British Isles originally began in France?

There was certainly a stone-monument-building culture in Brittany before one existed in the British Isles. Its oldest monument is the Cairn of Barnenez, an artificial mound, approximately 240 feet long, 80 feet wide, and 26 feet high. Built from around 14,000 tons of stone and containing eleven chambers entered by separate passages from the outside, it is a multiple burial mausoleum created in stages between 4500 and 4000 BCE.[8] Such monuments were common in Brittany until around 3500 BCE, but although the British Isles also had chambered tombs before and during the Megalithic period, they were of a very different design; for example, having single, not multiple, entrances. Furthermore, the Brittany tombs were decorated with simple glyphs, such as wavy lines and representations of axes and bows, which were completely absent in Britain or Ireland.[9] While it does indeed date from before the stone-circle-building society in the British Isles and its monuments are often confusingly described as "megalithic," there is little evidence that this culture in Neolithic Brittany had any influence on the Megalithic culture across the sea. Indeed, it seems to have been in decline well before the first stone circles were erected in the British Isles.

There *was* a tradition of building stone monuments in the British Isles just prior to the actual Megalithic period—the era of the stone circles. But this was confined to burial structures or tombs. Although modern humans have been burying their dead for at least one hundred thousand years, often along with grave goods, such as animal bones and various stone tools, until around twelve thousand years ago, interment was a simple procedure of burial in the ground, in a pit or trench. This may have been for reasons of hygiene, but the inclusion of grave goods implies additional motives such as religious practices, spiritual beliefs, and respect for the dead. Grave markers, such as small piles of stones or mounds of earth, didn't appear to any extent until the beginnings of agriculture —the deliberate cultivation of crops and domestication of animals as food sources—which started at the end of the last Ice Age, made possible by the warmer, wetter conditions that then occurred.[10]

The causes of ice ages, when global temperatures drop significantly, are still not fully understood, but they are thought to be due to various conditions, such as atmospheric composition altered by volcanic activity, comet or asteroid impacts, changes in ocean currents, and variations in solar output. The last ice age lasted from around 110,000 to 12,000 years ago, and at its height, some 20,000 years ago, permanent ice sheets, as much as 2.5 miles thick, covered much of northern Europe, Asia, and North America to below the Great Lakes; the British Isles were almost completely engulfed. The severe cold meant that even places such as the modern United States and southern Europe, which remained free from glaciations, were reduced to the kind of tundra conditions now found in northern Canada and Siberia. Not only were temperatures lower throughout the world, so was rainfall: a large part of the world's fresh water was tied up in ice. So during this long, cold, dry period, food supplies were scarce throughout much of the world, and put simply, *Homo sapiens* just didn't have the luxury to develop farming techniques. Humans remained as nomadic hunter-gatherers. Paradoxically, although the tropics remained warm, the plentiful food and game meant that the incentive to develop agriculture never really existed in those areas of the world. It was only when the Ice Age ended fairly abruptly around 12,000 years ago and the glaciers retreated above the Arctic Circle that the impetus to invent farming was initiated at higher latitudes.[11]

Large parts of the world that had been either uninhabitable or were places to barely eke out a living not only became vast new locations to live but also were highly fertile. The melting glaciers had left behind rich soils of sand, silt, and clay, deposited by the ice. Humans rapidly migrated into these areas, where fresh fauna and flora offered a new kind of life. Unlike in the tropics, where ecosystems were generally uniformly rich, with rain forests and savannas, the fertile areas of higher latitudes tended to center around water systems and coastal regions. This led inevitably to settlements, and while living together in larger numbers people began to work collectively, and the invention of farming soon followed. This was the birth of the Neolithic era (see chapter 2).[12]

Unlike the invention of bronze, the conception of agriculture occurred separately in various parts of the world, and with larger, permanent settlements came the more elaborate burials. Higher-status individuals tended to have their graves marked in various ways, by stones or earthen mounds, but these remained small and simple. Although Göbekli Tepe and Çatalhöyük in Turkey are remarkable early examples of the creation of stone-built temples and a brick-built town, they are enigmatic, isolated cases of sophisticated constructions that were both abandoned by 6000 BCE. Interestingly there is no evidence that the Göbekli Tepe structures were used as tombs, although the residents may have honored the dead in some way, while in Çatalhöyük the deceased were buried in simple graves. The next known man-made structures appear in France from around

4500 BCE—the elaborate, chambered burial mounds discussed above—almost all in Brittany.

But what was occurring in the British Isles? Geologists have determined that at the end of the Ice Age Britain was joined to continental Europe by a land bridge referred to as Doggerland, which stretched from southeastern England to the Netherlands and part of Germany. Humans are thought to have reinhabited the now ice-free Britain by following migrating herds of reindeer and then settling once they crossed Doggerland. Then around 6500 BCE rising sea levels submerged Doggerland, cutting off Britain to this day. At the time there were estimated to have been around five thousand hunter-gatherers living scattered throughout this newly created island. Some of these people also crossed to Ireland by dugout log boats and settled in small coastal communities, depending for much of their livelihood on the sea. The remains of such simple boats have been found conserved in mud and peat bogs in various parts of the British Isles.[13] Scientific examination of ancient pollen and vegetation preserved in prehistoric soil layers has determined that Britain and Ireland were much warmer and sunnier than they are today. In fact, the climate would have been more like that we would now find in parts of southern Europe: the kind of decent weather that so favored the development of Roman civilization millennia later. Indeed, this was the climate still enjoyed by the Megalithic culture that emerged some three thousand years after Britain was divided from the rest of Europe.[14]

The term "Neolithic" refers to the period when hunter-gatherers and people in simple fishing communities began to adopt farming techniques, deliberately growing and cultivating plants and domesticating animals. In some parts of the world this began soon after the end of the Ice Age, but in the British Isles this didn't really get going until around 4000 BCE, once the population had grown to around one hundred thousand people in Britain and forty thousand in Ireland. (The term often used for the period between the end of the Ice Age and the Neolithic is Mesolithic, meaning Middle Stone Age.)

It was not long after the Neolithic period commenced that the first tombs were built. They began with what have been called long barrows ("barrow" being an early English word for a mound). The oldest to survive is thought to be the West Kennet Long Barrow in south-central England, which dates from around 3600 BCE. It is an earthen and chalk mound approximately 330 feet long and 80 feet wide, rising to a height of over 10 feet. From one end, a passage, well over 6 feet high, with two pairs of alcoves off to the sides, leads to a 10-foot-square chamber about 40 feet inside the mound. The structure, still intact after 5.5 millennia, was made from large monoliths, standing upright or laid one above the other and joined by heavy lintel stones, before being covered with earth and rubble to form the grassy mound. Outside, the single entrance is flanked by further huge megaliths, the largest over 12 feet tall and weighing more than 20 tons. The barrow is thought to have contained the remains of around fifty people and was probably in use for many generations.

Such long barrows are found throughout much of southern Britain, like Wayland's Smithy, about 20 miles to the southwest of the West Kennet barrow. Dating from around 3500 BCE, it is smaller but of similar construction to that barrow: a rock-chambered tomb covered with earth, its entrance flanked by four shaped standing stones, the tallest over 10 feet high. The barrow is 43 feet wide and 185 feet long and is thought to have contained the remains of as many as fourteen bodies. (Its present name dates from the Anglo-Saxon period, over four thousand years after it was built, when legend told how it was created by Wayland the Smith, a mythical Anglo-Saxon figure who forged weapons for the gods.) There were many such long barrows, thought to have been built between around 3600 and 3300 BCE, scattered throughout southern Britain. Archaeologists have determined that the outside perimeters of such barrows were originally supported by drystone walls, but of particular interest is that for some unknown reason the burial chambers were limited to only one end of the barrow. About four times longer than wide, the mounds sloped away from the entrance to the lower end, and around two-thirds of the structure mysteriously contained no further chambers or evidence of burials or grave goods.[15] Long barrows seem to have been created as tombs for individuals of a special status. As they contained the remains of children as well as male and female adults, they were probably reserved for tribal leaders and their families.

As well as the long barrows, the same period saw the creation of far more, but smaller, portal tombs. These consisted of a close arrangement of standing stones, usually three or four, which supported a large capstone to form a burial chamber. The entire structure was then covered with earth to create a mound. Today, most of these burial mounds have eroded away, leaving only the skeleton of the original megaliths to appear something like a kind of giant stone table standing alone on the landscape. These exposed structures are commonly known as dolmens, a name thought to originate from an old Celtic term meaning "stone portal," from where the archaeological term "portal tomb" derives.[16]

Dolmens exist in considerable numbers throughout southern Britain and Ireland, one of the largest being in South West Wales. Called the Pentre Ifan (Ivan's Village) Dolmen, it consists of an 18-ton capstone that is 16 feet long, 8 feet wide, and 3 feet thick and is held 8 feet off the ground by three standing stones, while three other, smaller monoliths remain, which had once flanked and sealed the entrance when the structure was covered by a mound. Another typical dolmen, a 14-ton, 18-foot-long capstone supported by three 5-foot-tall upright monoliths, is Lanyon Quoit in the county of Cornwall, in the extreme southwest of England (*quoit* being another old name for such a monument). Also in the county of Cornwall, on Bodmin Moor, there stands Trethevy Quoit, which consists of a 12-foot long, 10-ton sloping capstone supported by five upright monoliths, the tallest about 9 feet tall. Poulnabrone Dolmen in western Ireland has a 12-foot-long, relatively thin capstone, held 6 feet above the ground by four monoliths. Spinster's Rock in the county of Devon, in England's West Country, has a 14-foot by 10-foot 16-ton capstone, supported 8 feet above the ground by three

Fig. 3.2. The locations of just some of the long barrows
and dolmens of the British Isles.

standing stones. In the county of Oxfordshire in central England, there stand the Whispering Knights, a collapsed dolmen consisting of four uprights, the tallest about 8 foot high, with its capstone now flat on the ground. And in the extreme southeast of England, in the county of Kent, is the quaintly named Kit's Coty House, which consists of three 8-foot upright stones supporting a capstone measuring 13 by 9 feet. These are just a few of the hundreds of dolmens that still survive in the British Isles; most of them, however, only remain as fallen stones.

These dolmens date from 3600 to 3100 BCE, a time frame similar to that of the long barrows, and seem to have belonged to the same culture. Archaeologists believe that the mounds that covered them were built to a design similar to that of the long barrows: much longer than wide, with the burial chamber situated at one end. Essentially, they would have been less elaborate long barrows with an entrance leading directly into the chamber rather than being accessed by a passage.[17] The reason long barrows have tended to survive as mounds, whereas the portal tombs have eroded, is that the barrow mounds were built from both earth *and* chunks of rock. These dolmens, or portal tombs, were probably built by smaller or poorer communities, where a lack of sufficient resources or labor prohibited the creation of the more elaborate constructions. Nonetheless, both structures would have been considerable undertakings. Large stones had to be quarried and shaped and then dragged to where they were erected, and the lintels and capstones were probably hauled into place once mounds of earth were stacked around them to form ramps.

Judging by their burial practices, it seems that the Barrow culture lived in stable communities where they planted crops such as wheat and barley and raised herds of sheep, pigs, and cattle. They had not yet learned to weave, so clothing would have been garments made from animal hide. From examination of the human bones of the period, it seems that the average life span was between thirty and thirty-five years. Permanent settlements were pretty much confined to coastal areas, where there was a plentiful supply of fish, while farming communities tended to move every so often. The intricacies of crop cultivation had not yet been mastered, so once the nutrients of a piece of land had been depleted, the settlement would move to some other fertile location nearby. After a while the land had lain fallow for long enough to regenerate, so the community could return to a previous settlement. For this reason buildings were made from wood, with stone structures being reserved for the dead.

Long barrows likely served a succession of generations whose settlements were moved regularly around them. The barrows and portal tombs probably served as the central point of a rotating community made up of just a few hundred people. Archaeologists have estimated that with the builders using simple Stone Age tools, construction of the West Kennet and Wayland's Smithy long barrows, for example, would have been extensive and backbreaking endeavors but could have been accomplished within around a decade. As these tombs had movable stone "doorways," it is possible that they were also used as shrines that could be periodically opened, not only for new interments but also for ceremonies concerning some kind of ancestor worship. It was not until around 3300 BCE that the people of the British Isles began to develop crop rotation, alternatively planting different types of crops in a system of divided fields so that the land would be replenished and remain fertile. This innovation had presumably occurred through trial and error, as it would be millennia before the chemistry of farming was understood. It led inevitably to permanent settlements of much larger populations—and, so it would seem, the beginnings of the Megalithic age.[18]

Over the years there has been much speculation concerning whether the Megalithic culture owes its origins to Brittany, although modern archaeology has pretty much ruled this out. We have already seen that the type of stone structures erected in Brittany were markedly different from those in the British Isles. Although there are chambered graves, often referred to as dolmens, in Brittany, they are also very different from those of the pre-Megalithic era in the British Isles. They consist of two parallel rows of upright stones, around ten on average, with a series of horizontal stones placed across the tops of them to form a tunnel, nothing like a portal tomb. There are one or two stone formations that do resemble dolmens, but these are of a later period, and the similarities could be coincidental, or they might even have been copied from those in Britain. The prehistoric culture in Brittany was indeed remarkable, having erected some of the world's oldest monuments. But it seems to have had nothing to do with Megalithic stone-circle-building culture in the British Isles. There are small arrangements of standing stones in Brittany known as cromlechs, of which there are just a few dozen. But these are stone ovals, horseshoes, and squares; in fact, there is not a true stone circle among them. This name has led to some confusion as it is also applied to dolmens in parts of Wales. The word "cromlech" actually comes from an ancient Celtic term meaning "a collection of standing stones," not a specific type of monument. The Bretons may have erected stone monoliths, as did other Stone Age people around the world, but they did not create the kind of stone circles, megalithic complexes, henge monuments, and the mysterious earthworks found exclusively in the British Isles (see chapter 1).

So the Barrow culture of the British Isles seems to have developed independently from the stone-monument-building culture in Brittany, as did the Megalithic era that followed. The question then is, Where *did* the Megalithic era begin? One might assume that it started in southern Britain, where the majority of the earlier long barrows and dolmens are found. It seems not. Astonishingly the first stone circle was built far away from both Brittany and southern Britain—on the Orkney Isles, off the northern tip of Scotland.

4

The Beginning

The Stones of Stenness

THE OLDEST DATED STONE CIRCLE in the British Isles is found approximately 700 miles north of Stonehenge, on an island called Mainland. With an area of about 200 square miles, it is the largest of the Orkney Isles, which lie some 10 miles off the northern tip of Scotland. Known as the Stones of Stenness (after the name of a nearby village), the monument now consists of four stones, up to 16 feet high, standing in a semicircle, with two smaller standing stones and a third lying flat grouped together just inside the arrangement. Now called the cove, these smaller stones were only erected in the early twentieth century as a tourist attraction. Wealthy sightseers would be told that the flat stone was an altar where human sacrifices were made. It was partly dismantled in the 1970s. However, archaeological excavations have determined that although the cove never formed part of the original megalithic monument, its stones were probably fragments of fallen monoliths from the ancient stone circle, rearranged to form the supposed altar in 1907. As with many stone circles over the years, stones have been toppled and broken up for building materials or smashed apart by religious zealots. In fact, in 1814 a newcomer to the Orkneys, one Captain Mackay, who leased the land on which the stones stood, deliberately attempted to remove the entire monument. Apparently, he was angered by local people who were performing "rituals" there. What kind of rituals is not recorded. Outraged, the islanders managed to put a stop to the demolition before the Stones of Stenness were completely destroyed.

From the radiocarbon dating of organic material found beneath the stones still standing, the circle seems to have been erected around 3100 BCE, and from telltale signs in the soil, it seems that it once consisted of twelve monoliths, equally spaced in a circle of just over 100 feet in diameter. Archaeologists have found evidence that a further stone, probably a king stone (see chapter 1), long since moved or destroyed, stood about 200 feet outside the circle to the southeast, which happens to align with the midwinter sunrise as seen from the center of the ring. These standing stones would probably have been between 16 and 20 feet high, but although they were as tall as some of the largest megaliths elsewhere in the British Isles, they would have been relatively light. The type of sandstone from which they are fashioned is known as flagstone, a sedimentary rock divided into natural layers, making it comparatively easy to quarry into slabs. The remaining monoliths are only about 4 feet wide and 1 foot thick, giving them an elongated, tablet-like appearance, different from the hefty look of monuments such as Avebury and Stonehenge. They are thought to have been quarried near what is now the village of Finstown, about 3 miles to the east, where, interestingly, a modern quarry still exists today. There are many other standing stones in the area (see chapter 6), but these have been dated to around five hundred years after the Stones of Stenness.[1]

The Orkney people who erected the Stones of Stenness also developed their own style of pottery, known as grooved ware. It gets its name from the characteristic grooved designs that decorated the rims of the unusual, flat-bottomed, straight-sided pots, the remains of which have been found in and around the Orkney settlements and monuments of the period. For some years scientists have been able to date ceramic material using a process called thermoluminescence. When pottery is fired it undergoes a change in crystalline structure that alters over sub-sequent time and can be measured to determine how long ago the item was made. However, thermoluminescence dating is only accurate to a limited extent: low levels of radiation from certain types of rocks or exposure to ultraviolet rays from sunlight, for example, can contaminate the sample and render testing unreliable. In recent years a new and far more accurate technique has been developed to date pottery. Called rehydroxylation dating, it measures how much water pottery has absorbed since the time it was fired.[2] By using a combination of these techniques archaeologists have now dated the first grooved ware to around 3100 BCE—the same time that the Stones of Stenness were erected. This has led to the name Grooved Ware culture being applied to the inhabitants of the Orkney Isles who built what appears to be the first stone circle.[3]

Grooved ware is found at other Neolithic sites in the British Isles, spreading quickly from north to south, over a period of around a century. This couldn't have been though invasion —the population of the Orkneys was too small to pose any kind of threat to anyone else—but rather it was the result of a rapid expansion of cultural influence. But it was not only the new type of pottery that was systematically adopted elsewhere in the British Isles but also the building of stone dwellings, and, more importantly, the creation of stone circles. Grooved ware ceramics have been found at nearly all of the earliest stone circles, very much implying that they were linked to the same cultural innovations that began on the Orkney Isles. Grooved ware pottery is actually found at Stonehenge, dating from around 3000 BCE, implying that those who built the first stone circle at the site (see chapter 1) had adopted the culture that began on the Orkneys only a century before.[4]

Since so many grooved ware pots—from small drinking vessels to the size of buckets—have been found at the earliest stone circles and in contemporary burial sites, it is likely that their design held some special, perhaps religious, significance. And as the oldest examples are found on the Orkney Isles, it would appear that this new thinking—spiritual, social, or whatever—that led to stone-circle building actually originated there. Some commentators have argued that such cultural innovation could not have originated in such an isolated area with a limited population. The argument is sound, but the problem is that there is, so far, no convincing evidence that it originated anywhere else. We have already discounted any direct influence from Brittany (see chapter 3).

As for the south of Britain: if Grooved Ware culture originated there, how did it spread through the British Isles, beginning in the far north? Although various exotic ideas have been proposed, such as seafaring migrants from the Mediterranean or the Middle East, perhaps the early Egyptians or Sumerians, the kind of dwellings, building techniques, ceramic ware, and monuments found on the Orkney Isles bear little similarity to anything from that contemporary part of the world. From a geographical perspective, the only reasonable possibility that it could have begun somewhere other than in the Orkney Isles is that it came from Scandinavia, about 300 miles across the North Sea to the east of the islands. However, nothing has been found in Denmark, Norway, or Sweden anything like the culture on the Orkneys. The contemporary Scandinavians are known as the Pitted Ware culture, named after the ornamentation consisting of horizontal rows of depressions that decorate their pottery. Not only do their ceramics bear no resemblance to anything found on the Orkney Isles, they also were chiefly a hunter-gatherer people, still in the Mesolithic age.[5] They certainly never built any stone circles. So even though it seems highly improbable that the Megalithic culture emerged on the isolated Orkney Isles, it has to have started somewhere and—at present—no other logical conclusion can be reached.

The Stones of Stenness seems to have been the first stone circle built anywhere in the British Isles. So what is known about it, historically? As the Romans never conquered this far north, we have no records from them concerning the Orkney Isles. The Vikings from Norway settled there in the ninth century CE, and when antiquarians began visiting and recording the stones during the eighteenth and nineteenth centu-

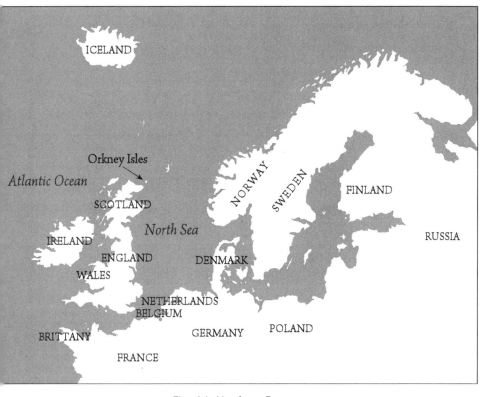

Fig. 4.1. Northern Europe.

ries, local people seem to have believed that the site had been a temple associated with the Norse god Odin. However, it dates from four millennia before the Vikings arrived.

Incredibly, a settlement that housed some of the very people who built the Stones of Stenness still survives, virtually intact, due to a storm that buried it in sand around 2500 BCE. Called Skara Brae, this Neolithic village stands on the coast, some 6 miles northwest of the stone circle. It has been uncovered by archaeologists and found to have consisted of a group of clustered stone wall dwellings, set into the ground with only their thatch-covered roofs visible above the surface. The layout of this astonishing underground settlement, with its houses connected by a series of tunnels, was a clever way to keep warm and dry in the cold, damp climate of the windswept Orkney Isles. Occupied from around 3100 BCE, it is the best preserved site of its kind anywhere in the world. Not only does it date from the same time as the Stones of Stenness, but scientific analysis also has shown that pottery found there precisely matches similar fragments excavated from beneath the circle's monoliths. This ancient village is unlike anything found anywhere else in the British Isles dating from before 3100 BCE. When Skara Brae was being established, the inhabitants of the rest of the British Isles had yet to create permanent, stone-built settlements; elsewhere dwellings were made primarily from wood (see chapter 3). Although such buildings occasionally had stone foundations, they were nothing remotely like those at Skara Brae.[6]

So who were these people? They certainly had no direct connection to the Barrow culture hundreds of miles to the south. Not only were they separated geographically from the inhabitants of southern Britain and Ireland, the distinctive long barrows and dolmen tombs of the period also are completely absent in the Orkney Isles or, for that matter, anywhere else in the northern British Isles.[7] DNA analysis of human remains from the period can tell us only so much, and that is that the people of the Orkneys were indistinguishable from the inhabitants of the rest of the British Isles at the time (see chapter 11). Archaeological work, though, does suggest that the Grooved Ware culture emerged among those formerly living on the Orkneys. Before the building of Skara Brae, the site was already occupied. The houses were built around mounds of human domestic waste known as middens, basically heaps of discarded shells, animal bones, and other items associated with past human occupation. Such settlements on the Orkney Isles, dating up to the building of Skara Brae, are located close to the shores, implying that the inhabitants made their living primarily from the sea. This is supported by excavations revealing that their diet consisted mainly of fish; mollusks, such as crabs and lobsters; and various shellfish, along with edible seaweeds, such as kelp, carrageen, and laver, while clothing was made from the skins of marine mammals, such as seal and walrus.

Although these people predated the Grooved Ware culture, they did build stone dwellings similar to those at Skara Brae.[8] The earliest stone houses built on the Orkney Isles—in fact, anywhere in the British Isles—are on the island of Papa Westray, to the north of Mainland Isle. The remains of this small settlement, called the Knap of Howar, now consist of two round-cornered, rectangular stone buildings, linked by passageways. The walls of their seaward-facing sides, where the entrances are situated, are aboveground, but the rest of the dwellings are built into the sloping hillside. They share many features found at Skara Brae but date from around five hundred years earlier. These are in fact the oldest preserved houses anywhere in northern Europe, dating from even earlier than the Barrow culture of southern Britain and Ireland. The Knap of Howar is the best preserved such site, but archaeologists have discovered evidence of clusters of other early stone buildings dating from 3600 to 3100 BCE dotted around the Orkney Isles.[9] They were occupied, it seems, by the very people who went on to build Skara Brae and the Stones of Stenness and to begin the Megalithic age.

The big question is, Why did the Orkney Islanders start building stone housing before anyone else in the British Isles? It may have been through necessity. While the islands are now largely treeless, archaeology has shown that until around 5,600 years ago the lower-lying areas were thickly wooded by hazel, birch, and willow trees, the remains of which now exist in peat bogs. However, the use of timber by humans gradually deforested the islands, starting with the smaller ones, such as Papa Westray. With no wood for creating dwellings, homes began to be built from stone. Eventually, trees virtually disappeared from all the islands, so stone buildings replaced the earlier wooden ones throughout the Orkneys.[10] When archaeologists first realized this, they were confronted by a mystery. What did the later islanders use for fuel? Recent excavations of Skara Brae and other Grooved Ware settlements on the islands have found evidence that fires were made from dried seaweed. Seaweed was probably also used to make roofs for the buildings. The Orkneys still had a plentiful supply of tough grasses, so straw rope could be made. Until the twentieth century, traditional roofing on the Orkney Isles consisted of ropes attached to stones, over which seaweed was thatched. It's quite possible that it was the same with the ancient dwellings.[11]

Those who began the Grooved Ware culture around 5,100 years ago were almost certainly the same people who had been living on the Orkney Isles for centuries. As they primarily made their living from the sea, they had long lived in stable, permanent communities, rather than moving around as nomadic hunter-gatherers. They were already used to living in one place and in larger numbers than most Mesolithic people. Once deforestation forced them to change, it would not have taken much to adapt their lifestyle to live in permanent stone dwellings. And the building of stone dwellings probably led to the construction of stone monuments. The regular quarrying of stone meant that they inadvertently developed the skills necessary to build stone circles. The islanders had gradually learned how to cut, move, and erect ever larger stones. Despite the sophistication of their society, they were still in the Stone Age. It would be centuries before the Bronze Age came to the British Isles. Rock would need to be quarried and shaped with stone, flint, and bone implements. But the natural layers into which the native flagstone was stratified made it comparatively easy. If they had only hard rock, such as granite, to work with, it's unlikely that the Stones of Stenness would ever have been erected.

This doesn't explain *why* the Orkney Islanders built the Stenness stone circle, but it does explain how they were able to erect such a monument before anyone else in the British Isles. Whatever their impetus was, the project would have required a great deal of time and effort by a large number of people working together for a common cause. None of this would have been possible without a relatively large population, a stable society, and a surplus of labor, freed up from the day-to-day tasks of survival. In other words, the Orkney Islanders were prosperous and well fed. There was a steep rise in the general standard of living by the time Skara Brae was built, which was due to the adoption of agriculture to complement an already decent livelihood from the sea. The island-ers had long been a boat-building people who made craft from dugout logs and hide-covered canoes from the skins of aquatic mammals, in which they not only fished and hunted seal and walrus but also traded between the islands and the mainland. Farming, in the form of animal husbandry, had reached northern Scotland by around 3500 BCE, and the Orkney Islanders began to copy these innovations, bringing back sheep, pigs, and cattle, which they bred successfully into their own live-stock herds. Archaeologists have found the bones of many such animals around such settlements as the Knap of Howar, occurring in increas-ing numbers over the decades leading up to the period the Stones of Stenness were erected. By the time Skara Brae was built, the Orkney Islanders were already a Neolithic farming society, growing crops such as barley, as ancient seeds have been excavated there and in other con-temporary settlements.[12] So by 3100 BCE the islanders had added agri-culture to their long-established living earned from the sea. Plentiful food led to a rise in population, and the limited area of living space afforded by the Orkneys meant the growth of settlements close by one another. This in turn would have necessitated a degree of cooperation between various settlements that would not be required on the British mainland. Accordingly we have the growth of an island-wide society more advanced than anything else in the British Isles at the time, some-thing strikingly revealed by the way they lived.

Skara Brae consisted of seven clustered dwellings composed of sin-gle, rounded rooms measuring an average of 400 square feet. Each was entered through a low doorway sealed with a stone slab that could be slid open and shut. The homes even contained pieces of furniture, such as closets, seats, and storage boxes, all made from stone, as were hearth areas; beds were created by a stone rectangle, which would probably have been filled with straw overlaid by animal hides. An eighth building has no such furnishings but was divided into cubicles and seems to have been used as a workplace for making tools, such as bone needles, stone axes, and flint knives. Amazingly a drainage system was incorporated into the overall design of the settlement, including a toilet in each house in the form of a stone-divided cubicle. It may not seem like much by today's standards, but compared with anything else in the British Isles at the time, this was the height of luxury.[13]

Skara Brae is thought to have been home to around fifty individuals at any one time. There were other contemporary villages on the islands, up to twice the size, but none have remained anywhere nearly as well preserved. Just to the north of the Stones of Stenness, on the shores of the Loch of Harry, is one such village. Called the Barnhouse Settlement, it was excavated in the 1980s to reveal that it originally consisted of around fifteen dwellings similar to those at Skara Brae.[14] There were probably dozens of such ancient Neolithic villages dotted around Mainland Island, each home to between fifty and one hundred people. The fragmentary remains of some of these settlements have been identified, but it is thought that, as most were built close to shore, many have been lost to the ocean due to rising sea levels and the erosion of the exposed coastline. Some, however, may still await discovery, buried beneath the ground. Today around twenty thousand people inhabit the islands, which is pretty much the same number of people who lived there when records began in 1801. However, it is impossible to tell just how many people lived on the Orkneys five thousand years ago, but it must have been a thriving population, with workers to spare.

By around 3100 BCE the islanders had presumably united as a single society with common aims, as they came together to create the Stenness stone circle. Such an undertaking would have required hundreds of people working in unison—quarrying, moving, and erecting the stones for the monument. Like the rest of the Neolithic British Isles, there is no evidence that the islanders tamed large mammals, such as oxen or ponies, to work as draft animals. No one had invented the yoke or harness, for a start. In fact, the use of animals as beasts of burden did not occur anywhere in the British Isles until the Bronze Age, over a thousand years later. So the islanders had to drag the huge stones themselves. They knew how to make rope, so large numbers of people could combine their efforts. But how did they drag stones weighing around 6 tons each? The general consensus concerning the movement of large megalithic stones in later mainland Britain, such as those at Stonehenge, is that they were dragged along on wooden rollers. It wouldn't need many such rollers, as each would be moved from back to front as the stone rolled forward.[15] But were there still enough large trees left on the Orkney Isles for rollers to be made? The same question would apply to the kind of heavy timber A-frames thought to have been used elsewhere in the British Isles to haul the stones into their final upright positions. Although the climate was warmer during the period in question, the far north of Britain would still have been snow covered in winter. It is therefore possible that the islanders actually impacted snow in front of the stones and managed to slide them along somehow. It is also possible that they built ramps from snow in order to raise the stones to be dropped down into their pre-dug holes.

Whatever compelled the Orkney Islanders to build such a monument, the Stenness stone circle is clear evidence that some kind of new thinking had occurred. Archaeology has shown that the people who erected the Stones of Stenness were well fed and lived comfortably. By 3100 BCE their lives were no longer dominated completely by the toil to survive. The islanders—certainly some of them—were enjoying something completely new: leisure time. They had time to think, create, and invent: a state of affairs rife for fresh ideas. The reasoning behind the building of the oldest known stone circle in the British Isles must have emerged from some kind of innovative religious or social concepts that consequently developed. And it's not only the Stones of Stenness that suggest the emergence of a new culture but also the contemporary change in ceramic style.

As we have seen, around the very time that the Stones of Stenness were erected, grooved ware pottery started to be made on the Orkney Isles. This is surely more than coincidence. Before 3100 BCE the style of pottery found on the islands was what is called unstan ware. Named after a site on Mainland Island where it was first discovered, it

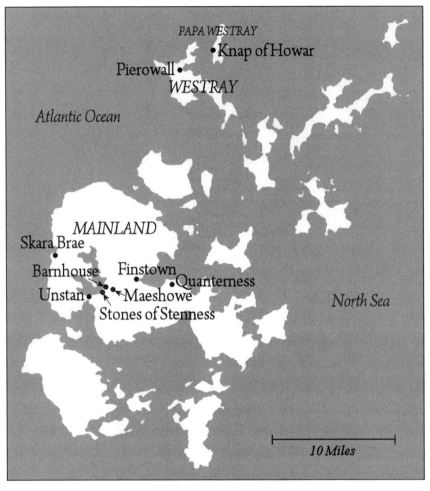

Fig. 4.2. The Orkney Isles.

is characterized by a rounded design, very different from the angular grooved ware that followed. Unstan ware has been found at the Knap of Howar and at other settlements throughout the Orkney Islands, dating from around 3600 BCE until the appearance of grooved ware some five hundred years later. It has also been found at numerous burial sites across the islands dating from this period, leading to the name Unstan Ware culture being applied to the islanders of this time. They were almost certainly the same people who became the Grooved Ware culture, as both buried their dead in distinctive round tombs not found anywhere else in the British Isles during the period in question. Unstan ware is actually named after one of these earlier such tombs. Called the Unstan Chambered Cairn, it lies two miles to the south-west of the Stenness Stones and is a typical tomb of the period from 3600 to 3100 BCE, consisting of a circular mound built over a central stone chamber, accessed by a long passageway. The shape, construction, and entire layout of these so-called passage tombs are completely different from those of the long barrows and dolmens in southern Britain and Ireland (see chapter 3). At the time, this style of burial mound was unique to the Orkney Isles. Elsewhere, tombs mounds were elongated rather than circular and lacked the low stone tunnels that led to the Orkney burial chambers.[16]

Although the Orkney tombs continued to have their unique, round external shape and the long entrance tunnels, the design of the central chamber abruptly changed around 3100 BCE. One of the earliest examples is the Quanterness Cairn on the eastern side of Mainland Island, which dates from that time. Its central chamber is surrounded by side chambers that are not found in earlier tombs. This distinctive change from the tombs of the Unstan period, with a single burial chamber, must have marked the same transformation in thinking that accompanied the emergence of grooved ware pottery and the building of the Stenness stone circle. Excavations at Quanterness in the 1970s uncovered the remains of 157 individuals of all ages, and it is thought that the tomb originally contained around 400 people buried over many generations. These new burial mounds, which continued to be used and built for over five hundred years, have been termed Maeshowe-style tombs, of which seven still survive on the Orkney Isles, although there were no doubt many more that have been lost to the sea. They are named after the best-preserved example, which stands about half a mile to the east of the Stones of Stenness. The Maeshowe mound is 115 feet in diameter and rises to a height of 24 feet. Its low entrance passage is 3 feet high and about 36 feet long, leading to a 12-foot-high square chamber, measuring about 15 feet on each side. Some of the larger stones used to create Maeshowe weigh over 3 tons. The central chamber is constructed of flat stone slabs, many traversing the entire sides of the chamber, with the top part of the walls constructed of overlapping slabs to create a beehive-shaped roof. In each corner is a cleverly designed buttress to support the ceiling, each made from stacked stones, together with a large standing stone about 8 feet high. Three side chambers, or cells, averaging about 6 feet by 5 feet and about 3 feet high, are accessed by 2.5-foot-square entrances, each built halfway along the side and rear walls, some 2.5 feet above the ground. Today, a large stone, thought to have been used to seal them, lies on the floor outside each of these cells.[17]

Maeshowe has been emptied by a variety of tomb robbers and souvenir hunters over the centuries, including the Vikings, who even left graffiti at the site. Nordic runes (the old Scandinavian alphabet) dating from the twelfth century are found all over the walls of the central chamber. Many tell us who carved them—such names as Vermundr, Thorir, and Haermund Hardaxe—while others include various lewd comments boasting of sexual exploits. Quite contrary to the notion that such places were once used as temples to Odin (see page 59), the Vikings clearly had no respect for the site. Interestingly, some of this age-old graffiti tells us that treasure was supposedly hidden there; the Vikings probably tore the place apart looking for it. Consequently, little in the way of human remains has survived for modern archaeologists to examine. Although a newspaper article in 1861 reported that two female "mummies" and the skeleton of a man over ten feet tall were found there in that year, few people, even at the time, took the claim seriously.[18] Nonetheless, enough has been discovered in recent years, such as shards of grooved ware pottery, to date Maeshowe to being around 5,100 years old. It is an astonishing architectural achievement for its time, and like the other Maeshowe-style tombs, it seems to have been a completely local innovation.

Estimates for the amount of time needed to build Maeshowe vary between forty thousand and one hundred thousand work-hours; either way, it required vast effort and enormous commitment. Of particular interest is that the long, straight entrance passage at Maeshowe is constructed to let the direct light of the setting sun illuminate the central chamber at the winter solstice (the shortest day of the year), around December 21. Undoubtedly, this was more than coincidence. Just like the Stones of Stenness, the structure was seemingly associated with some religious or other formal activity connected with midwinter. It therefore seems likely that the Maeshowe-style mounds were more than just tombs. Some scholars propose that they were used *primarily* as ceremonial sites, the burials being secondary, in a similar manner to how medieval cathedrals were principally places of worship, although they also contained crypts in which the dead were laid to rest. As the Stones of Stenness appear to have had a king stone aligned to the midwinter sunrise, it's possible that, on the shortest day of the year, a ceremony took place at the stone circle at dawn and another at Maeshowe at sunset. The two sites are about a mile apart, and an ancient Neolithic track, possibly a processional way, joins them together.

Some extraordinary examples of Neolithic art also accompanied the beginning of this new culture. During excavations at Skara Brae, a number of strange stone balls were found. About the size of tennis balls, they are carved with enigmatic grooves and bumps, with one covered in sixty-seven pyramid-shaped protrusions. Another similar object, of the same size but with six equally spaced round knobs, was found during excavations of another Neolithic settlement at the Ness of Brodgar near the Stones of Stenness. Referred to by archaeologists as petrospheres, they don't seem to have been used as any kind of tool, as they reveal no indication of the sort of wear and tear expected to be found on work implements. Such items, dating from around 3000 BCE onward, have been discovered elsewhere in the British Isles, at sites where grooved ware pottery is also found.[19] At present, their purpose remains a mystery, yet another enigma accompanying the birth of the stone-circle-building culture.

In 1981 among the remains of a badly damaged Maeshowe-style

passage tomb near Pierowall on the island of Westray to the north of Mainland, a new discovery was made: a megalith, about 4 feet long and broken in two. The first piece was found by workers at a local quarry and the second by archaeologists from Cardiff University who conducted an excavation following the discovery. It was determined that the stone was part of a larger lintel that was once set over the tomb's entrance. Known as the Westray Stone, it is now on display at the island's museum at Pierowall. Decorated with a series of double spirals and concentric circles, it dates from around the same time as the Stones of Stenness and is the earliest known example of such ornamentation found anywhere in the British Isles.[20] The carvings survived because the stone had remained buried for millennia, but it is thought that similar markings may have adorned the exterior stones of other passage tombs such as Maeshowe but have eroded away in the relentless wind and rain that batter the Orkney Islands.

So on the Orkney Isles we have the Grooved Ware culture, with its new types of passage tombs and dwellings developing from the simpler, earlier structures of the Unstan Ware culture. Around 3100 BCE there were unique artistic innovations in the form of pottery, the mysterious petrospheres, and the spiral designs carved into stone. And at the same time the islanders erected the Stones of Stenness. All the evidence suggests that what was to become the unique Megalithic culture of the British Isles began there. The same grooved ware ceramics, petrospheres, and spiral carving are found at subsequent sites throughout the British Isles, some of these sites also having circular passage tombs. And at all these locations we find the local people building their own stone circles. For whatever purpose they were erected, they must have been of immense importance to those who created them. Over a period of around a hundred years separate peoples, spread far and wide over 130,000 square miles, suddenly, and for some unknown reason, started to adopt the ways of the enigmatic Grooved Ware culture, and the Megalithic age was born.

5

Progression

*The Discovery of Stone Circles
throughout the British Isles*

AS NORTHEASTERN SCOTLAND IS THE CLOSEST region to the
Orkney Isles, we might expect this to be where the influence of the
Grooved Ware culture first spread. Many stone circles were built in this
part of Scotland, of which well over a hundred survive. The oldest of
them, however, date from around 2700 BCE, four centuries after the
Stones of Stenness (see chapter 6). The culture's earliest appearance in
Scotland, other than in the Orkneys, was on its northwestern islands,
the Hebrides, probably because the inhabitants shared a similar, island-
dwelling way of life, making their livelihood from the sea.

On the west coast of Lewis, the largest and most northerly of the
Hebrides islands, is the Callanish Stone Circle, often described as
Scotland's Stonehenge. Although it may be the best preserved of the
larger stone circles in the country, it does not have the arrangement of
lintel arches unique to the real Stonehenge. The circle, consisting of thirteen standing stones, ranging from 8 to 13 feet high, is about 37 feet in
diameter. The megaliths have a similar, elongated, tablet-like appearance
to the Stones of Stenness but are made of a local rock called Lewisian
gneiss, giving them a rough, craggy appearance. Rows of standing stones

radiate from the ring in a cruciform pattern, but these are thought to have been added later, possibly at the same time that avenues were incorporated into other megalithic complexes, around 2600 BCE (see chapter 1). There is also a collapsed chambered tomb within the circle that includes a further standing stone; there, fragments of so-called Beaker ware pottery have been excavated, ceramics that did not occur in the British Isles until after 2500 BCE (see chapter 9). Dating the Callanish Stone Circle has been something of a problem, as less in the way of datable organic material has been found beneath the stones than at Stenness. However, as well as the Beaker ware, fragments of grooved ware pottery have been excavated from the Callanish Stone Circle, which modern rehydroxylation methods (see chapter 4) have dated to as early as 3050 BCE. At present, the Callanish monument is thought to be the second oldest stone circle after the Stones of Stenness.[1]

The Callanish Stone Circle is somewhat smaller than the Stones of Stenness and originally had thirteen rather than twelve stones. It's difficult to tell whether there was a king stone standing outside the main circle, as ground-penetrating radar suggests that many of the later, outlying stones were moved on various occasions during the Neolithic period, leaving telltale signs of various holes that now add confusion to surveys. Some experts believe that the large stone that forms part of the collapsed tomb, which stands almost 16 feet high, might once have been set some distance outside the main circle to mark the midwinter sunrise. So far, no passage tombs of the Unstan or Maeshowe type have been found in the Hebrides, but neither have any settlements of the period when the Callanish Stone Circle was erected. The latest thinking is that the remains of tombs and villages of the early Neolithic era on the islands have been lost to rising sea levels. Whatever future discoveries might reveal, five thousand years ago the inhabitants of the Isle of Lewis were clearly influenced by the culture of the Orkneys, 130 miles to the northwest: within a century of the building of the Stones of Stenness, they had adopted the distinctive type of grooved ware pottery and erected their own stone circle.[2]

The remains of many stone circles are found on the Hebrides islands, but few have been excavated. The Lochbuie Stone Circle on the island of Mull, south of Lewis, is one. Dating from around 3000 BCE, it measures approximately 40 feet in diameter and consists of nine stones up to 6 feet high. They are much smaller than the stones of Callanish and Stenness, probably due to the difficulty in cutting and shaping the hard local granite from which they are fashioned, making them much thicker than the taller slabs of the Orkney and Lewis monuments. Some 130 feet to the southwest of the circle, there stands a 9-foot-tall monolith aligned with the midwinter sunset.

Another excavated stone circle in the Hebrides, dating from around the same time, is Cultoon Stone Circle on the Isle of Islay at the southern end of the archipelago, which now consists of three standing megaliths and a further twelve lying flat on the ground. The tallest of the still-standing monoliths is about 6 feet tall, and the fallen stones measure up to 9 feet long. Considering that around a third of such megaliths needed to be planted in the ground to keep them upright, it follows that the original circle consisted of fifteen approximately 6-foot-high stones and seems to have been about 15 feet in diameter.

Just to the south of the Hebrides proper is the Isle of Arran in the Firth of Clyde. There are six stone circles; the oldest, which archaeologists refer to as Machrie Moor 2, dates from around 3000 BCE. It originally consisted of a 45-foot-diameter circle of eight stones, of which three survive, the tallest being almost 15 feet high. Shaped from a type of hard sandstone, the monoliths have a similar appearance to the Stones of Stenness. Because later stones were erected in the area, it is now unclear whether there was an outlying king stone. So far, no passage tombs or villages similar to Skara Brae have been found on the Hebrides or the Isle of Arran, which might be explained by their loss to rising sea levels. Nonetheless, the islanders certainly embraced significant aspects of the Grooved Ware culture within around a century of the creation of the Stones of Stenness.[3]

The Grooved Ware culture and its practice of stone circle building spread quickly on the mainland to southwestern Scotland, where no fewer than sixty-one stone circles survive in the district of Dumfries and Galloway. The earliest, dating from around 3000 BCE, is known as the Twelve Apostles. Standing just outside the market town of Dumfries, it measures some 280 feet in diameter, making it the largest stone circle on the Scottish mainland. As its name suggests, it was originally composed of twelve stones, each about 6 feet tall, of which eleven remain. Geophysics has revealed that a further stone that aligned with the midwinter sunset stood about 200 feet to the southwest of the circle. Although the Twelve Apostles had the same number of megaliths as the Stones of Stenness, the particularly hard local Silurian rock from which its megaliths were cut made it difficult to shape them with Stone Age tools. They are therefore wider, thicker, and more crudely shaped than the monoliths of many other stone circles. As on the Hebrides, no passage tombs have been found in this region.[4]

Around 3000 BCE what is thought to be the oldest surviving stone circle in England was created. Castlerigg Stone Circle, near the town of Keswick in the district of Cumbria in the far northwest of the country, is about 100 feet in diameter and consists of thirty-eight stones up to 7 feet high, the largest weighing around 15 tons. About 300 feet southwest of the circle, a single 3-foot stone aligns with the midwinter sunset. An unusual feature of Castlerigg is a rectangle of smaller standing stones within the main circle, although this seems to have been added much later. The large number of stones at the site is thought to represent the greater population and relative wealth of the area, compared with the contemporary Hebrides and southwestern Scotland.[5] The same applies to the Swinside Stone Circle, some 30 miles to the south. Built around the same time, it has a diameter of 94 feet and consists of fifty-five stones up to 10 feet tall. As in Dumfries and Galloway, just to the north, many stone circles were built in Cumbria, of which some fifty still survive. Two further stones, set close together just outside of the southeastern side of the circle, are thought to have marked some kind of ceremonial entrance. As this aligns with the midwinter sunrise, it seems likely that an outlying monolith also stood in this direction. Not only has grooved ware pottery been found at the oldest of these circles, but examples of rock art identical to that on the Westray Stone from the Orkneys also still survive (see chapter 4). A 12-foot-tall monolith known as Long Meg, near the village of Langwathby, is actually decorated with a series of concentric circles and spirals, just like the Westray Stone, as are two stones from the nearby Little Meg Stone Circle. Once again, no passage tombs have yet been identified in the area.[6]

The earliest stone circles found in the English county of Lancashire, to the immediate south of Cumbria, date from a later period than those we have been examining, as do those on the mainland of North Wales. The next influence of the contemporary Grooved Ware culture we need to examine is actually found in Ireland. The seaside town of Portpatrick, in southwestern Dumfries and Galloway, is only 14 miles from the coast of County Down in northeastern Ireland. Intriguingly the culture may have taken root in Ireland at the same time, or possibly earlier, that it spread into Cumbria or even Dumfries and Galloway. The North Channel is less than 30 miles wide where it divides the Hebrides from Ireland, and archaeology has revealed that regular trading of various Stone Age implements across this strait was already established well before 3000 BCE, so it is possible that the Grooved Ware culture arrived directly from Islay, the most southern of the Hebrides.

Close to two hundred stone circles still survive throughout Ireland, in various states of preservation, the oldest of which is thought to be Ballynoe Stone Circle. Standing about 2.5 miles south of Downpatrick in County Down, Northern Ireland, it is approximately 150 feet in diameter and originally consisted of over fifty stones up to 6 feet tall, most of which still survive. Dating from around 3000 BCE, it is similar in design to the contemporary Swinside Stone Circle in Cumbria. But it was not only the stone circle tradition and the manufacture of grooved ware pottery that was adopted in Ireland but also the building of passage tombs.[7]

Across the border in the Irish Republic there stands the largest of

Fig. 5.1. Early stone circles and megalithic sites.

all such monuments in the British Isles. Newgrange, which lies 5 miles west of the town of Drogheda in County Meath on Ireland's eastern coast, is a mound about 250 feet across and 40 feet high, over twice the size of Maeshowe (see chapter 4). Various dates, ranging over a period of more than a century, have been estimated for the construction of Newgrange, with most tourist information providing the earliest date of 3200 BCE. If correct, this would make it older than the earliest passage tombs on the Orkney Isles. However, the dating should be treated with caution. The monument was in a severely dilapidated condition until it was restored in the late 1960s and early 1970s. Examination of organic remains from the site made before this time obtained a central date of around 3200 BCE, but it was only after Newgrange was reconstructed that a more reliable form of radiocarbon dating, incorporating a process called accelerator mass spectrometry, was achieved. The problem was that the rebuilding of the tomb meant that organic remains were contaminated, making it difficult to accurately date the structure with the more precise technique. It has therefore been left to rehydroxylation dating (see chapter 4) of pottery excavated at the site to determine its age, and this has resulted in a date of around 3100 BCE. All the same, Newgrange would still date from almost the same time as the Maeshowe-style tombs on the Orkney Isles.[8]

It seems that the Grooved Ware culture became firmly established in the Newgrange area even before it made a lasting mark in the Hebrides. The fact that Newgrange and other passage tombs have been found in Ireland but not in the western islands of Scotland or in northwestern England has resulted in speculation that the Groove Ware culture might have spread to Ireland directly from the Orkney Isles.[9] Archaeology has revealed that early Neolithic sea-trading routes between Ireland and the Orkneys did exist. For instance, items such as axes and knives, made from flint found on the east coast of Ireland, have been unearthed at Skara Brae. Voyagers from Ireland may have been inspired to build such tombs after visiting the Orkney Isles; alternatively voyagers from the Orkneys may have settled in Ireland, where they built monuments like

Maeshowe. Either way, the apparent absence of passage tombs at locations in between might imply that eastern Ireland was more prosperous than the Hebrides, mainland Scotland, or northern England and more able to dedicate the resources necessary to construct such mausoleums.

Although some researchers have gone so far as to propose that Newgrange was actually built *before* the passage tombs of the Orkney Isles and represents a separate tradition entirely, this is almost certainly wrong. There is a clear evolution of such monuments on the Orkneys, from Unstan-style to Maeshowe-style tombs, over a five-hundred-year period, whereas no such systematic development is found in Ireland. The skills required to create Newgrange had to have been learned by trial and error; it is so well put together that it could not have been the first of its kind. However, there are no known precursors to the monument in Ireland. The expertise had to have been developed somewhere, and at present, the only place where evidence of such a Neolithic learning curve has been found is on the Orkney Isles.

Although Newgrange is bigger than anything so far discovered on the Orkneys, it was constructed in a design similar to Maeshowe. The mound is entered by a 60-foot-long stone passage, averaging about 5 feet in height, which leads to a rectangular chamber with a corbeled roof, measuring 21 feet long, 17 feet wide, and 20 feet high. Like Maeshowe, it has three side chambers, one to the front and one on each side of the central chamber as viewed from the end of the passage. Also like Maeshowe, the passage is directly aligned so that the rays of the midwinter sun, on the solstice, around December 21, shine directly into the central chamber, although at Newgrange it occurs at sunrise rather than sunset.

During reconstruction of the tomb in the 1970s, irregular-shaped white quartz rocks, most less than a foot in size, which previously had littered the area around the front of the monument, were assembled into a 20-foot-high wall curving around the façade. The result is certainly impressive, but there is now considerable doubt among archaeologists that Newgrange originally had such a feature. It seems most unlikely that such a high, vertical wall of these stones could have been built five thousand years ago; those who created it in the 1970s needed to fix the stones in place with concrete to prevent the whole thing from collapsing. When the monument was originally built, the technology simply did not exist to fasten such a high retaining wall at such a steep angle. It is now thought that these quartz rocks were actually cobblestones that lined a terrace or plaza on the ground before the entrance. This was certainly the case at the nearby passage tomb of Knowth: similar in size to Newgrange, it was built to the same design a few centuries later. Most archaeologists now believe this terrace to have been a later addition to Newgrange, constructed around the same time as the Knowth tomb. Newgrange also has the remains of a stone circle around it, but this too was erected later, around 2500 BCE.

There can be no doubt that the Grooved Ware culture was responsible for the building of Newgrange. Not only is it a Maeshowe-style tomb, complete with grooved ware pottery, but a number of its large stones, both inside and around the entrance, are carved with the same concentric circles and spirals found on the Orkney Westray Stone and in Cumbria.[10]

Shortly after Newgrange was built, the Grooved Ware culture makes its first appearance in Wales, on the Isle of Anglesey. Evidence of trading across the 70 miles of the Irish Sea separating Anglesey from the east coast of Ireland exists from early Neolithic times, and it seems likely that the influence of the Grooved Ware culture, and its practice of stone circle building, followed the same route to this part of northwest Wales. It's doubtful to have first arrived from northern England, as there is no sign of grooved ware ceramics or stone circles along the northern coast of Wales or in Lancashire, immediately south of Cumbria, until some centuries later. Moreover, the practice of building passage tombs, which had been so eagerly embraced in Ireland but was absent in Cumbria, was also adopted in Anglesey. On the west coast of the island, 2 miles northwest of the village of Aberffraw, is the passage tomb of Barclodiad y Gawres. Until excavations in the 1950s it was in such a poor condition that it looked like a big pile of stones, which led to its name: in Welsh, *barclodiad y gawres* means "apronful of the giantess." Local legend tells how the mound was created when a lady giant dumped a stack of stones she had been carrying in her apron. Around 90 feet in diameter, with a 20-foot entrance passage leading to a chamber with three smaller chambers to the back and sides, the tomb is basically a scaled-down version of Newgrange. Its chambers have long since collapsed, and after the 1950s excavations a concrete roof was constructed to preserve the interior.[11] As at Newgrange, not only has grooved ware pottery been uncovered from the site, but five of its megaliths also are carved with the same circular designs found at the Irish tomb. Eight miles to the southeast of Barclodiad y Gawres are the standing stones of Bryn Gwyn (White Hill). Today only two remain, but at 13 feet high they are the tallest Neolithic standing stones in Wales. Archaeological excavation in 2008 and 2010 determined that they are what remains of a circle of eight stones, some 50 feet in diameter. Organic samples obtained from beneath one of the stones have been radiocarbon dated to around 3000 BCE, making the Bryn Gwyn monument Wales's oldest stone circle.

In Britain the practice of building passage tombs seems unique to Anglesey. However, the Grooved Ware culture spread to the county of Pembrokeshire in South West Wales at almost the same time as it appeared on that island. Strangely there is no evidence of stone-circle building in central Wales during this early period, so it's possible that the new culture was again spread by sea traders, either from Anglesey or directly from Ireland. The earliest dated stone circle in Pembrokeshire is the Gors Fawr (Great Marsh) Stone Circle close to the village of Mynachlog-ddu (Black Monastery), just south of the Preseli Hills. It consists of sixteen rather small standing stones, none of them much above 3 feet high, in a ring some 70 feet in diameter. To the northeast of the circle is a 6-foot-tall monolith, known locally as the Dreaming Stone, which aligns with the midsummer sunrise. A second stone of the same size stands nearby, although this is thought to have been a later addition.

Because of a five-hundred-year break in the sequence of pottery fragments found at the site, it seems to have been abandoned for some centuries soon after it was constructed before being used again. A newer and far more impressive stone circle might have been erected at Carn Menyn, 2 miles to the north in the Preseli Hills. This, in 2005, is what Professor Timothy Darvill of Bournemouth University identified as the location from where the Stonehenge bluestones came (see chapter 1). The latest theory is that the stones were not only quarried there, but the fifty-six bluestones, each approximately 6 feet high, 3.5 feet wide, and 2.5 feet thick, that formed the first circle at Stonehenge had originally been a stone circle in the hilly district of Carn Menyn.[12] Recent surveys by geologists Richard Bevins, Ph.D. (National Museum of Wales), and Robert Ixer, Ph.D. (University College London), identified the spotted dolerite rock from which the Stonehenge bluestones were cut as originating in a specific outcrop in an area called Carn Goedog. It actually retains evidence of quarrying in Neolithic times. Moreover, a number of cut stones were actually found at the site of the ancient quarry. It seems that these were partially shaped megaliths that had been accidentally broken and consequently abandoned. In 2015 a large team of geologists and archaeologists assembled by University College London not only confirmed the work of Bevins and Ixer, but by radiocarbon dating charcoal excavated from the Neolithic quarry workers' campfires, they also specifically dated activity to around 3000 BCE.[13] In 2008 excavations at Stonehenge, led by archaeologist Mike Parker Pearson, Ph.D., of the University of Sheffield, had previously dated the holes that contained the original bluestones to around this very time.[14]

These separate findings imply that the bluestones could not have remained in the Carn Menyn area for long. Although it's possible that they were quarried there specifically to be dragged all the way to Stonehenge, it now seems more likely that they originally formed a local stone circle that was considered important enough to be moved. Geophysics surveys around Bedd Arthur, an arrangement of standing stones half a mile south of Carn Goedog, have indicated that a large stone circle may once have stood there. The results suggest that a series of at least fifty holes had been dug in a ring about 280 feet in diameter, matching the size of the original bluestone circle at Stonehenge. At present, no archaeological excavation has been conducted to date the holes or to determine for sure if they had once contained stones, but they do seem to correspond to the size necessary to have held megaliths about 3.5 feet wide and 2.5 feet thick, the dimensions of the Stonehenge bluestones. As the only stones in the area are now the fourteen stones that make up the horseshoe arrangement of Bedd Arthur, none more than 2 feet high, it seems that if a circle of much larger stones once stood there, then it must have been moved away. Just why a stone circle might have been moved from South Wales all the way to southern England is a mystery.

Whether or not the Stonehenge bluestones originally formed a stone circle in the Preseli Hills, they were certainly quarried there. Either way, the Grooved Ware culture quickly spread into southern England, and the fact that the first stones at Stonehenge came from the Preseli Hills is the smoking gun to reveal that the culture's influence originated from that region. What's strange, however, is that there is no evidence of its taking root anywhere between Pembrokeshire and the Stonehenge area around 3000 BCE. Until now we have seen how the culture seems to have been spread primarily by sea-trading people, but Stonehenge is about 50 miles from the nearest sea, which is on England's west coast. It is over 130 miles—even as the crow flies—from the Preseli Hills, yet there are no stone circles or evidence of grooved ware pottery found anywhere between these locations in southeastern Wales and western England dating from this period. How could such a major cultural influence just jump between the two completely separate areas? The answer seems to be that it was spread by river traders.

During early Neolithic times, what is now the county of Wiltshire around Stonehenge was the richest area in the British Isles. It is where the most impressive long barrows, such as West Kennet and Wayland's Smithy, are found (see chapter 3). As remarkable as they

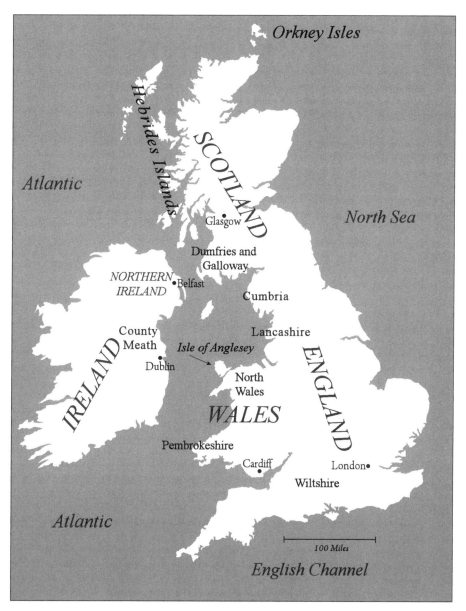

Fig. 5.2. Spread of the early Megalithic culture.

were, these tombs pale beside an astonishing contemporary construction near Stonehenge. Less than half a mile north of Stonehenge is a linear earthwork known as the Cursus. It consists of an area measuring about 400 feet wide and almost 2 miles long, completely enclosed by a rectangular embankment, originally about 10 feet wide and 4 feet high, which rose to over 10 feet at either end. During archaeological excavations conducted between 2004 and 2006, the remains of broken antler picks found in the rubble from which the earthwork was created were radiocarbon dated to around 3500 BCE—five centuries before even the first stone circle was erected at Stonehenge.[15] The name *cursus* comes from the Latin word for a racetrack; it was so-named in the eighteenth century as early antiquarians mistakenly thought it had been a Roman chariot-racing arena. Its true purpose remains a mystery, but as it was constructed along an east-west axis, it may have been a ceremonial enclosure associated with sunrise or sunset on the equinoxes, around the twenty-first of March and September, when day and night are of equal length. Whatever its function, it was created by the Barrow culture that built the West Kennet and Wayland's Smithy tombs (see chapter 3). Not only does it date from the same period, but a long barrow also was actually incorporated into the earthwork at one end. One thing is certain: it would have taken a vast amount of time and effort to construct—clear evidence of the area's sizable and prosperous population. Indeed, the largest Neolithic settlement so far identified in the British Isles lies just 2 miles northeast of Stonehenge. Called Durrington Walls, it is thought to have been inhabited by as many as four thousand people.

Excavations at Durrington Walls, conducted between 2004 and 2006, revealed that distinctive grooved ware pottery began to be used around 3000 BCE. Prior to this time, ceramics in southern Britain consisted of curved, round-bottomed utensils, rather than the flat-bottomed, bucket-shaped pots of the grooved ware style. Their decorations varied from place to place, presumably reflecting regional tribal traditions, making it relatively easy for archaeologists to determine what areas were trading with one another.[16] Distinctive bowl-style pottery from Pembrokeshire has been found at Durrington Walls, and vice versa, meaning that these two areas were in regular contact with each other before they were influenced by the Grooved Ware culture. As there is no evidence of Pembrokeshire pottery being found anywhere between these two areas, it seems likely that they were trading by water. It would have been possible to navigate the sea from the Pembrokeshire coast, up the Bristol Channel (separating South Wales from South West England), and then southwestward along the River Avon until it reaches Wiltshire at what is now the town of Bradford-on-Avon, just 20 miles from Stonehenge. Neolithic boats of the period included canoes made from hollowed tree trunks, and examples have been found preserved in marshes and river banks, some over 20 feet long.[17]

Various scholars now suggest that the bluestones were moved for most of their journey on a number of such boats that were lashed together to form a raft. It would then only have been a matter of dragging the stones about 20 miles, rather than the almost 250-mile route required to get around the intervening hills and the Bristol Channel overland. All the same, it would still have been an enormous undertaking. However it was done, the Pembrokeshire bluestones must have held a special importance, considering that there was equally good material from which to build a stone circle much closer to home: the later, much larger sarsen megaliths were quarried from the Marlborough Downs, just 20 miles north of Stonehenge (see chapter 1).

The people of Wiltshire, five thousand years ago, must have been massively influenced by their trading partners in Pembrokeshire. Whatever this influence involved—be it religious or something else— the inhabitants of Wiltshire, presumably those who lived in and around Durrington Walls, were so impressed by it that they not only copied the Grooved Ware culture of the Preseli Hills, they actually transported its stones back home. The inhabitants of Wilshire were far more populous and prosperous than the people of South West Wales, and they were already building impressive monuments of their own. Perhaps the Grooved Ware people of the Carn Menyn area decided to move to Wiltshire, where the locals, having adopted their culture, welcomed them with open arms. It seems most unlikely that anyone would be able to quarry the stone or, if the latest theory is right, move an already existing stone circle from the Preseli Hills without the cooperation of the local people. Exactly what may have happened, and why it was done, is something we shall be returning to later. Suffice it to say, by around 3000 BCE, just a century after the first stone circle was built on the Orkney Isles, another one had been erected at Stonehenge, 700 miles to the south.

So far, in examining the spread of the Grooved Ware culture, I have been referring to a period of *around* 3000 BCE. This is because radiocarbon is generally only accurate to within about one hundred years either way. Rehydroxylation dating has pretty much the same results for all the sites we have been examining in this chapter: somewhere between 3100 and 2900 BCE. From this alone, we cannot say with certainty in what chronological order the various monuments were built. Nonetheless, the proposed progression we have been examining stands to reason. We can see a systematic development of the culture on the Orkney Isles over a period of some five hundred years, such as the gradual advances made in the quarrying, cutting, and shaping of ever larger stones, beginning with the need to build houses out of something other than wood, whereas elsewhere there is no such evolution. The first areas to adopt the practice of building stone circles outside the Orkney Isles evidence no step-by-step developments in stonemasonry; they seem to have acquired their expertise ready-formed from others who had previously learned such skills, originally honed on the Orkney Isles.

In Scotland, Grooved Ware culture spread out from Dumfries and Galloway; in northern England, from Cumbria; in Ireland, from County Meath; and in southern England, from Wiltshire. (Strangely, it seems to have stalled in Wales, to be reintroduced some years later.) Although there is ample evidence that the ideas began in the Orkneys, the precise route of their geographical spread elsewhere is mainly conjecture.

Plate 1. *The east side of Stonehenge with lintel stones still forming the arches of the Sarsen Circle, erected around 2600 BCE. It is the only megalithic stone circle known to have had these distinguishing features.*

(Photography by Deborah Cartwright)

Plate 2. *The west side of Stonehenge with its fallen monoliths. The monument we see today was not the original. Erected around five thousand years ago, the original consisted of a larger ring but with smaller stones.*

(Photography by Deborah Cartwright)

Plate 3. The Trilithon Horseshoe at the center of Stonehenge. Lintel stones weighing as much as 8 tons were somehow positioned on top of the giant, 20-foot-tall megaliths. (Photography by Deborah Cartwright)

Plate 4. Some historians think that the megaliths of Stonehenge were moved from where they were quarried by lashing them to timber runners and sliding them along wooden rollers, as shown here. (Photography by Deborah Cartwright)

Plate 5. Thatched dwellings of the Neolithic period were made from wood frames covered with whitewashed mud. These reconstructions of the homes of the early Megalithic people of southern England can be seen at the Stonehenge Visitor Centre.

(Photography by Deborah Cartwright)

Plate 6. The 5,500-year-old long barrow of Wayland's Smithy in Wiltshire. Such tombs were built before the first stone circles.

(Photography by Deborah Cartwright)

Plate 7. *Bodowyr Burial Chamber on the Isle of Anglesey. Known as dolmens or portal tombs, such arrangements of stones, which date from before the era of stone circle building in the British Isles, were once covered by mounds of earth that have long since eroded away.*

(Photography by Deborah Cartwright)

Plate 8. *Bryn Celli Ddu on the Isle of Anglesey. Such Maeshowe-style passage tombs, typified by a series of central chambers accessed by a long stone corridor, date from the early Megalithic period, around 3000 BCE.*

(Photography by Deborah Cartwright)

Plate 9. The 3-foot-high, 36-foot-long stone corridor of the Maeshowe mound passage tomb on the Orkney Isles. It was constructed so that the direct light of the setting sun illuminates the tomb's central chamber at the midwinter solstice.

(Photography by Deborah Cartwright)

Plate 10. *The Stones of Stenness on Mainland Island of the Orkney Isles. Dating from around 3100 BCE, it is the oldest known stone circle in the British Isles.*

(Photography by Deborah Cartwright)

Plate 11. *Many stone circles had additional monoliths outside the main ring, aligned to the sunrise or sunset on the midsummer or midwinter solstice.*

(Photography by Deborah Cartwright)

Plate 12. *The Neolithic settlement of Skara Brae on the Orkney Isles, where some of the people who erected the very first stone circle at Stenness actually lived. Built around 3100 BCE, it is the best-preserved prehistoric village in the world.*

(Photography by Deborah Cartwright)

Plate 13. *The rooms of the five-thousand-year-old dwellings of Skara Brae still have their ancient stone beds, shelving, and washing facilities. The village was preserved by being covered with sand during a freak storm around 2500 BCE.*

(Photography by Deborah Cartwright)

Plate 14. The Nine Ladies stone circle in Derbyshire is typical of the hundreds of smaller stone circles erected throughout the British Isles.

(Photography by Deborah Cartwright)

Plate 15. Avebury is the largest stone circle in the British Isles. With a diameter of over 1,000 feet and a surrounding henge earthwork consisting of a 30-foot-deep ditch and a 20-foot-high embankment, it dwarfs the more famous Stonehenge, which lies 17 miles to the south

(Photography by Deborah Cartwright)

Plate 16. The Ring of Brodgar on the Orkney Isles is typical of the huge henge stone circles built from around 2600 BCE. (Photography by Deborah Cartwright)

Plate 17. The sixty stones that made up the 340-foot-diameter Ring of Brodgar were up to 15 feet high. There were dozens of similar, grand stone circles built in prehistoric Britain and Ireland. (Photography by Deborah Cartwright)

Plate 18. *Stone avenues, such as the West Kennet Avenue at Avebury, some running for miles, often joined the larger stone circles to other, smaller stone circles in the immediate area.*

(Photography by Deborah Cartwright)

Plate 19. *Silbury Hill, near Avebury, is 130 feet high and covers 5 acres. Such mysterious artificial mounds, containing no internal structures or burials, were constructed as part of an elaborate arrangement of monoliths and earthworks making up complexes of megalithic monuments.*

(Photography by Deborah Cartwright)

Plate 20. *The Rudston Monolith now stands in a medieval churchyard in Yorkshire. At 25 feet high, it is the tallest megalith in Britain, one of thousands of single, isolated standing stones, known as menhirs, found all over the British Isles.* (Photography by Deborah Cartwright)

Plate 21. *The Devil's Arrows are an alignment of monoliths, up to 22 feet high, that cross fields in the district of Boroughbridge in northern England. In 1921, the English archaeologist Alfred Watkins proposed that the menhirs had been deliberately placed to align for miles across the British countryside as part of a linear network of prehistoric monuments he called ley lines.*

(Photography by Deborah Cartwright)

Plate 22. *One of the inner stone circles at Avebury. Such additional stone circles may have been added to compensate for the apparent change in the positions of the stars with which the monoliths at such megalithic complexes were intended to align.*

(Photography by Deborah Cartwright)

Plate 23. *The Cove at Avebury, an arrangement of huge monoliths weighing up to 100 tons each, which may be the oldest part of the megalithic complex.*

(Photography by Deborah Cartwright)

Plate 24. The Callanish Stone Circle on Scotland's Isle of Lewis was in use for over three thousand years, during which time many of its monoliths were moved and new stones added, perhaps to accommodate for the gradual shift in the Earth's axis of rotation. (Photography by Deborah Cartwright)

Plate 25. *The Iron Age burial chamber inside the Callanish Stone Circle. Such tombs—built inside stone circles for up to one thousand years after 500 BCE—reveal that the Celts venerated stone circles as passionately as did their forebears.*

(Photography by Deborah Cartwright)

Plate 26. *The two 10-foot-tall monoliths at the Bridestones in Cheshire once formed part of a stone circle that stood just behind their present position. It may have been Britain's last stone circle, built about 450 CE, some 3,500 years after the first stone circle was built at Stenness in the Orkney Islands.* (Photography by Deborah Cartwright)

Plate 27. *The Bridestones box cairn. These unusual burial chambers, once covered by mounds, were the tombs of the Druids. This one may have been the final resting place of the last of the ancient Druids.* (Photography by Deborah Cartwright)

Some of the details regarding the proposed migration of the Grooved Ware culture could, of course, be wrong. For example, it might have reached Ireland from northern England, rather than Scotland. However, the routes suggested would seem to be the most logical. One thing seems fairly certain: it arrived in Wiltshire directly from Pembrokeshire, as implied by the origin of the bluestones.

From around 3000 BCE the practice of building stone circles continued to spread. It became so prevalent in the British Isles that it is no longer accurate to refer to the stone circle builders after this time as the Grooved Ware culture. For a start, some of those who adopted the practice continued to use other types of pottery. The idea might have started on the Orkney Isles and spread to the Hebrides, southwestern Scotland, North West England, eastern Ireland, and into Wales, but by the time it reached Stonehenge it had taken on a life of its own. From this point onward, we should refer to those who built stone circles as the Megalithic culture.

6

The Phases of Megalithic Construction

BEFORE MOVING ON, we should assess what we know so far. The first people to build stone circles in the British Isles also adopted grooved ware pottery, most likely because it was a far more practical design than anything already in use, with its flat rather than curved bases. You might be wondering why no one had thought of that before. They probably had, but coming up with the idea and implementing it are very different matters. The skill set necessary to make straight-sided, flat-bottomed pots that didn't fall apart upon firing probably had taken years to master. Apart from anything else, it required hotter and more efficient kilns,[1] and these were something that the people of the Orkneys had managed to create in their villages, such as Skara Brae. They likely developed them over time, by trial and error, while seeking more effective ways of heating the stone-built homes (see chapter 4). Pottery has so many applications: drinking, eating, cooking, storage, carrying, and use as ceremonial vessels. Flat-bottomed ceramics are taken for granted today, but imagine how much easier life would suddenly become if you had never had such items before. The Grooved Ware culture probably spread so rapidly and so widely because its ceramic innovations were so beneficial.

Crucially, there must also have been something just as important as improved pottery about their stone circles, as they too were replicated with equal enthusiasm. Are the stone circles perhaps evidence of some compelling new religion? Had the Neolithic people in various parts of the British Isles been motivated to adopt the cultic practices that began with the Grooved Ware culture on the Orkney Isles? If so, then we would expect to see evidence of widespread changes in various other conventions, such as burial practices and artistic expression. But apart from a few early examples, these are just not found.

Long barrows and portal tombs (dolmens) were no longer being built in Britain by 3000 BCE; instead bones or cremated remains were, for the most part, being buried in simple pits. This didn't change, apart from the passage tombs that were only adopted for a while in a small part of Ireland and on Anglesey.[2] (There is one kind of rare, anomalous burial monument, known as a box tomb, that continued to be built throughout the Megalithic era, but we shall be examining that in chapter 12.) Ancient religions are usually identified by specific funerary practices; the fact that the majority of those people who built the early stone circles throughout the British Isles didn't change their burial traditions in any way suggests that their basic religion remained the same. Neither did the majority of the early stone circle builders inscribe their stones with spiral or concentric circle designs, such as those found on the Westray Stone, which presumably held some sacred significance. Examples are found in Cumbria, Ireland, and Anglesey, but not in the Hebrides, Dumfries and Galloway, Pembrokeshire, or at Stonehenge. And then there's the pottery. The Grooved Ware style of straight-sided, flat-bottomed vessels may have been copied in many areas, but their engravings—which presumably held religious or cultural meaning—invariably remained unchanged.[3] We can't know for sure, but it would certainly appear that whatever enigmatic function the stone circles served, it was something other than just religious. As with the grooved ware pottery, the people may have copied the practice of erecting stone circles for some *practical* purpose. What this might have been, we shall be considering later, once we have a fuller picture of the Megalithic culture, its creations, its extent, and its development. Nevertheless, we already have *some* interesting clues to ponder.

For whatever reason the stone circles were created, the monoliths were equally spaced around the rings, but the number of stones, their sizes and shapes, and the diameters of the rings varied considerably. Here are the approximate dimensions of the stone circles we have examined so far.

STONE CIRCLE	NUMBER OF STONES	HIGHEST STONE IN FEET	DIAMETER IN FEET
Stenness	12	20	100
Callanish	13	13	37
Lochbuie	9	6	40
Cultoon	15	6	15
Machrie Moor 2	8	15	45
Twelve Apostles	12	6	280
Castlerigg	38	7	100
Swinside	55	10	94
Ballynoe	50	6	150
Bryn Gwyn	8	13	50
Gors Fawr	16	3	70
First Stonehenge	56	6	280

As we can clearly see, the erecting of standing stones in a circle, regardless of size or number, seems to have been the critical factor. However, something that many of the early stone circles, built between about 3100 and 3000 BCE, do have in common is solar alignments. So also do the contemporary passage tombs. As discussed, some scholars believe that the Maeshowe-style tombs may not have been used only for burials but also as shrines or places of ceremonial activity (see chapter 4). As such, an important ceremony might have been performed inside them at a specific time of the year, when the direct rays of the sun illuminated the central chamber. On the Orkneys, at Maeshowe, this occurs on the midwinter solstice, around December 21. Of the dozen Maeshowe-style tombs so far identified on the Orkney Isles, some have their passage aligned to the midwinter sunrise, rather than sunset, such as the South Cairn on the Isle of Papa Westray and Quoyness on Sanday Island. Others, such as Cuween Hill and Quanterness on Mainland Island, have passages aligned eastward, possibly to face the sunrise on the equinoxes, around March 21 and September 21, when day and night are of equal length. On the Orkney Isles these solar alignments appear to have been a new innovation accompanying the beginning of the Grooved Ware culture, as the earlier Unstan-type tombs (see chapter 4), built between 3600 and 3100 BCE, don't seem to have favored any such orientations.[4] We find the same in Ireland. The earlier Neolithic graves, dating between 3600 and 3100 BCE, are sometimes confusingly referred to as passage tombs. Although they do have entry passages, these are much shorter than those in the Maeshowe-style tombs, and their inner chambers are smaller and much less elaborate. They are, in fact, far more similar to the contemporary long barrows and dolmen tombs found across the Irish Sea in Britain.[5] Although various solar orientations have been proposed for some of these earlier monuments, for the most part their passages lie in various, seemingly random directions. Conversely, as on the Orkney Isles, most of Ireland's Maeshowe-style tombs, built from around 3100 BCE, *do* have what appear to have been deliberate solar alignments. Ireland's passage tomb of Dowth in County Meath has its passage aligned to the midsummer sunset, while at the nearby tomb of Newgrange it aligns with the midwinter sunrise. At Knowth, another of the passage tombs in County Meath, the passage faces in an easterly direction, possibly to align with the sunrise on the equinoxes, perhaps the spring equinox, which many ancient cultures regarded as the start of summer. And in Wales, on the Isle of Anglesey, where the only Maeshowe-style tombs are known to have been built other than on the Orkneys and in Ireland, we find similar alignments. Although at Barclodiad y Gawres (see chapter 5) the passage is aligned almost due north, meaning it was not aligned to the sun at any time of the year, at the contemporary tomb of Bryn Celli Ddu, on the island's southeast side, the passage is aligned to the sunrise on the summer solstice, around June 21.[6] Regarding the early stone circles, most of them had a freestanding monolith, the so-called king stone (see chapter 1), erected some distance outside the circle and aligned to the midwinter sunrise or sunset as seen from the center of the ring. At Stenness, Callanish, Swinside, and Ballynoe, this appears to have been the sunrise, while at Lochbuie, the Twelve Apostles, and Castlerigg, it was the sunset.

There can be little doubt that the sun held important significance to the Grooved Ware culture people who built the Maeshowe-style tombs and the first stone circles, but whether this involved sunrise or sunset varied from site to site. In most cases the time of year concerned is the midwinter solstice, around December 21, while a few involved the equinoxes. However, once the culture reached Wales the custom involved mainly midsummer. Not only was the passage of Anglesey's Bryn Celli Ddu aligned to the sunrise on the summer solstice, so was the king stone of the Gors Fawr Stone Circle in Pembrokeshire. The first bluestone circle at Stonehenge may also have had a king stone marking the sunrise on the midsummer solstice. The later ring of sarsen stones included the outlying Heel Stone (see chapter 1), which was aligned to the midsummer sunrise; an original bluestone could well have stood in its location.

Theories as to why these solar alignments were created abound. Some may have been to mark important dates associated with agriculture. The spring equinox occurs around the beginning of the growing season, and the fall equinox occurs around the time of the harvest. But the majority of these alignments involve the solstices: the middle of winter and summer. Some scholars who believe that the monuments were primarily religious shrines have proposed that a solar deity needed to be thanked at the height of summer or appeased in the heart of winter.

Others have suggested a more elaborate interpretation to account for the sun-aligned passages of the Maeshowe-style tombs. The structures, they suggest, represented the womb of an earth goddess; the rays of light that penetrated the passage symbolized the power of the sun god annually fertilizing Mother Earth. A similar theory has been proposed for stone circles: the king stone represented the phallus of the sun god, and the stone circle the womb of the earth goddess. At sunset, it is suggested, the shadow of the king stone would grow longer and penetrate the circle, emulating sexual union. The notion concerning the passage graves would make sense, but not the majority of stone circles, in which the king stone is aligned to the sunrise, when the shadow would grow shorter, not longer. Moreover, although it is easy to see how a passage tomb might resemble a womb, the same cannot be said of a stone circle.

One way or another, the passage tombs ceased to be built after the early Megalithic period, and they never were built outside the Orkneys, Anglesey, and parts of Ireland. The Megalithic culture that ultimately spread throughout the British Isles is typified by its stone circles, and it is the mystery of *these* we hope to solve. At this stage in our investigation it is too early to make any meaningful conjecture concerning what purpose the stone circles may have served, be it religious, practical, or a combination of the two. Next we need to examine how the practice of building stone circles spread, following its beginnings with the Grooved Ware culture between around 3100 and 3000 BCE.

Archaeologists have estimated that as many as 5,000 stone circles may have ultimately been erected in the British Isles. Only around 1,300 survive in various states of preservation: the official figures are just over 500 in Scotland and its islands, almost 400 in Ireland, approximately 300 in England, and some 80 in Wales. If these numbers are right, then it seems that around three-quarters of them have been lost over time. Some were broken up for readily available building materials, and others were destroyed by religious fanatics, but for the most part they have been obliterated by the building of towns, cities, roads, and a myriad of other forms of infrastructure, and more recently to make way for modern farming techniques. Those that remain are mainly in sparsely inhabited districts, such as hills, mountains, and moorlands. Consequently the majority have survived in the uplands of England and Ireland and the highlands of Scotland and Wales. Almost none can now be identified in heavily populated regions such as central and southeastern England. Fortunately in the locations where they still exist we have enough evidence to determine the chronological expansion and development of the Megalithic culture.

The early Megalithic period can be divided into two stages. The first, from its beginnings on the Orkney Isles to the building of the original stone circle at Stonehenge, we have already examined. The second is from approximately 3000 to 2600 BCE. Strangely in some of the first areas where grooved ware pottery was adopted, stone circle building never occurred during this period. For example, in the north of mainland Scotland, where the new ceramic style was embraced fairly early on, no stone circles are known to have been built for the next four hundred years.[7] In some areas where early stone circles *were* built, the practice seems to have been abandoned. In Ireland, despite the building of elaborate Maeshowe-style tombs such as Newgrange, which was even bigger than anything on the Orkney Isles, and the creation of Ballynoe, one of the largest of the early stone circles in the British Isles, the Megalithic culture seems to have stalled completely soon after it began. No more stone circles appear to have been built for almost a thousand years, until the practice was reembraced around 2000 BCE. The same seems to have happened throughout Wales, but for only a few hundred years, despite the construction of passage tombs in Anglesey and the enormous undertaking of moving bluestones all the way from Pembrokeshire to Stonehenge. Even on the Orkney Isles, where the whole thing began, no new stone circles appear to have been erected during this second Megalithic phase. Other than the Stones of Stenness, only one other stone circle is known on the Orkney Isles, and that dates from around 2600 BCE. However, in this case it might be explained by the single monument adequately serving the islands' limited population. During this period, the main areas in which the Megalithic culture did flourish were four separate regions: the Hebrides and the Isle of Arran, Dumfries and Galloway, the adjacent Cumbria, and southern and South West England.

In the Hebrides at least eight other stone circles were erected on the Isle of Lewis at regular intervals between 3000 and 2600 BCE, and on the Isle of Arran it was around eleven, while a number of other stone circles were built close to the shores on the nearby mainland. The remains of around sixty-four stone circles survive in the district of Dumfries and Galloway, of which eleven are still in a reasonable state of preservation; around half of them appear to date from 3000 to 2600 BCE, the earliest being the Twelve Apostles (see chapter 5). A typical circle built in this district shortly after the Twelve Apostles is the Torhouse Stones, about 38 miles to the southwest. It consists of nineteen stones between 2 and 5 feet high, in a ring measuring 70 feet in diameter. A further stone, about 6 feet tall, stands approximately 130 feet to the southeast of the circle in the direction of the midwinter sunrise. Some thirty stone circles have been identified in Cumbria, of which fifteen are in a reasonable state of preservation. As we have seen, what is believed to be the oldest stone circle in England, Castlerigg, is among them. Once again, around half of them were built between 3000 and 2600 BCE, typical being the Blakeley Raise Stone Circle in the district of Kinniside; it consists of eleven stones, up to 4 feet high, in a ring some 60 feet in diameter.

It was in the South of England that there occurred what has been the most studied development of the second phase of Megalithic culture. After the creation of the first ring at Stonehenge, ring building quickly spread through southern Britain. Evidence of megalithic monuments has been largely eradicated in the heavily built-up and industrial areas to the south and east of Stonehenge, but to the southwest it thankfully survives. In the county of Dorset, to the immediate west of Wilshire, where Stonehenge is situated, around half a dozen stone circles survive from the period between 3000 and 2600 BCE. For example, in the hilly Dorset Downs, on the western edge of the village of Winterbourne Abbas, there stands the Nine Stones Circle. As its name suggests, nine of its stones survive, but it is thought that it originally consisted of ten, up to 7 feet high, the largest weighing approximately 8 tons, in a ring about 27 feet in diameter. During the eighteenth century, a coach road was built across the northwest side of the circle, making it impossible to tell if a king stone once stood in the direction of the midsummer sunset. West of Dorset is the county of Devonshire (Devon for short), where some sixteen stone circles survive, and in the extreme southwest of England is the county of Cornwall, where a further seventeen stone circles can still be found. Approximately half of the circles in these two counties appear to date from before 2600 BCE. For example, the Scorhill Stone Circle, near the village of Gidleigh in the bleak Devonshire uplands of Dartmoor, consists of thirty-eight stones, up to 7 feet tall, in a ring approximately 90 feet in diameter. It does not seem to have had a king stone, but the tallest monolith has a distinctive jagged point, above which the midsummer sun sets as viewed from the center of the ring. A Cornish example, on the windswept slopes of Bodmin Moor, is Fernacre Stone Circle, just over a mile northeast of the village of St. Breward. It was originally composed of over eighty stones, of which sixty-nine survive, thirty-eight still standing in a ring about 150 feet in diameter. The monoliths are badly weathered, none above 4 feet high, but a fallen stone, 7 feet long, lies to the southeast of the circle and may have marked the midwinter sunrise. And on the rugged Penwith Peninsula, just 5 miles from Land's End, the most westerly point of England, is the Merry Maidens Stone Circle. Thought to be complete, it is about 80 feet in diameter and consists of nineteen standing stones, ranging between 3.5 and 4.5 feet tall. About 1,000 feet outside the circle stand two much taller stones. Over 10 feet high, they both align to the northeast of the Merry Maidens in the direction of the midwinter sunrise.

Just like the earlier stone circles, those built in the areas of Britain where the Megalithic culture flourished between around 3000 and

2600 BCE varied considerably concerning the number of stones, from about ten to as many as ninety, as do their diameters, from less than 30 to over 150 feet. So too did the size of the monoliths, from less than 3 feet to over 10 feet high. The size of the stones and the diameter of the circles may represent the extent of the local population, but the considerable variation in the *number* of stones is intriguing. Once more, the outlying stones varied too, sometimes aligning to the sunset or sunrise at both midwinter and midsummer, and some circles have no evidence of a king stone at all, while others have two or more such outliers. It would seem that for whatever reason the stone circle obsession caught on, it was evidently not considered necessary to precisely copy the design.

The lifestyle of those who created these stone circles during this second Megalithic phase continued largely unaltered from earlier Neolithic times. Dwellings remained unchanged. The elaborate stone buildings of the Orkney Isles were not copied elsewhere, probably because of the availability of trees, which were not as scarce as they had on these northern islands. Homes at settlements such as Durrington Walls (see chapter 5) were basically single-roomed, circular, wickerwork constructions fashioned from tree branches with dried-mud walls and thatched roofs. Dwellings in more forested areas were rectangular log structures divided into two or more chambers with roofs overlaid with turf, not dissimilar to the simple cabins of the early European pioneers in the American West. None of these have left traces to be seen today, but they have been identified by archaeologists using geophysics equipment to detect signs of ancient postholes in the ground and dated by identifying and radiocarbon dating decomposed timber remains in the soil.[8]

Archeological finds do not directly record evidence of weaving, as fabrics would long since have rotted away; however, their use can be discerned from the discovery of implements used in their manufacture, such as bone spindles, whorls, needles, and stone weights for twining thread. Also, remarkably, imprints of fabrics have actually been found on pottery, where clothing or matting pushed against the clay before it was fired. From such evidence, it is known that the Neolithic people of the period in question had woven straw mats, plant fiber carpeting and probably wall hangings, and woolen blankets and clothing. Most garments, however, were almost certainly made from animal hide sewn together with sinew.[9] From various Stone Age tools discovered at Neolithic settlements of the time, we can also tell that they made baskets, ropes, and nets. And most adornments consisted of simple necklaces or bracelets of bone, teeth, and shells. Interestingly, only a handful of figurines, carved from bone or stone or made from clay, have been found from the Neolithic period in the British Isles. Even these were crude representations of animals difficult to identify. It would seem that if the early Megalithic people did venerate a sun god or a mother goddess, they apparently saw no need to represent them in the form of anthropomorphic statuettes, although they may have carved such effigies from wood. The only seemingly ritual carvings known to have been made were the mysterious petrospheres, of which over four hundred have been discovered at sites all over the British Isles (see chapter 4).

For those who wish to see how the people of the era actually lived, five Neolithic houses, complete with replica pottery, tools, simple wooden furnishings, and various artifacts, have been reconstructed outside the visitor center at Stonehenge. They are of the wickerwork frame type, with the interior walls whitewashed with ground chalk, thought to have been designed not only to make the dwellings brighter but also to reflect warmth from the fire. The outside walls are also whitewashed to reflect the heat of sunlight in the summertime. On certain occasions reenactors actually dress up in Neolithic styles and perform ancient daily activities in and around the dwellings.

For some four centuries the Megalithic culture seems to have continued pretty much unchanged, merely building more of the same stone circles in the three areas we have examined. The most northerly point the culture stretched in southern England was over 250 miles south of the stone-circle-building area in Cumbria. There is no evidence of its appearing anywhere between these two locations during the period between 3000 and 2600 BCE, and no further stone circles seem to have been built in Wales or Ireland during this time. In the North, English Cumbria adjoins what is now the Scottish district of Dumfries and Galloway, but no such political boundary existed at the time, making these combined parts of northwestern England and southwestern Scotland a single Megalithic region. The other area where stone circle building continued was on the Hebrides and the nearby Isle of Arran. The northern coast of Dumfries and Galloway is only about 30 miles from the Isle of Arran, so perhaps all these northern areas should also be regarded as a single Megalithic region. This still leaves us with two geographically isolated locations where the same culture seems to have continued unabated for four centuries.[10] What happened next, however, is *really* strange: an identical, simultaneous revolution in megalithic construction suddenly occurred in these widely separated locations and also on the Orkney Isles off the far north of Scotland. (It may have been noted that I have not been referring to Ireland regarding the creation of the megalithic complexes. That is because the stone-circle-building tradition seems to have been abandoned in Ireland for about a thousand years, until it was readopted around 2000 BCE. See chapter 10.)

The third phase of Megalithic culture in the British Isles was the sudden building of dozens of huge henge stone circles that began around 2600 BC (see chapter 1). The word "henge" refers to a circular ditch and embankment that surrounded these new stone circles. Intriguingly the ditch was invariably built inside the embankment, the opposite way around for the earthwork to have been created for defensive purposes, so why they were built still remains a mystery. Based on the number and size of the various Neolithic sites identified, archaeologists estimate that by 2600 BCE the population of Britain was somewhere around two hundred thousand people (about the modern population of Salt Lake City spread throughout an area the size of the entire state of Utah). By far the most densely inhabited area was what is now the

Fig. 6.1. Isolated regions of stone circle building
between 3000 and 2600 BCE.

county of Wiltshire, which may have been home to as many as thirty thousand people.[11]

And it was in Wiltshire that the first of these new creations was built: at Avebury, 17 miles north of Stonehenge. With a diameter of over 1,000 feet, the Avebury Stone Circle is the largest such monument in the entire British Isles. By far the biggest stone circles built before this time were the first Stonehenge and the Twelve Apostles, with diameters only a quarter this size (odd that Avebury is far less famous than the much smaller Stonehenge). The Avebury circle originally consisted of about a hundred stones made from sarsen rock, the same type of hard sandstone from which the later Stonehenge was built (see chapter 1), of which twenty-nine remain, ranging from 9 to 20 feet high, the largest weighing as much as 40 tons. Due to intensive farming and the village that grew up in and around the stone circle, it is now impossible to tell if it had an outlying king stone. The entire circle was encompassed by a truly enormous henge earthwork: a ditch about 30 feet deep and 60 feet wide, surrounded by an embankment some 20 feet high and 40 feet thick. Its outer diameter is about 1,400 feet and encloses an area of almost 30 acres; that's a circumference of over half a mile. The henge's construction would have been an immense undertaking. Using nothing more than antler picks and stone axes, the builders had to cut through over 3 million cubic feet of solid bedrock—almost 200,000 tons of the stuff—to create the ditch and then pile up the rubble to form the embankment, originally some 100 feet from top to bottom. It has been estimated that to construct the henge as well as to cut and shape the megaliths where they were quarried, 2 miles away on the Marlborough Downs, and then drag them to and erect them at Avebury would have taken as many as 1.5 million work-hours. The creation of the Avebury monument must have been of extraordinary importance.[12]

The latest radiocarbon dates obtained from organic material found beneath the stones and in the embankment at Avebury have arrived at a central date of around 2600 BCE, which is the same dating as that of another huge henge monument built 700 miles to the north on the

Orkney Isles. Around a mile to the northwest of the Stones of Stenness is the Ring of Brodgar. This stone circle is about 340 feet in diameter and was originally composed of sixty stones, of which twenty-seven remain, ranging in height from 7 to 15 feet. They have the same slab-like appearance as the Stenness stones and were probably quarried in the same place, near Finstown, about 3 miles to the east.[13] The Ring of Brodgar is set within a 400-foot-diameter circular ditch, about 10 feet deep and 30 feet wide, the outer embankment now having eroded away due to its setting, exposed to the relentless Atlantic weather. Around 450 feet to the east of the circle is a 6-foot-tall outlying monolith known as the Comet Stone. It is actually a few degrees south of true east, as seen from the center of the ring, so it does not seem to align with the equinox sunrise. (The stone's name has no connection to an ancient cometary alignment; it was only coined in 1920 to commemorate the appearance of Halley's Comet. It was previously called the Oil Stone, seemingly due to a local tradition to smear it with wax for good luck.)

Far away to the south, in the county of Dorset a mile from the village of Wimborne St. Giles, is the site of another such monument. There the ruins of a solitary medieval church stand right in the middle of a 330-foot-diameter megalithic henge. Aptly known as Church Henge, the enclosing ditch and its outer embankment are both approximately 30 feet wide. Although now considerably eroded, they are thought to have originally been over 10 feet high and deep. Not much smaller than the henge of the Ring of Brodgar, it is thought to have encompassed a stone circle consisting of around fifty monoliths. Sadly, none of the stones any longer survives, as they were broken up and used to build the church in the twelfth century.

Not all of these newer and much larger stone circles built around 2600 BCE were surrounded by these enigmatic henge earthworks. In Cumbria, for instance, is one of the largest stone circles in the British Isles. Quaintly known as Long Meg and Her Daughters, it originally consisted of around seventy monoliths, of which fifty-nine remain, set in a circle approximately 340 feet in diameter. Some 20 feet to the southwest of the circle is another 12-foot-tall standing stone aligned to the midwinter sunset as seen from the center of the ring.

About the same time as these new giant stone circles were being erected, the practice of building the usual, smaller stone circles was spreading to other parts of Britain where they had not been built before. A typical example is the Nine Ladies stone circle in the county of Derbyshire. Standing on a hill in Stanton Moor, it remains remarkably complete: nine stones about 3 feet high, in a ring just over 30 feet in diameter, with a similarly sized king stone 130 feet to the southwest in the direction of the midwinter sunset. In many of these areas the big henge monuments were also erected at virtually the same time as circles such as Avebury, Brodgar, and Church Henge. Around 35 miles west of Stonehenge, in the county of Somerset, for example, the Stanton Drew Stone Circle stands just outside a village of that name. At 370 feet in diameter, it is the second largest stone circle in the British Isles after Avebury, the Ring of Brodgar, at 340 feet, being the third. Surprisingly for such a large ring, it only seems to have had around thirty stones, of which twenty-seven survive. Heavily weathered and measuring between 6 and 10 feet high, many of them are now fallen.[14] The ring is enclosed by a circular 23-foot-wide ditch, over 440 feet in diameter. No outer bank is now visible, but it is thought to have eroded over the years, as the site lies within the periodic floodplain of the Chew Valley. Around 1,000 feet north-northeast of the circle lies a fallen stone called Hautville's Quoit, all that remains of a 13-foot-tall monolith that originally stood a little to the south of where it is now, where it may have marked the midsummer sunrise before being dragged to its current location by farmers in the eighteenth century. And in central England, 2 miles south of the village of Monyash in the county of Derbyshire, is Arbor Low. A henge about 290 feet in diameter, its outer embankment, 30 feet wide and 7 feet high, and inner ditch, 7 feet deep and 30 feet wide, surround the fallen remains of a stone circle that originally consisted of about fifty monoliths between 8 and 10 feet high. A large broken stone that now lies in the middle of the circle may have been an outlying king stone that was moved there some time in the later Megalithic era.[15]

The fourth phase of megalithic monument building occurred around 2400 BCE, with the addition of avenues to the larger stone circles, usually the henge monuments. These were parallel rows of stones or embankments that led to the stone circles. Just as with the henge stone circles, the creation of these avenues seems to have occurred simultaneously far and wide throughout Britain. To give just a few examples: at Avebury, an 80-foot-wide avenue of parallel monoliths was added to the southeast of the circle. Referred to as the West Kennet Avenue, it originally consisted of about a hundred pairs of stones spaced at intervals of about 50 feet, which followed a relatively straight course for about 1.5 miles to the nearby River Kennet. Today, twenty-seven of the stones, between 4 and 13 feet high, remain standing for the first half mile of the avenue, the remainder having been removed when the village of West Kennet and its surrounding roads were built since the eighteenth century.[16] At the same time the faraway Callanish Stone Circle on the Isle of Lewis, 500 miles to the north, had a more modest 20-foot-wide, 270-foot-long avenue added to the north-northeast of the ring. It is thought to have consisted of about fifty stones up to 11 feet high, of which nineteen survive. And in Cornwall, 130 miles to the southwest of Avebury, geophysics surveys have revealed that a 140-foot-diameter stone circle called the Hurlers, which originally consisted of twenty-eight monoliths, of which fourteen survive, had a 100-foot-long avenue of stones erected, also to the north-northeast of the ring. At some of the larger stone circles, these stone avenues were erected on newly constructed embankments, such as one, 130 feet long and 30 feet wide, leading to the northeast of Stanton Drew. Two parallel ditches lie outside the banks, on top of which stood the rows of monoliths averaging between 4 and 6 feet high. As there were gaps in the henge structures where the avenues met the circles, it is thought that these stone rows may have acted as processional walkways for people entering the main monuments on special occasions. However, not all experts agree:

Fig. 6.2. Some of the many megalithic complexes built
between 2600 and 2000 BCE.

few of the avenues actually align with the sunrise or sunset at occasions such as the solstices and equinoxes, as we might imagine if they were ceremonial walkways; they also seem to have been unnecessarily wide for such a purpose.

The fifth phase of megalithic construction around the large stone circles, somewhere about 2200 BCE, involved the building of further rings or other arrangements of monoliths at the ends of the avenues, and sometimes the addition of a second avenue. At Avebury, for instance, the West Kennet Avenue was extended in a curve some 800 feet to the east to reach Overton Hill, where it ended at a newly built stone circle, approximately 130 feet in diameter and consisting of about forty stones, known as the Sanctuary. The stones have long since vanished, but today concrete blocks mark where archaeologists have determined their positions to have been. During this phase of building, a second avenue of stones was created to the southwest side of the main Avebury circle. Called the Beckhampton Avenue, only one of its monoliths still survives, as they were broken up for buildings in the village of Beckhampton over the last three centuries.[17] In the year 2000 excavations and geophysical surveys conducted by the University of Southampton revealed evidence of parallel rows of holes that once contained standing stones in a similar pattern to the West Kennet Avenue. It is thought to have followed a curved route for about a mile to end in an arrangement of four huge megaliths that were recorded in the eighteenth century as the Longstone Cove.[18] Only one of the Longstone Cove monoliths survives. Going by the name Adam, it weighs an estimated 62 tons. (Nearby there is also a stone called Eve, the only surviving stone from the Beckhampton Avenue.)

Another example is Stanton Drew, where almost exactly the same modifications occurred. An approximately 100-foot-diameter stone circle, probably consisting of twelve 6-foot-tall monoliths, of which eight survive, was added just off center of the end of the avenue built two centuries earlier. The avenue itself was then extended about another 200 feet to the banks of the River Chew; nineteen of these avenue monoliths still survive, the largest being just over 11 feet tall. As at Avebury, a second stone avenue was added at this time, to the south-southwest side of the main circle. It was about 500 feet long and built to the same specifications as the first avenue, leading to a third stone circle some 140 feet in diameter, which is thought to have consisted of twelve stones, of which eleven survive, the tallest being about 6 feet high.[19] In many cases the new complexes consist of extra stone circles close by, often within 300 feet of the originals, without being joined by avenues, such as Church Henge in Derbyshire, the Hurlers in Cornwall, and at Machrie Moor on the Isle of Arran, although these were added later, periodically, over a period of many centuries (see chapter 12).

A further building phase at these stone circle complexes occurred around two centuries later—about 2000 BCE—with the addition of nearby artificial hills. Three-quarters of a mile south of the main circle at Avebury, for example, pretty much midway between the ends of the stone avenues, stands Silbury Hill. At about 130 feet high and covering some 5 acres, it is the largest artificial mound in the British Isles. Archaeologists have estimated that it would have taken around four million hours of work to build from over 0.5 million tons of material, mainly solid chalk hacked from the surrounding land. Astonishingly although it has been both thoroughly excavated and exhaustively scanned with geophysics equipment, there is no indication that any chambers or burials exist within.[20] In the county of Flintshire, North Wales, 145 miles to the northwest of Avebury, stands Gop Cairn, the second largest of these megalithic artificial hills. It is a 40-foot-high mound, over 300 feet wide, standing about half a mile northwest of the village of Trelawnyd, where it is believed a megalithic stone circle complex once existed before being obliterated when the village was built during the Middle Ages. Just as with Silbury Hill, archaeologists have found the hillock to have no internal structures such as burial chambers. A further 400 miles to the north, on the Orkney Isles, a similar construction was built around the same time. Called the Salt Knowe (Scottish for "knoll"), this 130-foot-wide, 20-foot-high artificial mound stands some 450 feet southwest of the Ring of Brodgar.[21] As with Silbury Hill and Gop Cairn, extensive archaeological research has revealed that absolutely nothing resides inside it: no chambers, no monoliths, not so much as a single human bone. These and dozens of similar, single artificial mounds were added to the megalithic stone circle complexes throughout Britain all around the same time. They were clearly not tombs or temples, neither do they contain ceremonial chambers; they can only be described as fake hills that would have taken vast resources to construct. Why they were created is yet another intriguing megalithic mystery.

These, then, were the major phases of construction of the megalithic monuments of the British Isles, from the building of the first stone circle in the Orkneys around 3100 BCE until the creation of the mysteri-

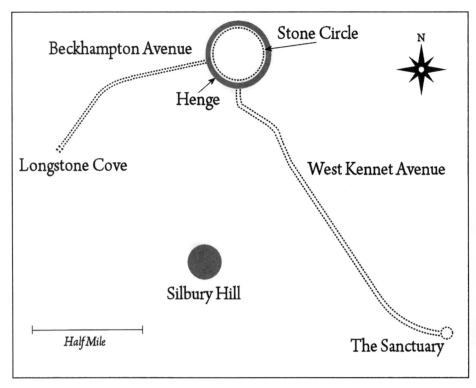

Fig. 6.3. The Avebury megalithic complex.

ous artificial hills around a thousand years later. Once the stone circle obsession had become established throughout many parts of Britain by around 2600 BCE, four further periodic stages of development—large henge monuments, the addition of avenues, the addition of paired stone circles, and artificial hills—each occurred simultaneously in communities that appear to have lived completely independently of one another, right across the length and breadth of the country, at two-hundred-year intervals. There was a degree of trading and no doubt travel between these areas, but there is no archaeological evidence that these ancient Britons were united into any kind of overall kingdom or had any type of central authority. They were divided into dozens, if not hundreds, of separate tribal entities, each a law unto themselves (see chapter 1). Yet somehow, and for some unknown reason, they were nearly all involving themselves in precisely the same monument-building projects, requiring immense amounts of time, enormous manpower, and vast resources. But at one location in particular where these episodic developments occurred, the local inhabitants seem to have been determined to outdo everyone else—and that was at Stonehenge.

7

Rivalry among
the Megalithic Complexes

THE GIANT STONE CIRCLES, often surrounded by henge earthworks and accompanied by outlying monoliths, artificial hills, and avenues leading to smaller rings, are collectively referred to as megalithic complexes. They were built in specific stages that occurred simultaneously throughout many parts of Britain:

Circa 2600 BCE: The building of the grand, larger-scale stone circles, usually enclosed by massive henge constructions

Circa 2400 BCE: The attachment of long avenues of standing stones and parallel linear embankments

Circa 2200 BCE: The creation of smaller satellite stone circles, sometimes at the end of existing avenues, sometimes involving extensions to or the addition of further avenues

Circa 2000 BCE: The building of enormous artificial hills near the grand stone circles

In Ireland, however, the Megalithic culture seems to have been abandoned during this period, until it was readopted around 2000 BCE (see chapter 6).

Avebury may have been the largest such complex, but it was not the most elaborate. That distinction belongs to Stonehenge. It is not its diameter, or the size of its stones, that so distinguishes it among this new generation of stone circles, but its extraordinary design. Stonehenge seems to have started life during the very first phase of stone circle building, around 3000 BCE. It is thought to have originally consisted of fifty-six stones, averaging about 6 feet high, set in a ring some 280 feet in diameter (see chapter 1). As such, it had more monoliths than any of the early stone circles and by far the greatest circumference apart from the Twelve Apostles in Scotland, which was about the same size (see chapter 5). It is also unique, in that the stones from which it was created—the bluestones—came from so far away: from Pembrokeshire in South Wales, where there is evidence that they had previously formed an already existing stone circle in the Carn Menyn district of the Preseli Hills. As stone circle building seems to have ceased throughout Wales for some centuries after it briefly became established around 3000 BCE, it's possible that there was migration into southern England, where the Welsh merged with the population of settlements such as Durrington Walls and, astonishingly, brought one of their own stone circles with them (see chapter 5).

At Stonehenge, in 2008, excavations led by archaeologist Mike Parker Pearson, Ph.D., of the University of Sheffield dated the pits, the so-called Aubrey Holes (see chapter 1), thought to have contained the first ring of bluestones, to around 3000 BCE. The erection of the much larger sarsen stones, quarried from the Marlborough Downs, 20 miles north of Stonehenge, occurred around four hundred years later, the same time that other henge circles, such as Avebury, Stanton Drew, and the Ring of Brodgar, were being built. However, this new circle at Stonehenge was very different from any of its competitors. Called the Sarsen Circle, it was composed of thirty standing stones, each some 13 feet high and weighing around 25 tons, spaced just over 3 feet apart, with a further thirty 6-ton blocks placed on top of them to create a continuous ring of rectangular arches 108 feet in diameter.

Despite how Hollywood often depicts ancient stone circles with lintel stones joining the monoliths to form such arches, no other stone circle in the British Isles is known to have had anything like them. There were lintel megaliths incorporated into various burial structures, such as long barrows, dolmens, and passage tombs, but they are not found linking the monoliths of any stone circle other than at Stonehenge. It certainly wasn't a lack of resources in other locations that left Stonehenge unique in this respect. The work needed to create much larger monuments such as Avebury would have required vastly more people toiling significantly longer than was needed to create the famous Sarsen Circle, no matter how impressive it appears. We have already noted that the specific diameter of any particular stone circle, its size, and number of monoliths do not appear to have been regarded as essential aspects of whatever primary function the stone circles were meant to serve (see chapter 6). The same reasoning must also apply to the arches of Stonehenge. As the arrangement was evidently never copied elsewhere, the addition of lintel stones could in no way have been considered a necessary feature for stone circles generally, in order for them to serve the mysterious purpose for which they were built.

Although circles of standing stones were ultimately erected all over the British Isles, we do find a few minor regional adaptations: for example, the recumbent stone circles of northern Scotland. Around 2700 BCE, the stone-circle-building tradition was adopted on the mainland of the far north of Scotland, mirroring the expansion of the Megalithic culture elsewhere in Britain at this time as it spread out from its earlier enclaves in the Orkneys, northwestern Britain, and southwestern England. The only difference with the stone circles in this part of Scotland is that they are typified by the incorporation of a large monolith lying horizontally between two of the ring's standing stones: the "recumbent stone," from which the monuments get their name.[1] As many of these horizontal monoliths are found on the southwest side of the recumbent circles, the direction of the midwinter sunset, they may have served a similar purpose to king stones elsewhere (although some scholars have suggested the possibility of lunar alignments).

In the far southwest of Britain, another slight variation is found. In Cornwall, some stone circles have a standing stone set inside the ring, such as at Boscawen-Un (old Cornish for "elder farm field") near the village of St. Buryan, where it seems to have been deliberately positioned at an angle pointing northeast, the direction of the midsummer sunrise. Once again, this might be a local variant of the outlying king stones, while in Devon, some stone circles, such as Down Tor Circle on Dartmoor, have single-stone rows, rather than double-stone avenues, leading up to the rings. This is also found on the Isle of Lewis, where the main Callanish Stone Circle had no fewer than three single-stone rows added to complement its existing avenue. Perhaps Stonehenge's Sarsen Circle was a similar local embellishment on a much grander scale,[2] so grand, in fact, that it was never repeated. The precision workmanship required to shape stones to the exact dimensions needed to create such a monument may simply have been considered too much of an unnecessary extravagance to be replicated by anyone else.

But it was not only the lintels that so distinguished Stonehenge; its surrounding henge is also unusual in that the embankment lies *inside* the ditch. At other megalithic henge monuments the embankment was built *outside* the ditch, which is a perplexing arrangement. During the later Bronze and Iron Ages, when regional feuding seems to have occurred in Britain—possibly due to colder, less fertile conditions and a consequent decline in food production—large fortifications were created around settlements. Commonly referred to as hillforts, as many were built on the summit of hills, they consisted of circular ditches and embankments on top of which timber stockades were erected. The hillfort ditches were dug outside the embankments, meaning that attackers would need to descend into a deep, wide trench before climbing a steep embankment to reach the primary fortifications. Very often the ditch would fill with water to create a moat, or at the very least to become a muddy quagmire, bogging down the enemy. The whole thing was constructed to slow and tire adversaries so they could be more easily picked off by spears, arrows, and other projectiles hurled from atop the defensive stockade.[3] If the ditch had been built *inside* the embankment, the ramparts would not only be considerably less effective, they would be self-defeating, hampering defenders within the fort. Intriguingly, this bizarre inside-out arrangement was exactly how nearly all the megalithic henge earthworks were constructed, with the ditch on the inside of the embankment. Whatever function they served, it was clearly not defensive. However, Stonehenge is an exception. There the embankment, about 6 feet high and 20 feet wide, was built inside the ditch of approximately the same dimensions, as would be expected for defensive reasons.

Intriguingly the henge at Stonehenge seems to have existed even before the first stone circle was built: the bones of deer and oxen excavated from the bottom of the ditch have been radiocarbon dated to around 3100 BCE, about a century earlier than the bluestone circle.[4] It is uncertain whether the stones of the original ring were left standing when the Sarsen Circle was erected, but most archaeologists think that they were removed and initially dragged away. The henge is about 360 feet in diameter and stands just outside the first stone circle, which measured some 280 feet in diameter. The Sarsen Circle, with a diameter of only 108 feet, stands well inside the encircling ditch and embankment, implying that the henge was already there when the new circle was erected—otherwise it would have been built closer to the sarsen stones. And if the dating is right, the first bluestone circle was built inside this already existing feature.

The area around Stonehenge was a well-populated region by 3100 BCE, and its people had already built some impressive earthworks, such as the 400-foot-wide, 2-mile-long Cursus, less than 0.5 mile to the north, which dates from around 3500 BCE (see chapter 5). Like the Cursus, might the Stonehenge ditch and embankment have been created for some ceremonial purpose before the stone-circle-building tradition was adopted in southern England? There are a few isolated examples of Neolithic henge earthworks that appear to have lacked stone circles or any accompanying monoliths. For example, in Cumbria there stands the romantically named King Arthur's Round Table, just outside the village of Eamont Bridge, an approximately 300-foot-diameter circular embankment, 35 feet wide and 6 feet high, with an internal ditch 45 feet wide and 5 feet deep. And in the county of Derbyshire, near the town of Buxton in north-central England, there is a monument called the Bull Ring (although it never was one). It is a roughly 200-foot-diameter circular embankment, originally about 7 feet high by 30 feet wide, with an inner ditch around the same depth and width. The former has never been conclusively dated, but the Bull Ring seems to date from around the time that Avebury and the other henge monuments were being built. These, and a handful of other henges without stones, may represent the abandonment of a site before completion, but some scholars argue that such earthworks are rare but complete monuments in their own right.[5] One way or the other, unlike these earthworks, at Stonehenge the ditch is on the outside of the embankment. Not only does it appear to date from five hundred years before the other henge monuments were created—even before the very first stone circles were built—it also is consistent with a defensive structure and unlike a true henge. On balance of evidence, therefore, it would seem that the ditch and embankment at Stonehenge were originally built to protect some kind of existing shrine or settlement, the evidence for which has been eradicated by the extensive remodeling of the site over many centuries. Although the Sarsen Circle was indeed one of the imposing new stone circles created around 2600 BCE, it may share more in common with the few grand stone circles where a henge was not constructed, such as Long Meg and Her Daughters in Cumbria (see chapter 6). It is more likely to have been happenstance that the first circle at Stonehenge was built inside preexisting defensive ramparts that superficially resembled a henge. Ironically it would seem that, despite its name, Stonehenge is not actually a *henge* monument at all.

Because radiocarbon dating is not a precise art, we can only say that

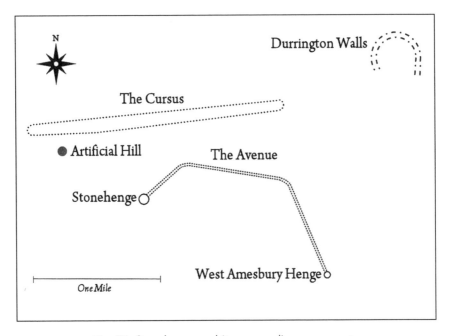

Fig. 7.1. Stonehenge and its surrounding monuments.

the grand stone circles were erected *around* 2600 BCE. In what order they were built is a matter of guesswork. Which came first: Stonehenge, Avebury, Stanton Drew, the Ring of Brodgar, or one of the others? Some researchers believe it was Stonehenge. The builders of the other monuments, it is proposed, may have been unable to replicate Stonehenge's imposing arches, but the surrounding ditch and embankment arrangement *was* copied. This notion, however, seems most unlikely. Those who built the henge monuments went to extraordinary lengths to create them. If they were following the lead of Stonehenge, why build them the wrong way around? Those who built the grand stone circles around 2600 BCE clearly did not duplicate Stonehenge's apparently defensive ramparts. Its surrounding ditch and embankment may have been older, but it must have served a different purpose to henge earthworks such as Avebury and cannot as such be regarded as evidence for Stonehenge's being the first of what were to become the splendid megalithic complexes. Others have suggested that Stenness, dated at about 3100 BCE, was the first stone circle to be surrounded by a true henge. Although there is little visible evidence of it today, excavations indicate that at one time the monument did have an encircling bank and ditch. If this was contemporary with the monoliths—seemingly the oldest stone circle of all (see chapter 4)—then it would indeed be the first henge stone circle in the British Isles. However, due to weathering and movement of the soil over time impairing radiocarbon tests, it is difficult to tell when the Stenness earthwork was actually created. It may have been added much later, around 2600 BCE, in an attempt to turn the Stones of Stenness into a henge monument before the Ring of Brodgar was built nearby (see chapter 6). As things stand at present, all that can be said with any degree of certainty is that the large stone circles, most with henges, all began to appear around the same time. Where the idea started is far from clear.

Returning to Stonehenge, as its Sarsen Circle was built at the same time as the true henge monuments and the other grand stone circles, it does fit into the overall picture of the synchronous development of megalithic complexes as a whole. This also applies to its later accompaniments, such as an avenue built around 2400 BCE, the same period as the first avenues were created at Avebury and elsewhere. The original avenue at Stonehenge consisted of a pair of parallel banks, originally about 6 feet high and 20 feet wide, set about 70 feet apart, with a ditch outside them, which ran straight for about 1,500 feet. Geophysics surveys conducted in the 1980s indicated that uniformly spaced standing stones ran along these embankments: about fifty in each row. As the avenue runs directly in line with the Heel Stone (see chapter 1), as viewed from the center of the circle, in a northeasterly direction, it has been suggested that it may have marked a processional way aligned to the midsummer sunrise. Around two hundred years later the earthen avenue was extended at an angle for three-quarters of a mile to the east, before bending around to follow a relatively straight course for a farther three-quarters of a mile in a southeasterly direction.[6] Due to severe erosion, it is not known whether this extension included standing stones like the original avenue. As at so many other megalithic complexes, a further stone circle was erected at the end of the lengthened avenue at this time.

Excavations conducted in 2008, led by Parker Pearson, uncovered evidence that a long-vanished stone circle, about 30 feet in diameter, consisting of about twenty-five monoliths, had been erected on the spot; further work the following year by Timothy Darvill of the University of Bournemouth and Geoff Wainwright of the Society of Antiquaries provided evidence to date the monument to around 2200 BCE.[7] It is now referred to as West Amesbury Henge.

Like many of the other megalithic complexes, Stonehenge also seems to have had an artificial hill erected nearby about 2000 BCE. Stonehenge is surrounded by many artificial mounds, but these are later burial tumuli (see chapter 9). However, some half a mile northwest of Stonehenge, in an area referred to by archaeologists as Amesbury 50, there are the remains of what seems to have been an earlier man-made hillock. It is now just a circular rise, about 65 feet in diameter and just a couple of feet high, but a land survey of 1913 records it as being very much larger. The exact size is not revealed, but it was referred to as a "hill," which it could in no way be called today. Archaeologists reckon that it was originally over 20 feet high, but it seems to have been leveled by farmers in the mid-twentieth century to create an open field. Excavations and geophysics surveys conducted in 2010, initiated by the University of Birmingham and the Ludwig Boltzmann Institute for Archaeological Prospection and Virtual Archaeology of Vienna, revealed it to have likely been an artificial hill without internal structures, similar to Silbury Hill at Avebury and built about the same time.[8]

By around 2000 BCE there may have been as many as fifty megalithic complexes throughout Britain. Based on their distribution in regions where evidence of them still survives, it seems that the complexes were the principal monuments of the tribal district they served. Due to the astonishing diversity of topography in such a small country, the tribes of Britain appear to have been tiny by international standards—nothing like the huge Native American nations, the tribes of Africa, or the Germanic peoples of the Roman era. Even when the Romans invaded Britain in 43 CE, what is now England, Scotland, and Wales was divided into at least forty major tribes. From excavations of Neolithic settlements, archaeologists believe that there were around fifty primary tribal regions in Britain during the Megalithic era, which tallies with the estimated number of complexes. By 2000 BCE, the population of Britain is thought to have risen to around three hundred thousand, an average of six thousand per tribe. However, these tribal regions varied considerably in size. Some fertile areas around sites such as Avebury might have had populations as large as thirty thousand, while others, in harsher districts such as Dartmoor in Devon, had tribal groups consisting of less than a thousand people. This is typified by the size of monuments. For example, the Scorhill Circle, the principle stone circle of Dartmoor's Gidleigh Moor megalithic complex, is only about 80 feet in diameter, compared to Avebury's enormous 1,088 feet, while its stones average just 4 feet tall, as opposed to Avebury's average of 15 feet. In addition to these complexes there were thousands of smaller, individual stone circles spread throughout the countryside.[9] We could perhaps compare the megalithic complexes to the city cathedrals of medieval England, each catering to a diocese (a clerical district) approximating a modern British county. Every diocese had many individual parishes—towns and villages—all having their own local church, which might be compared to the ordinary stone circles. During the Middle Ages parishioners would regularly attend their home chapel, but on special occasions, such as Christmas and Easter, they would make a pilgrimage to the cathedral. We can only assume that, broadly speaking, this is how the stone circle culture functioned, although whether the religious context of this analogy is appropriate remains to be seen.

Something that the two most impressive megalithic complexes certainly seem to have shared with medieval cathedrals is their rivalry. During the Middle Ages, there was intense competition between the two senior figures of the Church in England: the archbishop of Canterbury, who held jurisdiction over the South, and the archbishop of York in the North. Their cathedrals were the most splendid in the country, and over a period of some four centuries, between 1100 and 1500 CE, a succession of these archbishops made ever more elaborate embellishments to their respective buildings in the hope of gaining the greater prestige. It seems that something similar occurred during the late Neolithic era between Avebury and Stonehenge. Although it all began on the Orkney Isles around 3100 BCE, by 2600 BCE the Wiltshire area had become the thriving heart of megalithic activity. Stonehenge and Avebury were both situated in this region, only 17 miles apart, and the communities they served seem determined to outdo each other. When the Sarsen Circle was erected at Stonehenge, it was a far more sophisticated structure than any other stone circle in the British Isles. Being so close, the Avebury community may well have feared they would lose their "congregation" to the lure of the more impressive monument of their immediate neighbors to the south. Perhaps, lacking the know-how to construct a lintel circle, they decided instead to impress by sheer size. In diameter, Avebury is almost ten times larger than the Sarsen Circle at Stonehenge, and its surrounding henge was enormous compared to its rival's diminutive ditch and embankment. It could of course have occurred the other way around. It might have been the people of Avebury deciding to create the largest henge circle ever built that began this megalithic pride race, with those at Stonehenge reacting to this gigantic undertaking by opting for magnificence over size and constructing something never before accomplished. Even with the most modern dating techniques, it is still impossible to know exactly which of the stone circles was built first. The dating of the various phases of Stonehenge has been made relatively easy due to the monument's isolation. Avebury, on the other hand, is in the middle of a village.

By the Middle Ages a sizable farming community had grown up around the Avebury stones, complete with a parish church, and during the early fourteenth century the priest instructed his parishioners to destroy what he considered to be a heathen monument in their midst. The villagers began to systematically pull down the stones and bury them in pre-dug pits where they fell. After much work, a fatal accident occurred. While one of the huge 13-ton megaliths was being toppled, it collapsed early, crushing one of the workers to death. As the monolith could not be lifted, the corpse remained beneath the stone until it was moved by archaeologists in 1938. Underneath was the skeleton of a man together with the belongings he had with him the day he died. These included three silver coins dating from the 1320s, along with a pair of rusted scissors and a razor. Because of these items he is thought to have been a barber, and after the monolith was re-erected it became known as the Barber's Stone. The destruction of the megaliths appears to have ceased after the death of the "barber." Perhaps the local people feared the curse of the stones more than the wrath of their own priest.

Sadly the Barber's Stone incident was not the last religious vandalism that Avebury endured. In the mid-1600s the Puritan régime of Oliver Cromwell seized power in England, and the destruction of the megalithic complex resumed with a vengeance. This time the stones were smashed to pieces with sledgehammers, their fragments used to construct and repair buildings in and around the village.[10] Even though the Puritans only ruled England for a short while, once people started breaking up the stones for building material it didn't stop. Nearly all the stones that still stood were destroyed by the end of the eighteenth century. By a strange irony, however, a reasonable number managed to survive: those that the medieval priest had ordered to be buried. Today they have been uncovered and re-erected by archaeologists, but because they are no longer in situ it is impossible to obtain reliable dating from organic or ceramic remains that lie beneath them.

So what do we know? There does appear to have been some kind of monument at Avebury at the time the first bluestone ring was built at Stonehenge, although it was not a stone circle. Well inside the Avebury ring there are two particularly large stones—the tallest, a bulky megalith 14 feet high—standing close together. Called the Cove, these stones somehow managed to escape the vandalism and remained standing without disturbance. (There were originally three monoliths in the group, in a triangular formation, but one of them was broken up in 1713.) Consequently it has been possible to date them to around 3000 BCE, the same period as the original stone circle at Stonehenge. Avebury and Stonehenge, therefore, both appear to have been ceremonial sites well before their grand stone circles were created. Although dating the monoliths of the Avebury stone circle is problematic, its henge *can* be dated. Antler picks excavated from the embankment—presumably the remains of the tools used to create it—have been radiocarbon dated to around 2600 BCE.[11] As this is the same period that the other great henge monuments were being constructed, it is fairly safe to assume that the stone circle was a contemporary undertaking. Archaeologists have also been able to establish the layout of the Avebury stone circle by using both excavations and geophysics surveys, determining that it originally consisted of about a hundred stones, of which thirty survive. Judging by the remaining monoliths, they averaged about 13 feet in height and, being much bulkier than the Stonehenge megaliths, weighed as much as 40 tons (as opposed to the Sarsen Circle's 25 tons). So we can say with a fair degree of certainty that the Avebury henge and its grand stone circle did date from the same period as the Sarsen Circle at Stonehenge, and it is quite possible that the builders of each site were attempting to outdo each other: one community with sheer size, the other with splendor.

In addition to the usual accompaniment of avenues, outlying stone circles, and artificial hills found at other megalithic complexes, the builders of Stonehenge and Avebury made further modifications to their respective monuments not found elsewhere. The most amazing accomplishment of this stone-raising contest occurred with the erection of even larger rectangular arches at Stonehenge. Soon after the Sarsen Circle was created, its builders erected some mammoth constructions inside this ring: five pairs of massive sarsen megaliths, each over 20 feet high and weighing up to 50 tons, on top of which were set 8-ton lintel stones. Called trilithons, these five separate freestanding arches were arranged in an open-oval shape, some 45 feet across at its widest point,

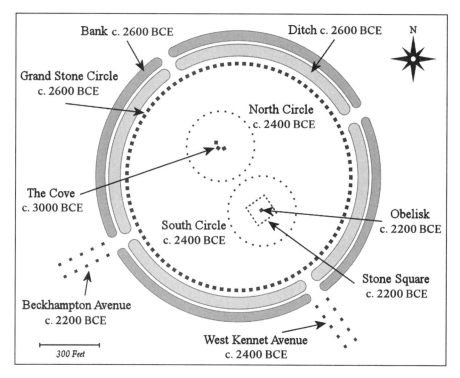

Fig. 7.2. Avebury stone circle by 2000 BCE.

facing toward the Heel Stone (which was probably erected around the same time). Called the Trilithon Horseshoe, it towers over six feet above the surrounding Sarsen Circle.[12]

At Avebury, geophysics and subsequent excavations have revealed that two further stone circles were created, one to the north and one to the south, inside the main ring. Approximately the same size and measuring well over 300 feet in diameter, they each consisted of about thirty stones up to 10 feet tall. Four and five stones survive, respectively, from these northern and southern inner circles, but as with the main circle, dating has proved difficult as they were re-erected, having been toppled centuries ago. Nevertheless, it has been possible to date them indirectly. Today, twenty-seven stones stand upright for the first half of the West Kennet Avenue (see chapter 6). Although most have been re-erected, four of them managed to survive the carnage of the past, probably because they stood well outside the village, and still remained standing when the Scottish archaeologist Alexander Keiller excavated the site in the 1930s. Animal bones unearthed from beneath these stones, thought to have been used to line the pits into which the stones were set, were later radiocarbon dated to provide a central date of around 2400 BCE. As similar organic remains dating from the same period have been excavated from a hole that originally contained one of the inner circle's monoliths, it is thought that both features were contemporary. If so, then Avebury's inner circles were created a century or two after trilithons at Stonehenge.[13]

By this time, Stonehenge saw the creation of its own inner circle: 80 feet in diameter, it consisted of thirty stones, averaging about 6 feet high, set between the 108-foot-diameter Sarsen Circle and the Trilithon Horseshoe. Known as the Bluestone Ring, it was not made from newly cut monoliths, but from the bluestones that are thought to have once formed the original circle at the site, presumably having survived being discarded somewhere nearby. Later, around 2000 BCE, another feature was added within the Sarsen Circle. Made from a further twenty of the original bluestones, it was an open-oval arrangement inside the Trilithon Horseshoe. Called the Bluestone Horseshoe, it measured some 35 feet across and matched the arrangement of the trilithon formation.[14]

If Stonehenge, with its extraordinary arches, had once bettered Avebury, it seems that by 2000 BCE circumstances had reversed. These new features at Stonehenge, the Bluestone Ring and the Bluestone Horseshoe, had no lintel stones and required none of the work and ingenuity needed to create the earlier Sarsen Circle and the trilithons. As existing monoliths were employed, these new features did not even necessitate the quarrying, cutting, and hauling of new megaliths. At Avebury, on the other hand, the builders were still going strong. Not only had they created two long avenues, rather than Stonehenge's one, but they also had built a completely new type of feature in the middle of the southern inner circle. Geophysics surveys in the summer of 2017 revealed that at the center of the ring about twenty new stones had been erected in a 100-foot-square arrangement, surrounding what is estimated to have been a huge, 20-foot-tall obelisk.[15] This giant freestanding megalith dwarfed the 6-foot-tall monolith, now confusingly called the Altar Stone (see chapter 1), erected in the center of Stonehenge by this time. And when Silbury Hill, the largest artificial mound in the British Isles, was added to the Avebury complex around 2000 BCE, the people of Stonehenge were just not up to the competition. Silbury is enormous, 548 feet in diameter, compared to Stonehenge's artificial hill of just 65 feet across. The Stonehenge mound would probably not have been much more than 20 feet high, whereas Silbury was a gigantic 130 feet high.

Although at Stonehenge and Avebury we find the same synchronous developments that occurred at the other megalithic complexes, like the addition of avenues, satellite circles, and artificial hills, the significant internal embellishments, such as the large-scale and elaborate arrangement of other monoliths, are limited to these two sites. There are a few isolated examples of inner rings being added to some smaller stone circles. For instance, the 90-foot-diameter Gunnerkeld Stone Circle in Cumbria, consisting of forty 5-foot stones, had a 30-foot-diameter ring of thirty stones erected inside it sometime around 2600 BCE, which might have been an attempt to outdo the nearby, similarly sized Castlerigg Stone Circle, about 18 miles to the west. Apart from Avebury and Stonehenge, of all the thousands of stone circles that would have existed in Britain, less than thirty are known to have had inner rings, and most of these were small monuments with stones less than a couple of feet high, and they were erected during the later Bronze Age, after 1500 BCE. Hence, it is difficult to interpret the exceptional embellishments found at Stonehenge and Avebury as anything other than evidence of local rivalry.

So by 2000 BCE we have around fifty large megalithic complexes all over Britain, the most imposing being Stonehenge and Avebury, each perhaps serving a particular tribal region in which there were hundreds of simple stone circles. But there is another type of monument that survives from the Megalithic era, and there are thousands of them. These are the solitary monoliths known as *menhirs* that stood alone and isolated from the stone circles. These lone standing stones are just as mysterious as anything created during Neolithic times, perhaps more so. Their existence has ignited one of the greatest controversies concerning the prehistoric British Isles: the enigma of the infamous ley lines.

8

Long Stones and Ley Lines

THE TERM FOR AN ISOLATED, freestanding monolith from the Neolithic period is "menhir," an old Celtic word meaning "long stone," coming from *maen* (stone) and *hir* (long). This may have been what the Celtic people called these enigmatic solitary megaliths, but the Celts didn't arrive in Britain until the late Megalithic era (see chapter 9). As with the stone circles, we have no idea what these single standing stones were called by the people who first erected them or, as archaeologists have found no evidence that they were grave markers, what purpose they originally served. They vary from just a couple of feet to over twenty feet high and, as their name implies, are generally tall and slender—the average being about 8 feet high, 3 feet wide, and 2 feet thick—and they tend to taper toward the top. However, there are numerous examples of other, different shapes and sizes. It is impossible to know just how many once stood throughout the British Isles, but some researchers have suggested there may have been over twenty thousand. There is no official estimate of how many *still* exist, but it has to be in the thousands.

Like the other megalithic monuments, surviving menhirs are found mainly in less populated areas such as the boggy uplands of Dartmoor in the county of Devon. There, many remain, such as the Beardown Man, the Loughtor Man, and the Harbourne Man, ranging between 8 and 11 feet tall, which all stand alone on the windswept moors. These are examples where the word "man" has replaced the earlier word "maen" for such stones, but in nearby Cornwall, where the Celtic language was spoken longer than elsewhere in England, the old name for the isolated standing stones is still found, such as Boswens Menhir, near the town of St. Just; Trevorgans Menhir, near the village of St. Buryan; and Try Menhir, near the village of Newmill, all about 8 feet high. The tallest of Dartmoor's menhirs is a 4-foot-wide, 14-foot-high megalith called the Bone, which stands in a misty vale aptly known as Drizzlecombe. But this was not the largest standing stone to have stood on Dartmoor. Many of its historically recorded menhirs have been destroyed, such as one on Hart Tor. (*Tor* is an old English word for a hill or rocky peak). Sadly, this 25-foot-tall monolith was broken up for building rubble in the late 1800s.[1]

These solitary standing stones can be found all over the British Isles. In England, in the county of Hereford, for example, we find a variety of different shapes, typifying the diversity of such monoliths found elsewhere. We have the usual tall, slender ones, such as the Pentre House Stone, which measures 10 feet tall, 3.5 feet wide, and 2.5 feet thick, now lying flat and overgrown in woodland close to the village of Bredwardine. Then there are shorter ones, such as the 4-foot-high, 1.5-foot-wide Wergins Stone, near the town of Hereford, which stands in the middle of an open meadow, surrounded by a rather ugly metal framework for its protection, and bulky ones, such as the Queen Stone in a farmer's field near the town of Goodrich: over 7 feet high and 5 feet wide, this squat megalith is heavily grooved by millennia of rainfall.[2]

Hundreds of menhirs survive in Wales too. In North Wales, near the town of Criccieth in the county of Gwynedd, is the Betws Fawr (Big Chapel) standing stone. Around 8 feet tall, it stands serenely among grazing cattle in a grassy pasture. In Mid Wales, in the bleak mountains of the Brecon Beacons, stands the 12-foot-tall Maen Llia, which is Llia's Stone in English; it still retains its Celtic name, as modern Welsh is derived directly from the ancient Celtic tongue. And in South Wales, on the edge of a scenic forest in the valley of the River Usk, near the

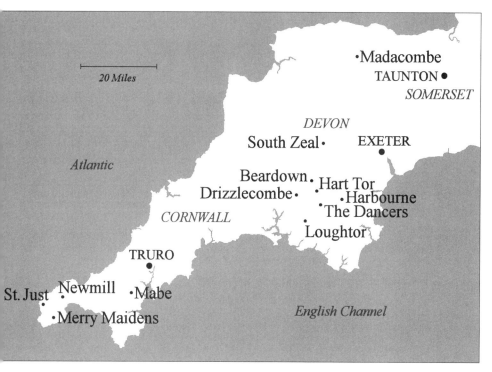

Fig. 8.1. Southwestern England sites discussed in this chapter.

village of Llangynidr, is the aptly named Fish Stone: 14 feet high and 4 feet wide at its broadest, it is shaped like an enormous fish standing upright on its tail.[3]

Because of its extensive regions of wilderness, Scotland probably has more surviving menhirs than any other part of Britain. Typical of the more accessible examples are the 9-foot-high, 4-foot wide Airthrey Stone, which stands beside a playing field on the campus of the University of Stirling; the 10-foot-tall Macbeth's Stone on the grounds of Belmont Castle near Dundee, named after the famous eleventh-century Scottish king who is reputed to have killed a sworn enemy nearby; and an 11-foot-tall menhir that stands right beside the busy A949 road near Loch Ospisdale in the north of Scotland: called Clach a'Charra, Gaelic for "stone of vengeance," it is said that enemies of the local clan were hanged on a tree that once stood beside it.[4]

There are also hundreds of menhirs in Ireland, but as the Megalithic culture seems to have been abandoned there around 3000 BCE before being readopted about a millennium later, it is a special case we shall be examining later (see chapter 11).

These are just a few examples of the menhirs that still survive. The vast majority have been obliterated over the years, and not just in well-populated areas. In sparsely inhabited districts, solitary standing stones were broken up to repair walls or farm buildings as late as the twentieth century, before being protected under law. In Cumbria, for instance, only one of six menhirs recorded in the area around the village of Cumwhitton during the 1800s now survives. Even in a really remote location such as the Isle of Lewis, megalithic standing stones were being destroyed for building material well into the modern era. Scotland's tallest monolith is Clach an Trushal (the Stone of Compassion) at Ballantrushal on the northwestern side of the island. About 5 feet wide, it stands almost 19 feet high and is the last of at least ten similarly sized menhirs documented in this part of the island during the eighteenth century. The last of these others was only removed in 1914 to be used as a lintel stone for a new building. We do, however, sometimes find menhirs that have managed to survive in the most unlikely locations. At South Zeal in Devon, one particular standing stone was used to support the wall of a medieval priory erected around it. The building is now a pub called the Oxenham Arms, where the 14-foot-tall monolith can still be seen in the corner of the bar, standing in the same location where it was originally erected thousands of years ago.[5] Some such stones have even survived in the middle of busy conurbations. Just off the main shopping street of the bustling harbor town of Gourock on the Firth of Clyde in Scotland, for example, there stands a 6-foot-tall menhir called the Granny Kempock Stone, protected by an ornate set of railings. For centuries, local sailors believed it was good luck to touch the stone before setting out to sea. So seriously did townsfolk take the superstition that in 1662 a local woman was, somewhat ironically, burned for witchcraft when she tried to have it removed. In more recent times it was said that no one dared move the megalith as they feared being cursed by the spirit of the alleged witch (oddly, the same woman who wanted it moved).

Often such stones managed to survive because they stood in what became Christian cemeteries. When Christianity first became established in Britain, at the end of the Roman era (in the mid-fourth century), many megalithic monuments were still being revered by the native Britons, although the Megalithic era ended there three hundred years before (see chapter 10). As was their practice throughout the newly Christianized late Roman Empire, the Catholic Church, rather than demolishing existing pagan shrines, tended to build their places of worship on ground already considered hallowed by the local population without destroying their preexisting shrines. And these often included stone circles. More elaborate medieval churches were later erected on the sites of these earlier chapels, usually with no attempt to demolish the surrounding megalithic rings, the reason being that land immediately around the church had been consecrated as a graveyard. We have already seen an example of this: Church Henge in southern England, where the ruins of a medieval church stand inside what was a 330-foot-diameter stone circle (see chapter 6). A Welsh example is found in the tiny hamlet of Ysbyty Cynfyn (King Cynfyn's Hospice) in the county of Ceredigion. There, the church of Saint John the Baptist stands in the middle of a stone circle whose megaliths, up to 11 feet high, survive in its surrounding wall. And in Scotland, a remarkably well-preserved recumbent stone circle survives in the graveyard surrounding the church at Midmar in the county of Aberdeenshire. It consists of seven upright monoliths, the tallest over 8 feet high, and a huge, 14-foot-long, horizontal megalith, weighing an estimated 20 tons, in a circle about 55 feet in diameter. Likewise, there are numerous examples of churches being erected next to single menhirs, and many of these stones still survive in their ancient graveyards. In the extreme southwest of the British Isles, for instance, there is one in the graveyard of Saint Laudus Church in the village of Mabe in Cornwall, and in the far north there is one in

Strathblane churchyard in Scotland. Most are no larger than 8 feet tall, but some are very much bigger. The largest of all surviving menhirs in the British Isles stands in the graveyard of All Saints Church in the village of Rudston in the county of Yorkshire: at 25 feet high, it dwarfs the Christian tombstones around it.

Interestingly there are many examples of menhirs having been erected in what were clearly intended to be alignments. The largest such stones are found in North Yorkshire: five monoliths, up to 22 feet high, stood in a straight line about 200 feet apart, crossing fields in the district of Boroughbridge. Called the Devil's Arrows, only three now survive, the others having been pulled down to be used in the construction of a nearby bridge in the eighteenth century. Such alignments were created from megaliths that were erected relatively close to one another, but in 1921 the English amateur archaeologist Alfred Watkins proposed that even the solitary menhirs had been raised at locations that formed straight lines across the British countryside. In his book *The Old Straight Track,* published in 1925, he advocated that menhirs were created as markers, set along age-old trackways.[6] Although such monoliths usually stood alone, miles apart, Watkins believed that on maps they could be shown to fall in alignments linking ancient settlements. They either acted as marker stones, he argued, or were erected as sacred obelisks along the archaic roads that the Neolithic people once traveled, similar to the way that shrines to saints are found along modern roads in Catholic countries such as Ireland. Watkins found that many of his supposed menhir alignments ran through places containing the syllable *ley* in their names, such as the villages Amberley, Bowley, and Foxley in his native Herefordshire, and concluded that this may have been the original word for the ancient roads. Accordingly he called his alignments "ley lines" (pronounced "lay"), and the name stuck. The academic community was not convinced. The suggested alignments, it was countered, were down to pure chance. One particular opponent plotted the locations of post offices on maps in an attempt to show that they fell in straight lines with just as much probability. Whether or not menhirs were deliberately erected in straight lines, modern archeology has shown that Watkins' reputed alignments have no link to ancient tracks. Apart from the fact that aerial surveys, geophysics, and excavations have failed to find evidence that they followed the course of Neolithic roads, many of the proposed "old straight tracks" ran right across huge obstacles, such as rivers, estuaries, marshes, and even mountains, and not around them, as would be expected with trackways.

Although archaeologists were loath to accept Watkins' ideas, the hippie movement in the 1960s came to embrace them with a passion. The notion that ley lines had been roads or trading routes was abandoned, and instead they were seen as channels of mystical power. The first person to write about the new theory, and possibly the one who initiated it, was British author John Michell. In his book *The View over Atlantis,* published in 1969, Michell advocated that ley lines marked conduits of "spiritual force" that ran through the Earth and were tapped by ancient priests, similar to the concept of *feng shui* in China.[7] According to this hypothesis, ley lines were—or were thought by their creators to be—the ancient equivalent of electric power lines, conducting some kind of supernatural energy through the Earth. These lines had been sensed by Neolithic dowsers, it was proposed, and the menhirs were erected to mark their course, with stone circles being built where ley lines crossed, marking locations where the power was at its strongest. Further elaborations to this theme were proposed by other researchers, with the eventual, most popular idea being that standing stones could somehow tap into this energy, in the way that acupuncture needles allegedly manipulate the so-called meridian channels of the human body. The energy of ley lines, it is argued, had been used to heal the sick, fertilize the land, gain spiritual enlightenment, commune with deities, and induce heightened states of mind.

Today, New Agers still congregate at stone circles and solitary menhirs in the belief that they can, even now, experience or manipulate this magical power. The notion of ley lines as some kind of paranormal power grid has found popularity around the globe, many people believing that they exist throughout the world. In this modern rendering of the theory, originally propounded to account for the apparent alignment of British menhirs, ancient cultures all over the Earth built sacred monuments on ley lines. Regardless of whether or not such psychic contours actually exist, the important question we need to address here is this: Do the megalithic standing stones of the British Isles really fall in straight lines as Watkins first proposed?

The big problem with ley lines is that, since Watkins' time, it is not only monuments from the Megalithic era that have been used to plot them. As we have seen, many old churches were built within stone circles or beside standing stones, and Watkins drew attention to this, often using them as his ley markers. Subsequent ley line enthusiasts jumped to the conclusion that *all* medieval churches ended up being built where stone circles or individual monoliths once stood and consequently included them as feasible ley markers. Additionally as Watkins had surmised that *ley* had been the original name for such alignments, many "ley hunters," as they came to be known, also included any locations with that syllable in their name, as well as its apparent variants, such as *lay, lea,* or *leigh*. From the 1960s all sorts of ancient sites that had nothing to do with the Neolithic period were added to the list of locations to pinpoint when plotting ley lines: Iron Age hillforts, medieval moats, holy wells, natural springs, even castles and ruins of any kind, to name just a few.

Watkins himself had included holy wells in his list, and one of his proposed ley lines, on the Malvern Hills in the county of Worcestershire, ran from Saint Anne's Well, through several natural springs and two other holy wells and only passed through two actual menhirs.[8] Natural springs are precisely what their name implies, places where an underground stream bubbles to the surface as a consequence of the terrain, while holy wells were built around such springs and dedicated to saints during the Middle Ages, when they were thought to be have miraculous healing properties. Such wells and springs were often venerated by the Celts before the Christian era and may also have been considered sacred by the Megalithic people, but their locations were set by topography, and they were not deliberately created to mark out tracks or lines of any kind. Some researchers have argued that "energy-carrying" ley lines were in part created by such springs, which seems to be a rather self-defeating argument, as nature does not fashion water systems in straight lines.

Fig. 8.2. Sites in Wales and western England discussed in this chapter.

If we really wish to determine whether megalithic monuments actually do line up more than would be expected by chance alone, then we should only include sites known with a fair degree of certainty to date from the Megalithic age. These would include stone circles, menhirs, stone rows and avenues, passage graves, henge earthworks, and artificial mounds such as Silbury Hill and Gop Cairn. Ley hunters tend to include *all* ancient burial mounds when plotting ley lines. However, long barrows and dolmens date from before the Megalithic era (see chapter 3), while round barrows—usually marked on the map as "tumuli" (singular *tumulus*)—date from the right period but are far too numerous to help draw any real conclusions concerning alignments (see chapter 9). For some reason ley hunters also include ancient military structures, such as castles, hillforts, and moats, as ley markers. Not only were these created centuries after the Megalithic era had ended, but they also were specifically built at readily defendable sites, compelled by the landscape; these were seldom the same kind of locations chosen by the Neolithic people for erecting *their* monuments.

When we examine many proposed ley lines—even those most cited by ley hunters to support their case—they don't really stand up to scrutiny. There are hundreds of proposed ley lines all over Britain, but let's concentrate on the area with the most elaborate megalithic monuments: the county of Wiltshire, which includes Avebury and Stonehenge. If there are going to be genuine ley lines anywhere, then surely it's going to be there. One of the most cited alleged ley lines in the British Isles is the so-called Stonehenge Ley, an approximately 19-mile alignment said to follow the course of the original 1,500-foot-long avenue at Stonehenge.[9] It is delineated by eight sites. Drawing a line on the map from the center of Stonehenge, along the avenue, and continuing in a northeasterly direction, it passes through Sidbury Camp, an Iron Age hillfort about 7 miles away, and ends a mile farther on with two tumuli in fields called Barrow Plantation. In the other direction, the ley is defined by a further tumulus, a second Iron Age hillfort called Grovely Castle, and an old pond thought to have been sacred to the Celts, and it ends at yet another Iron Age hillfort called Castle Ditches, some 11 miles from Stonehenge.

Out of these eight sites, only Stonehenge and its avenue are megalithic stone monuments. Three of them are forts, built on hilltops for defensive reasons centuries after the Megalithic period had ended, and three are Bronze Age tumuli. Although stone circles and other megalithic monuments were still being erected during the Bronze Age, so it could be argued that their locations might have been influenced by the same considerations that dictated where standing stones were erected, there are literally hundreds of such burial mounds in the Stonehenge area (see chapter 9). Draw a line virtually anywhere on the map around Stonehenge and it is difficult to avoid its passing through a number of them. One of the apparently ancient sites on this purported ley line is actually a duck pond, which may or may not have been considered sacred at some point in the past, leaving us only with Stonehenge itself as a site worthy of consideration in any serious attempt to determine whether megalithic monuments were deliberately aligned. All we can say with certainty about this supposed ley line is that Stonehenge did have an avenue of standing stones leading in a northeasterly direction. At present no evidence has been found for the existence of any other megalithic *stone* monuments anywhere along this line.

Another famous ley line in the area, known as the Old Sarum Ley, includes six sites and runs in a roughly north-south direction for approximately 20 miles, between a tumulus just to the north of Stonehenge and Frankenbury Camp on the edge of the New Forest.[10] It passes through the stone circle and on for 5 miles to ancient earthworks called Old Sarum before continuing through Salisbury Cathedral and Clearbury Ring to end at Frankenbury Camp. Frankenbury Camp is an Iron Age hillfort, and so is Clearbury Ring (although, confusingly, its name sounds as though it might be a stone circle). Old Sarum consists of various earthworks on and around a hill, some 2 miles north of modern Salisbury, which include Anglo-Saxon and medieval defensive embankments. Archaeologists have determined that the site *was* occupied during the Megalithic era, but it was a Neolithic village and extensive excavations have uncovered no evidence for any kind of megalithic monument ever having been erected there. As for Salisbury Cathedral, it was certainly not built on a pre-Christian sacred site. The original cathedral stood elsewhere and was re-erected in its present location during the thirteenth century, on land belonging to the wealthy bishop who initiated the project. If, as before, we also exclude the tumulus, due to the sheer number of them in the district, we are again left with only Stonehenge as a known megalithic monument on this celebrated ley line.

As discussed, ancient churches were often built within or beside stone circles and next to menhirs, but ley hunters tend to include *all* old churches when plotting alignments. The problem here is that although pre-Christian shrines were often the locations where the first chapels were built, the majority of such sites would not have been megalithic monuments, but pagan temples of the later Romans, Anglo-Saxons, and Vikings, and during the Middle Ages (from around 1100 to 1450 CE) many churches were built in completely new settlements. Without knowing for sure that Neolithic standing stones existed at the site of an old church, it would be unwise to include it as a proposed ley marker. Nevertheless, many assumed ley lines include medieval churches, regardless of their history.

Another famous ley line in southern England is the 22-mile Glastonbury Ley, running through Glastonbury Tor in Somerset, a hill that local legend holds was the mystical land of Avalon, and Gorsey Bigbury, a 130-foot-diameter henge monument some 11 miles to the north.[11] There are seven sites on the proposed ley line: it begins at Saint Nicholas's Church in Brockley, 18 miles north-northwest of Glastonbury, passes through Holy Trinity Church at Burrington, the Gorsey Bigbury henge, Westbury Camp, a small stone at a crossroads in the village of Yarley, through the ruins of Saint Michael's Church, which stands on top of Glastonbury Tor, and ends at Saint Leonard's Church at Burleigh, some 3 miles farther to the south. Westbury Camp is an Iron Age hillfort, and the stone at Yarley is a medieval boundary stone. As for the churches, all four date from the Middle Ages, after the eleventh century, and only one of them, Saint Leonard's, is known to have been erected on the site of an earlier church, dating from before this period. And at none of these churches is there evidence of a stone circle, henge earthwork, or menhir nearby. The Glastonbury Ley actually consists of only one known megalithic site, Gorsey Bigbury, and doesn't even include Glastonbury itself. Glastonbury Tor is a natural hill, not an artificial mound like Silbury Hill, and although it does appear to have been occupied as a settlement during Neolithic times, despite extensive archaeology, no evidence of a stone circle, menhir, or any other megalithic monument has been uncovered.

Enthusiasts draw attention to the syllables *ley* and *leigh* being found in the locations Brockley, Yarley, and Burleigh along this supposed ley line. We have seen how Watkins had proposed that the frequency in which these and similar syllables were found in the names of sites along his plotted alignments implied that *ley* or *leigh* was the original name of his "old straight tracks." He was, however, completely wrong. The origin of this word has nothing to do with trackways, let alone mystical power lines. The suffixes *-ley, -lea, -lay,* and *-leigh,* found in English place names, all derived from the Old English word *leah,* which referred to a woodland clearing.[12] And there are thousands of them. Randomly place a pin anywhere on a map of England and you will inevitably find a place bearing this suffix somewhere nearby.

Another often-cited ley line is the so-called Silbury Hill Ley, said to go through Avebury and Silbury and to terminate at Marden Henge approximately 6 miles to the south.[13] These three sites are indeed megalithic structures, but if the line is drawn through the center of Avebury and the summit of Silbury Hill, it misses Marden Henge by about half a mile. To get them to line up, going through the summit of Silbury Hill, the proposed ley only touches the western edge of the Avebury ring and the eastern edge of Marden Henge. The premise of ley lines, originally proposed by Watkins, is that they were marked out by menhirs, just a few feet in width. Marden Henge is more than 200 feet in diameter, and Avebury is over 1,000 feet. Critics say that unless an alignment goes through the center of a monument it can hardly be used as a ley marker; if we start using sites that cover such a large area, rather than just employing the middle of them, then we can draw ley lines just about anywhere.

Fig. 8.3. Sites in Scotland and northern England discussed in this chapter.

The other famous ley line said to pass through Avebury, known as the Avebury Ley, joins an ancient settlement on Windmill Hill, about 2 miles northwest of the stone circle, with another settlement on Martinsell Hill, 6 miles to the southeast of Avebury.[14] Windmill Hill was occupied in Neolithic times, although no evidence of any kind of megalithic monument has been found there, while Martinsell Hill was the site of an Iron Age hillfort. Nevertheless, even if we choose to use them as ley markers, of the other five sites on the alignment, one is a tumulus, one is a long barrow dating from before the Megalithic period, and another is a crossroads (at Bayardo Farm) where there is what appears to be a *natural* stone buried in a bank. The remaining two are linear features: the Ridgeway, an ancient road, and Wansdyke, a long defensive ditch and embankment. The Ridgeway is thought to be the oldest track in England and does date from Neolithic times, but Wansdyke was built by the Britons to hold back the invading Anglo-Saxons during the fifth and six centuries CE. But even if we use these features as ley markers, they cross the proposed alignment and run for 80 and 20 miles, respectively. Clearly, this stretches the size of ley markers way beyond the width that makes any kind of logical sense.

If ley lines really do exist as alignments of megalithic sites, then surely there would be one between Avebury and Stonehenge, the two best known and most elaborate megalithic monuments in Britain. They lie only 17 miles apart, which is the usual sort of length of proposed ley lines found in most books and websites dedicated to the subject. A straight line drawn on the map to join the center of these two monuments passes through six of the kind of sites generally used by ley hunters to plot their alignments. However, none of them are confirmed megalithic monuments. We have the West Kennet Long Barrow, which dates from before the period in question; Saint Mary's Church at Alton Barnes, which, although over a thousand years old, retains no evidence of standing stones in its vicinity; Casterley Camp, an Iron Age hillfort; a couple of late Bronze Age tumuli near Stonehenge; and the Cursus (see chapter 5), dating from around four hundred years before the Megalithic era. But if we suspend disbelief and accept that this might represent a deliberate alignment of ancient monuments, do six such sites falling between two stone circles represent something that would occur more than by chance alone? Typical of ley lines are the two we have examined that are said to cross at Stonehenge: the Stonehenge Ley, an approximately 19-mile alignment consisting of eight sites, and the 20-mile Old Sarum Ley consisting of six sites. It would seem that finding six to eight ancient sites along an approximately 20-mile line is considered convincing evidence by most ley hunters. So let's try an experiment.

On a detailed map, I have just drawn a completely arbitrary 19-mile line passing through Stonehenge. It runs from the summit of Knowle Hill, near the village of Bowerchalke, to a tumulus beside the A342 road in the district of Everleigh. Starting with Knowle Hill, 12 miles south-southwest of Stonehenge, these are the sites and features—the same as those generally employed by ley hunters—the line passes directly through:

1. It follows, almost perfectly, the course of an old track called Stoke Down for nearly 2 miles. (Ley lines are said to follow the course of old roads and footpaths.)
2. A tumulus three-quarters of a mile west of Hunts Down.
3. A Neolithic earthwork of unknown purpose called Cross Dykes, south of the village of Burcombe.
4. Saint John's Church, Burcombe, built on the foundations of an Anglo-Saxon chapel dating back at least 1,100 years.
5. A tumulus 1.5 miles west of Upper Woodford.
6 and 7. Two round barrows on Normanton Down.
8. Stonehenge.
9. The middle of the Cursus to the north of Stonehenge.
10. A tumulus near Baden Down Farm.
11. The tumulus at Everleigh, which is actually one of three ancient burial mounds, built close together in a line crossing our alignment.

If we leave out Knowle Hill, which is just the starting point, by pure chance we have no fewer than eleven typically employed ley features on a 19-mile line drawn completely at random: three more than the Stonehenge Ley and five more than the Old Sarum Ley, both approximately the same length as our totally imaginary alignment. And these are two of the most cited ley lines in Britain. It seems to me, at least, that the notion of ley lines being alignments of megalithic monuments—or for that matter any ancient monuments—fails to stands up to scrutiny.

Watkins began the whole idea by proposing that his "old straight tracks" were delineated by alignments of menhirs, so it is curious that so few actual standing stones are found along the famous ley lines we have examined. However, although long-distance alignments may be down to pure chance, it does seem that individual monoliths were sometimes deliberately aligned close to stone circles. The largest series of stones of such an alignment are found in North Yorkshire. Five menhirs, up to 22 feet high, stood in a line, about 200 feet apart, crossing fields in the district of Boroughbridge: the Devil's Arrows mentioned earlier in this chapter, on page 132. If we continue this line about 5 miles to the northwest, it passes through the Cana Barn and Hutton Moor henge monuments. Five standing stones and two huge henge circles, falling in a line running only 5 miles, does seem more than just coincidence. Another example is found at the other end of England, in Cornwall. There, we find that a line drawn from the center of the Merry Maidens Stone Circle, near the village of St. Buryan, passes through two aligned stones called the Pipers to the northeast and runs through at least three other standing stones before reaching the sea at Merthen Point, which would seem beyond a fluke for a line less than 1.5 miles long. There are many examples of single rows of megaliths falling in straight lines where the stones are placed fairly close together, within a few feet of each other. On Dartmoor in Devon there are dozens, the longest being a line of more than eight hundred monoliths, up to 8 feet tall, stretching over a mile between the Dancers Stone Circle on Bledge Hill and a Neolithic artificial mound at Green Hill to the north. Shorter single-stone rows are more common, such as an alignment in South Wales consisting of eight stones up to 9 feet tall (two are fallen and two have been removed since the nineteenth century), which runs for 120 feet near the village of Llanychaer, and the Madacombe stone row on Exmoor in Somerset, now consisting of twelve relatively small standing stones, which archaeologists have determined was originally made up of an alignment of many more, almost 1,000 feet long.

Local alignments aside, what exactly was the purpose of the solitary menhirs? Did they serve as some kind of shrine in places with populations too small or not prosperous enough to build a stone circle? Did

Fig. 8.4. Ley lines around Stonehenge and Avebury.

they serve some astronomical function, like various stone-circle monoliths, such as king stones, seem to have served? Where they, perhaps,
giant sundials to mark the course of the year? Menhirs were not unique
to the British Isles. Similar, isolated, freestanding monoliths are found
in great numbers across the English Channel in Brittany. There are

hundreds of lone megaliths in this historical French region, where they are also known as menhirs, as a variant of the Celtic language is still spoken in Brittany today. The largest menhir in the British Isles is the one in the Rudston churchyard in Yorkshire, which stands 25 feet high. At least a dozen French menhirs are taller than this, the largest being the now fallen Er-Grah monolith at the coastal town of Locmariaquer. It is about 67 feet long and broken into four fragments and is estimated to have weighed an astonishing 342 tons. The tallest one that is still standing is the 37-foot-tall Menhir de Kailhouan in the district of Plésidy.[15]

The Breton menhirs are generally bigger and older than those in the British Isles and seem to date from the cairn-building period between 4500 and 3000 BCE (see chapter 3), whereas the earliest of those dated in Britain were erected after this period and were contemporary with the stone circles. As the practice seems to have died out in Brittany before it was adopted in Britain, it would seem unlikely to have been a tradition copied from France. Erecting single standing stones is not unique to either country. They exist all over Europe and beyond and date from Neolithic until medieval times. In diverse cultures they were erected for a variety of reasons: as the simplest form of monument to commemorate an event, honor an ancestor, or venerate a god, or for a whole host of other reasons. Perhaps the solitary menhirs should not be considered monuments directly related to stone circles at all.

9

The Migration of
the Beaker People
and Other Cultures

IN BRITAIN, THE MEGALITHIC AGE lasted for over three thousand years before it ended with the Roman invasion of the mid to late first century CE. There had, however, been four earlier large-scale migrations from continental Europe through which the use and building of stone circles continued unabated. In fact, the monuments became ever more elaborate. Astonishingly whatever purpose the stone circles served, it seems to have appealed to a succession of completely different cultures.

The first mass influx of foreigners into the Megalithic British Isles came from what is now the Netherlands. Beginning around 2600 BCE it was driven by rising sea levels flooding this low-lying region. No one knows what the migrants called themselves, but archaeologists have termed them the Bell-Beaker or simply Beaker people, named after a distinctive type of bell-shaped pottery vessel, or "beaker," found in their graves, graves that were very different from the kind of burials being practiced by the contemporary Britons. After a brief period of building passage tombs in a few areas, the Megalithic culture seems to have abandoned elaborate interments, opting instead to bury their dead, either intact or as cremated remains, in simple pits, unmarked by any kind of lasting monument (see chapter 6). The Beaker people, on the other hand, buried their departed beneath round barrows.[1] A group of wonderfully preserved examples are the Nine Barrows near the village of Priddy in the county of Somerset. This cluster of 4,500-year-old, circular earthen mounds, averaging about 65 feet in diameter and rising to about 10 feet high at the center, stands close together on a high ridge of land to be seen for miles around. These are the same kind of mounds that exist in the hundreds around Stonehenge and Avebury, usually marked on the map as "tumuli" (see chapter 8). The round barrow was nothing like the long barrow or dolmen of the pre-Megalithic era or the passage tomb of the early Megalithic age, as it contained no inner chamber. It was a solid construction of earth and rubble: a circular hillock surrounded by a ditch from which the material was excavated to build the mound over a simple grave.

The Beaker people first settled in southern England, but within a century they had established a presence as far north as the top of Scotland. However, this was clearly not an invasion. No archaeological evidence has been found that the Beaker people and the native population engaged in fighting to any discernible extent. No defenses were erected around settlements, and no human remains have been unearthed exhibiting the kind of injuries sustained in battle. On the contrary, the two peoples seem to have lived and worked harmoniously together, while at the same time retaining their cultural identities.[2] Specific burial customs usually reflect a society's religious traditions, and in Britain, for both groups, these remained unchanged. Archaeological excavations in and around Durrington Walls, the largest known contemporary settlement in Britain (see chapter 5), for example, have revealed that both pit and round-barrow burials occurred side by side for centuries following the newcomers' first arrival.[3] That they should seemingly have maintained their religious differences is strange indeed, when the evidence reveals that they were both involved in the continued building of stone circles. Far from ending or watering down the Megalithic age, the influx of the Beaker people appears to have initiated its most extravagant phase.

The first stone circles, erected between 3100 and 2600 BCE, had generally been straightforward rings of monoliths, with nothing more than an outlying king stone located in the direction of the sunrise or sunset at a specific time of the year. Then, around 2600 BCE, the grandiose, larger-scale stone circles, often enclosed by massive henge constructions, suddenly began to be built (see chapter 6): an abrupt development that coincided precisely with the arrival of the Beaker people. Archaeologists believe the reason that these much larger, more elaborate monuments were suddenly erected was due in part to the increase in population and consequently the workforce necessary to create them. Today few scholars doubt that the construction of the Sarsen Circle and the subsequent developments at Stonehenge were joint efforts by the native and Beaker people living together at settlements such as Durrington Walls.[4] Another reason for concluding that the newcomers were actively involved in creating these monuments is a unique variation found at some of their larger round barrows. In addition to the surrounding ditch, they were encircled by an outer embankment—exactly the same as a henge earthwork. That this was adopted by the Beaker people only *after* they had settled in Britain, and at exactly the time that identical earthworks began to be created around stone circles, indicates that the henge was a collective innovation.[5] Most archaeologists are in agreement that Avebury, for instance, was a collaborative undertaking by both cultures living alongside one another at nearby settlements, such as one on Windmill Hill, about a mile northwest of the site. But such combined enterprises did not end with Stonehenge and Avebury. Evidence of the same kind of cooperation in constructing stone circles is found all across Britain, and it continued right through the extraordinary period of megalithic monument building between 2600 and 2000 BCE.[6] This is the era that saw not only the creation of large-scale henge circles but also the building of stone avenues, linear embankments, satellite rings, and enormous artificial hills (see chapter 6).

Clearly these illustrious stone circle complexes were not a new idea brought to Britain by the Beaker people: they never constructed such monuments themselves on the continental mainland.[7] The native Britons, on the other hand, were already building stone circles—and had been for five hundred years. All the evidence points to the new, more elaborate megalithic structures being created through a mutual endeavor by the two cultures. Yet if their burial customs are anything to go by, both retained their separate religious practices. Ancient cultures seldom opted to build temples to foreign gods unless they were enslaved or conquered, and as we have seen, this certainly was not the case during the period the Beaker people and the native Britons were living peaceably together. And it was not only larger monuments that were built; transformative new elaborations also were added to stone circles once the newcomers arrived. All this would seem to suggest that these monuments were something other than religious shrines. They may have served some *practical* function that was beneficial to both groups. Such reasoning is further supported by the fact that cooperative work on megalithic complexes ultimately involved yet another cultural group.

Around 2000 BCE there was a new influx of people into Britain, this time from what is now Belgium. Known as the Wessex culture, after the region of south-central England where their remains were first identified, they brought with them the beginnings of the British Bronze Age. Bronze is made by mixing copper with a small amount of tin, forming an alloy that is much harder and more useful than either metal alone. It seems to have first been made in Mesopotamia around 3300 BCE, leading to the rise of the Sumerian civilization shortly after, and was soon adopted in Egypt and the Indus Valley (see chapter 3). Knowledge of bronze manufacturing had spread northwestward into Europe, and it was being produced by the Wessex culture at the time they came to Britain. However, unlike the first civilizations of the Middle East and India, they had not developed the technology to make the alloy in the quantities necessary to revolutionize daily life. Bronze was a rare and valuable commodity, and its use was pretty much restricted to the making of ritual objects. Although bronze axes, arrowheads, and even swords have been found dating from the late Neolithic period in Britain, these seem to have been made for a privileged few, probably the tribal leaders. For the most part implements continued to be Stone Age items made from flint, bone, and wood. The British period from around 2000 BCE is often referred to as the Early Bronze Age, but for all practical purposes the Bronze Age did not really begin in Britain until the widespread use of the alloy for the regular making of tools occurred around 1200 BCE.[8]

It was the ornamental bronze artifacts that the Wessex culture made that distinguish their graves. The Beaker People interred their dead with simple pottery vessels, whereas the newcomers' burials included a variety of bronze grave goods, such as decorative knives, bowls, pots, bracelets, and various amulets. The richest of them included items also made from gold. These grave goods, along with the human remains, were buried in what is called a *cist* or cistvaen, a simple rectangular box dug into the earth and lined with flat stone slabs, with a capstone placed over the top. The more lavish examples also had a mound built over them. Such tombs were nowhere near as large as the dolmens of a thousand years before. The word *cist* comes from the Latin *cista,* meaning "chest," which is basically what these small constructions were, rather than actual burial chambers. Although these cistvaens were first identified in south-central England, they are found all over Britain.

One such tomb, called Bryn yr Ellyllon (Goblins Mound), near the town of Mold in North Wales, dates from about 1900 BCE. It contained a single skeleton buried with about three hundred amber beads, various sheets of bronze, an ornate urn, and, most spectacular of all, a shoulder adornment made from pure gold. Known as the Mold Cape, the item is a collar adornment designed to fit over the shoulders, upper arms, chest, and back. It was beaten out of a single piece of gold and intricately decorated with rings of abstract ornamentation. Because of its shape and size, it is thought that the person buried there was a high-ranking woman, possibly a priestess. Now in the British Museum, it is one of the most magnificent pieces of prehistoric art yet found in the British Isles.[9]

Another such cist tomb, dating from around 1700 BCE, in the far southwest of England, is Rillaton Barrow on Cornwall's Bodmin Moor. In its little stone compartment, measuring about 6 feet long and 3 feet wide, which survives almost intact, human remains were found, along with a bronze dagger, stone beads, pottery, and a handled gold cup about 3.5 inches high.[10] These are particularly rich cistvaens, but many others, with less luxurious grave goods, have been found all over Britain, dating from 2000 to 1200 BCE.

As with the arrival of the Beaker people over five hundred years earlier, there is no evidence of fighting between the Wessex culture and the indigenous population. The practices of native pit burials, Beaker tumuli, and Wessex cistvaens continued alongside one another in communities all over the country. Just like the Beaker people before them,

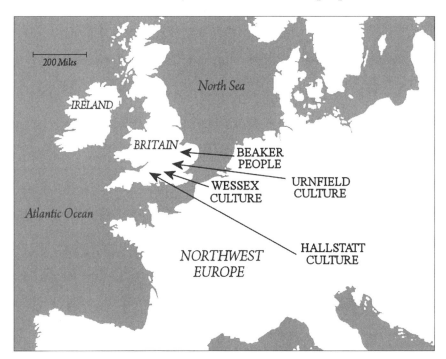

Fig. 9.1. Migrations to the British Isles
between 2600 and 700 BCE.

the Wessex culture seems to have embraced the stone circle tradition, though, once again, retaining their own religious customs, as evidenced at megalithic complexes created after their arrival. One such undertaking at Merrivale, on Dartmoor in the southwest of Britain, consisting of a stone circle, stone avenues, and an artificial hill, is surrounded by a number of contemporary cistvaens, as well as Beaker tumuli and native pit burials. An example from the far north of England is the Moor Divock megalithic complex in Cumbria, which includes a primary circle and two smaller rings originally joined by avenues. A nearby settlement has been excavated to reveal all three types of burials, dating between 2000 and 1500 BCE. And during this same period in Scotland, the Callanish Stone Circle (see chapter 5) was transformed into an elaborate complex consisting of stone rows, avenues, and an artificial hill. As well as both Beaker barrows and pit burials, some of the largest cistvaens in the British Isles have been excavated there. These, and many similar sites, provide pretty conclusive evidence that all three cultures, although continuing with their distinctive funerary practices, worked together on the megalithic monuments, which continued to be created right up until around 1200 BCE.[11] But with the next wave of migration into Britain, things drastically began to change.

The Beaker people and Wessex culture migrations seem to have been driven by rising sea levels affecting their homelands in the low-lying coastal areas of the Netherlands and Belgium. Since the end of the Ice Age, the waters had been continuously rising, slowly but surely, due to higher temperatures. However, the migration of a new people, originally from an area that now includes Austria and Germany, seems to have been triggered by the sudden onset of *colder* weather. Until around 1200 BCE the British climate was warmer than it is today, more like we would now find in the South of France. But then, quite quickly, the overall climate changed from what is known as the Subboreal to the sub-Atlantic climatic age, when temperatures dropped significantly. This has been determined by the remains of vegetation unearthed by archaeologists from the relevant levels of human occupation, showing at that time the local extinction of certain warm-weather flora and a marked increase in the kind of plants and trees that favor colder conditions.[12] Various theories have been proposed for this climatic change, involving shifting ocean currents, volcanism, and an alteration in the sun's activity. Whatever the cause, it was to have dramatic consequences for the inhabitants of northern Europe.

In Austria and Germany a cultural revolution was already taking place. This was the beginning of the true Bronze Age, when the alloy was being produced in sufficient quantities to make a real difference to daily life. Bronze tools, such as more efficient spades, axes, knives, and farming implements, were replacing more fragile Stone Age ones. On the one hand this was fortunate, because the longer, colder winters meant that producing enough food was becoming ever more problematic. But with harsher conditions came protectionism. In order to safeguard their precious resources, settlements began to be fortified, and the new bronze tools made it easier to build much bigger earthen structures, such as defensive ditches and embankments, and to work lumber into wooden stockades.[13] Around 1200 BCE fortified hilltop settlements were replacing the open communities of the lowlands. Generally referred to as hillforts, these new communities consisted of a cluster of dwellings on a relatively flat-topped hill around which a ditch was dug, together with an internal embankment surmounted by timber ramparts and fortified gatehouses to guard the entrance. Inevitably, this siege mentality, together with the new bronze technology, led to the development of weapons of war, such as swords, battle-axes, daggers, and metal-tipped arrows and spears.[14] A completely new kind of warrior culture was being born, a people the Greeks later referred to as the Keltoi. Today we know them as the Celts. The Celts proper, with their distinctive art, customs, and tribal structure, did not come into being until a few centuries later, in the Iron Age, when they came to occupy large parts of central and northeastern Europe. But their culture began with the peoples of Austria and Germany at the end of the second millennium BCE. The kind of tumuli and cist burials prevalent before this time were obviously too much of an extravagance for the sort of pragmatic society that had emerged. Instead, the dead were cremated and their ashes placed in pottery urns buried in fields, leading to the name by which archaeologists refer to these early Celts: the Urnfield culture.

Regular crop failures and food shortages, due to the climate change, impelled the Urnfield people to push westward into Belgium and the Netherlands, and from there they mounted raids across the English Channel to pillage the coastal settlements of southeastern England. Initially the people of Britain were totally unprepared for such incursions. The raiders were armed with bronze weapons from which the Britons had almost no defense. What began as raids soon turned into a mass migration by disparate warrior bands that brought to an end the peaceful, two-thousand-year-old Megalithic age.

By around 1000 BCE the whole of mainland Britain had changed. The building of megalithic monuments had ceased, and hillforts and fortified settlements appeared in every part of the land. What happened cannot really be described as an invasion, however, as the Urnfield culture consisted of numerous separate tribes. Besides which, the Britons swiftly adapted to the new situation and soon copied the bronze-making skills of the newcomers. They also created hillforts. Although Urnfield cemeteries are found in parts of Britain, the majority of graves excavated from this period are those of the preexisting population. Modern DNA analysis has shown that by this time the Neolithic, Beaker, and Wessex people had, for all intents and purposes, merged into a single culture that no longer buried their dead in a lavish way. For the most part, funerary customs had been reduced to simple graves and pit burials for all the inhabitants of Britain.[15] Moreover, their lifestyle became almost identical to that of the Urnfield culture, apart from the Germanic mode of urn burials, which continued for a while in parts of eastern Britain. Even this had changed by 900 BCE. British culture during this era is classified as Late Bronze Age, a period when ethnic groups are virtually indistinguishable from one another. Most Britons, no matter what their ancestry, were simply being buried in the ground, cremated or otherwise, without cists, grave goods, or identifying mounds. Archaeologically visible burial rites had all but disappeared. Times were harder; the new way of life just didn't lend itself to time-consuming and costly burials. A divisive ethos had descended on Britain. Local areas were controlled from hillfort settlements, and small regional clans covetously guarded what they possessed.

By around 700 BCE the new Britons may have felt relatively safe from one another in their hillforts, but an external and far more powerful foe was arriving in the southeast of England. For a hundred years or so, the Urnfield culture in continental Europe had been transformed by the Iron Age, when iron replaced bronze for the making of most common utensils, tools, and weapons. The melting point of iron is just over 1,500 degrees Celsius (2,732 degrees Fahrenheit): around 1,300 degrees higher than tin and nearly 500 degrees more than copper, the primary components of bronze. Its industrial production therefore occurred much later than that of these other metals. It is generally thought to have begun in the Hittite Empire, centered on what is now Turkey, although this is still a matter of scholarly debate. One way or the other, the Iron Age by 800 BCE had reached Austria, where it rapidly changed the entire nature of the Urnfield culture and initiated a new period of Celtic expansion.[16]

Although steel (a later-developed alloy made from iron and other elements, primarily carbon) has vastly superior tensile strength than bronze, the kind of iron used during the Iron Age was no harder and had no greater capacity to hold an edge. The reason for iron's superiority is that once the process of its smelting has been mastered, it can be produced in much greater quantities: iron-ore-bearing rocks are considerably more common than those of copper and tin. The kind of skirmishes and armed conflicts that occurred during the Bronze Age involved only a few participants actually wielding metal weapons; the majority were still fighting with Stone Age paraphernalia. Once the Iron Age took hold, most warriors could be armed with iron weaponry. A further disadvantage of bronze is that it was made from two metals rarely found in the same place. Tin and copper mines were usually miles apart. In Britain, for example, the main tin-mining area was in the southwest of England, while the primary copper mines were far away in northern Wales. Bronze production required continued trade between separate tribal regions. Once an Iron Age enemy had severed these trading routes, the supply of bronze was cut off. It was for these reasons that once the Urnfield culture in Austria and Germany had mastered the secrets of iron production, they quickly assumed control of much of central and northwestern Europe.[17] This new Celtic phase is known as the Hallstatt culture, named after a site near Salzburg in Austria, close to the modern border with Germany, where a huge cemetery of the period was excavated during the nineteenth century.

From around 700 BCE, metal farming implements, such as the iron-tipped ploughshare, made the cultivation of heavy soils possible in areas previously difficult to farm. The advances in metalworking also brought about a huge increase in the number of household utensils, decorative objects, and various ritual items being produced, such as bracelets, brooches, torcs (neck rings), amulets, cauldrons, and other artifacts, along with more lavish ornamentation of weapons belonging to high-status individuals, such as daggers, shields, and swords. Celtic art is typified by gold, silver, and bronze artifacts decorated with intricate designs incorporating scrolling, cording, and elaborate maze-like patterns, as well as lifelike representations of fauna and flora, which have survived to be seen today. Other advances during the Iron Age included the introduction of the potter's wheel, the lathe for woodworking, and the rotary quern for grinding grain. All of this resulted in larger communities where society was divided into factions: smiths, artisans, farmers, and manufacturing workers, together with the full-time armed defenders needed to keep them safe. Inevitably this led to social stratification and the emergence of a rigid cultural hierarchy previously unseen in northern Europe.[18]

The transformation of Britain from the Bronze to the Iron Age began with the Hallstatt culture settling virtually unopposed in the East of England. However, once the knowledge of iron working reached

Fig. 9.2. Prehistoric British sites discussed in this chapter.

this country, the practice quickly spread and the native population rapidly adopted the ways of the invaders. During the early Iron Age, the people of Britain were effectively absorbed into the new form of Celtic culture that had developed on the Continent (mainland Europe), largely without a fight. The new technology was of benefit to all, and enhanced food production resulted in a substantial population increase, reaching a million for the first time. Somewhere around fifty separate tribal regions seem to have existed throughout Iron Age Britain, each controlled by a series of hillforts.[19]

To protect these additional people, many new fortifications were built, but often existing Bronze Age hillforts were expanded and reinforced, sometimes with multiple ditches and embankments. The earthen remains of around 2,500 Iron Age hillforts exist throughout mainland Britain, most having two such ramparts, but some, probably the tribal capitals, having more. Maiden Castle, in the county of Dorset in southern England, for example, developed from a 16-acre, single-rampart Bronze Age settlement into a triple-ringed stronghold with ditches and embankments about 30 feet deep and high surrounding a central plateau nearly 50 acres in size. Some hillforts, such as Old Oswestry in the county of Shropshire in central Britain, were protected by four such earthworks. The immediate countryside in the protective shadow of these fortified settlements was peppered with small farming communities set within an ordered landscape of fields and livestock compounds and joined together by trackways. The standard Iron Age dwelling was the roundhouse, a circular building with low walls made from timber or stone, with a wooden-framed thatched roof. In the hillforts, many of these buildings served as workshops, and larger ones acted as both the residence and court for chieftains or district rulers.[20]

The common funerary practice for most people in Iron Age Britain seems to have been cremation; inhumation (the burial of bodies) was reserved for the higher-ranking members of society, who were interred in pits along with their possessions, such as jewelry and weapons, as well as household and ritual objects. These high-status individuals seem to have been buried clothed, as textiles have been found remarkably well preserved in graves dug in the anaerobic conditions of peat bogs. From such finds, it is thought that women wore dresses, tunics, and skirts, and men wore breeches with lower-leg wrappings, all made from woven wool, often multicolored. People kept warm with woolen shawls and capes made from animal hide worn with the fur facing inward, and footwear was laced and made from leather. Even hair has been preserved in such graves, showing that the preferred style seems to have involved braiding and top knots for both genders.[21]

The domestication of horses had begun during the Bronze Age, as trappings used to harness the animals to wagons have been found at various archaeological sites dating from 1200 BCE. There is, however, a lack of bridle gear, which would be evidence for horses being ridden, before the Iron Age. Horses were not only ridden in Britain after the arrival of the Hallstatt culture, but chariots also make an appearance. Small, light, wickerwork versions have been found in many graves from the Iron Age, having been dismantled and buried with their owners.

To recap, no fewer than five different cultures had merged to become the ancient Britons the Romans would eventually encounter:

3100 BCE	Neolithic Britons
2600 BCE	Beaker people
2000 BCE	Wessex culture
1200 BCE	Urnfield culture
700 BCE	Hallstatt culture

By 500 BCE, Britain was a very difference place from what it had been during the earlier Megalithic era. Although the country was divided into separate tribes, each controlled by a chieftain and ruling warrior elite, the domestication of horses meant that there was regular travel and extensive trading between the separate regions, all sharing a common Celtic culture. And it was a culture that can be considered much

closer to a true civilization than anything that had gone before. The tribal regions were each overseen from a fortified capital and controlled by armed warriors, trackways for riders and wagons joined communities together, and a priesthood (which we shall be examining in the next chapter) seems to have wielded a degree of overall authority that united the tribes into something of a single entity.

Although most people were either cremated or buried in simple pits, the leading members of society, chieftains of both sexes, were often interred beneath mounds, a practice that had not been seen in Britain for centuries. These mounds were built either from earth, giving them a similar appearance to earlier tumuli, or from large piles of stones, known as cairns. Many excellent examples have survived in Wales, such as the so-called Red Cairn, which is one of a group of burial mounds at the Garn Goch Iron Age hillfort in the district of Llandeilo in the Brecon Beacons, just to the south of the village of Carmel in the county of Carmarthenshire, and three huge stone cairns that stand in a row inside the early Iron Age hillfort of Foel Drygarn in Pembrokeshire. The best-preserved examples of high-status Iron Age burials have been excavated in Yorkshire in northern England. The site, on the land of Arras Farm near the town of Market Weighton, included a number of burial mounds up to 25 feet in diameter containing the bodies of men and women interred with splendid funerary goods, such as pendants, brooches, bracelets, rings, necklaces, and horse trappings, four of them containing entire chariots.[22] The most elaborate Iron Age burial sites, however, are box tombs, a kind of scaled-up cist, but built above ground level rather than in a pre-dug pit and covered by a cairn (large pile of stones) rather than a simple mound of earth and rubble. These rare tombs, also known as box cairns, seem to have been reserved for the priesthood (see chapter 11).

Intriguingly such Iron Age burial mounds reveal that, although few *new* megalithic monuments were created, the old ones were still being used: the Celts were deliberately building these tombs inside or right next to the ancient stone circles. For example, in the far south of

England the Yellowmead Stone Circle, near Sheepstor in Devon, had an Iron Age burial cairn constructed inside it, as did a stone circle known as Fingal's Cauldron on the Isle of Arran in Scotland. At Castlerigg in Cumbria an Iron Age burial mound, which now survives as a rectangular arrangement of ten stones, was built within the stone circle, and at Callanish on the Isle of Lewis a 20-foot-diameter chambered mound was erected inside the ring as late as the first century BCE. In some places excavations have revealed that entire megalithic complexes continued to be used: the organic remains of ritual feasting have been found at such sites, dating from throughout the Iron Age. At Llanidan on the Isle of Anglesey, for instance, the 180-foot-diameter henge circle of Bryn Gwyn continuously served as a ceremonial center until the area was overrun by the Romans in 60 CE.

The archaeological evidence clearly shows that, far from being abandoned around 1200 BCE, in many parts of Britain stone circles and other megalithic monuments continued to hold some special significance for the local population throughout the Celtic era. Most remarkably Stonehenge itself seems to have been used by the Celts right up until the time of the Roman invasion in 43 CE. The oldest historical reference to Stonehenge is thought to be by the Greek writer Diodorus Siculus in his *Bibliotheca Historica* (Library of History), written around 50 BCE, shortly after Julius Caesar led an abortive campaign to Britain. He refers to an island to the north of what is now France (presumably Britain) having a round temple sacred to a sun god where an influential priesthood regularly performed rituals. The devotees of this god, we are told, lived in a city close by. Stonehenge could indeed be described as a circular temple, and we have seen, it was aligned to the midsummer sunrise, perhaps giving foreign visitors reason to associate it with the worship of a solar deity.[23] In 2008 archaeological excavations at Stonehenge unearthed evidence of ritual feasting at the site dating to this very period.[24] And just over a mile to the east of Stonehenge is one of the largest Iron Age settlements in Britain, possibly the nearby "city" referred to by Diodorus. Now called

Vespasian's Camp, it was continuously occupied from the Bronze Age until Roman times.

The people who were using Stonehenge and other megalithic sites when the Romans came to Britain were not the same people who built them. However, as the Celts continued to revere these ancient stone circles, they may well have inherited knowledge concerning their original purpose from their predecessors. Perhaps they were using them for the very same reason. Culture after culture appears to have been transfixed by these unique monuments of the British Isles and to have continued to venerate them regardless of their ethnic differences. No contemporary texts reveal how any of these people themselves regarded the megalithic monuments: none of them, even the Celts, developed their own form of writing—that is, until the Romans arrived. It is therefore to Roman writings concerning the Celtic Britons and their beliefs that we now turn in our quest to understand just why the enigmatic stone circles were built.

10

Celtic Inheritance and the Roman Invasion

SO FAR, OUR INVESTIGATION into the stone circle mystery has relied on archaeological discoveries. Now, however, we have reached the point in British history when written records were compiled by the Romans. In 55 and 54 BCE, Britain was subjected to campaigns by Julius Caesar, and a century later, under Emperor Claudius, the island was successfully invaded. As we have seen, megalithic monuments were still being used at this time. So do Roman authors tell us what function the stone circles actually served? There survive a number of primary historical sources that include events relating to this period in Britain.

- *The Gallic Wars* by Julius Caesar, his own account of campaigns in northwestern Europe, which provides a wealth of detail concerning the culture of the Celts in general, including Britain, during the 50s BC
- *The Annals, The Histories,* and *The Life of Julius Agricola* (usually referred to collectively as *The Agricola*) by the Roman senator Publius Cornelius Tacitus, who wrote around 100 CE
- *The Twelve Caesars* by Gaius Suetonius Tranquillus, commonly

known as Suetonius, a Roman historian who wrote during the
early second century CE

- The *Roman History* by Cassius Dio, a Roman statesman of Greek
  origin who wrote around 200 CE

Before considering what these sources might reveal concerning how
the Britons regarded the megalithic monuments, we need to examine
just why the Romans were impelled to occupy Britain at all, bearing
in mind the kind of problems the invasion entailed. It all involved the
very people who were still using the stone circles: an enigmatic Celtic
sect called the Druids.

The Roman war machine was unlike anything seen before: a full-
time, professional army of trained soldiers, separated into military units
akin to a modern fighting force. It consisted of legions, comparable
to brigades, made up of about five thousand men commanded by a
legate, the equivalent of a modern colonel. Each legion was designated
by a number (the 1st, 2nd, and so on) and divided into ten cohorts of
around five hundred men, similar to a modern battalion, commanded
by a *praefectus cohortis,* the equivalent of a lieutenant colonel. In turn,
the cohort was made up of units known as *centuriae* (singular *centuria*),
or centuries, which originally consisted of a hundred men (hence the
name), but by the time Britain was invaded they numbered around
eighty. These were commanded by a *centurion,* the equivalent of a modern captain, and the smallest unit was the *contubernium,* corresponding
to a modern squad, consisting of eight men led by a *decanus,* similar
to a sergeant. In the first century CE the entire Roman army stood at
around thirty legions, but during campaigns each five-thousand-strong
legion was enhanced by up to the same number of auxiliaries. These
were recruited from foreign peoples, such as the Germanic tribes or
those from already occupied lands. Their Latin name, *auxilia,* means
"reinforcements," but for all intents and purposes they were mercenar-
ies, providing extra manpower and specialized fighting techniques.
Auxiliaries were less armored, hence more mobile than legionaries, and

were often used to attack enemy positions or pursue retreating opponents. Like the Roman soldiers themselves, these warriors were not conscripts but paid and skilled volunteers.[1]

Depending on the rank and function of individual soldiers, armor included metal helmets with back guards and side panels to protect the neck and face, coats of chain mail, metal or leather breastplates, shoulder armor, and shin guards. The front-line infantry carried sturdy, rectangular, vertically curved shields that were made from two sheets of wood glued together, covered with canvas or hide, and reinforced with a central metal boss. Known as *scuta* (singular *scutum*), they were about 3.5 feet high and 2 feet wide, and they were designed to be locked together to form a defensive wall in front of and above the combatants when they were arranged in what was called a *testudo,* or "tortoise," formation (as the configuration resembled the animal's protective shell). These soldiers were virtually invulnerable to enemy arrows, while the lengthwise, outward curve of the shield was designed to deflect spears. The opposition was thus forced to engage them at close quarters, which was exactly what the Romans wanted. The legionaries were armed with a short stabbing sword called a *gladius,* which could be thrust into opponents between narrow slits in their shield wall. Behind the front line were troops hurling javelins called *pila* (singular *pilum*). Around 6.5 feet long, their wooden shafts were joined to a 2-foot shank made from a softer iron than the head, causing it to bend upon impact, rendering it useless for the enemy to throw back. Most of Rome's opponents had simple, flat wooden shields; once these had a long, weighty, twisted javelin sticking out of them, they became heavy, unwieldy, and almost useless until the item was removed. And while attempting to pull it out, the warrior was defenseless against further javelins and showers of arrows launched from behind the Roman front lines. The Romans also had cavalry trained to guard the flanks and to break enemy formations, as well as deadly artillery. The *ballista,* a kind of giant crossbow, was a highly accurate weapon able to launch large projectiles, such as darts, stones, or iron balls, at targets up to 1,500 feet away. As well as being used as siege devices, the ballistas also were employed to pick off individual opponents, such as tribal leaders; some were specially mounted on carts to create a type of light, mobile field artillery. Then there was the heavy artillery: various types of huge catapults for demolishing fortifications.[2]

Just like modern armed forces, the Roman military was a standing army. When they weren't fighting the soldiers spent their time training, over and over, to prepare for all eventualities. The Britons they were to face were woefully unprepared for such foes. They were no single entity like the Roman war machine but were divided into separate tribes with only a few full-time warriors: local militia whose main purpose was to keep law and order and to defend their land against incursions by adjacent tribes. No Celtic population, in any part of Europe, is known to have employed a regular military set up as we would understand it today. Organization was according to status. Only the warrior caste would be fully armed and protected by chain mail, helmets, and decent armor; the majority of those engaged in the fighting—usually farmers and other workers conscripted at the last minute—would have no protection at all, apart from a small shield. Some would have swords and some spears, but many would be armed with little more than makeshift weapons adapted from farming implements, such as axes, sickles, and pitchforks. But even the Celtic swords—long, unwieldy, slashing weapons—were virtually useless against the testudo formations employed by the Romans. British horsemen were few and uncoordinated, far removed from effective cavalry. The Britons mainly used their horses to pull chariots. These were nothing like the huge metal carriages with knives attached to the wheels and drawn by multiple horses that were imagined by the Victorians and sometimes portrayed in the movies, but small, single-horse-drawn wicker carts with a driver and a warrior aboard, armed with a bow and spears. They were deployed in rapid hit-and-run maneuvers, usually aimed at slaying officers or harrying the less defended soldiers behind the front lines. These caused problems for Julius Caesar when he campaigned in Britain in the mid-50s BCE, but a century later, during the successful invasion, the Romans had adapted to counter this threat. The Britons had archers, of course, but the Romans' testudo formations, their armor, and their military tactics meant that their soldiers were either well protected or out of range. Crucially, the Britons had no long-range weapons or artillery. Roman artillery, however, made short work of the wooden stockades surrounding Celtic hillforts. It was all pretty much one sided. When the Britons were on the offensive, their only option was basically to charge head-on at the enemy, which might have worked well when fighting among themselves, but against the Romans it was invariably a rush to slaughter. So successful was the Roman army in Britain that, in one battle fought in 61 CE, Tacitus relates how eighty thousand Britons fell with the loss of only four hundred Romans.[3]

The Romans, however, did have a weakness: they were badly prepared to fight in mountainous or forested regions. In 9 CE, for example, Emperor Augustus sent three legions to invade Germany east of the Rhine. There, they were forced to march through dark woodland, along narrow tracks and through ravines, in columns stretched out for miles. The campaign was a short-lived disaster. The army was continually ambushed by the Germans. Small bands of warriors repeatedly sprang from the thick forest to cut down the passing troops, while spears and arrows rained down from the cover of trees and rocks. Roman soldiers were trained to fight in open land, in large, tight-knit formations, and caught in file, they were in complete disarray. Over a period of three days they were cut to pieces, and the last survivors of three entire legions were hunted to extinction. Many, including their commander, Varus, chose suicide rather than fall into enemy hands.[4] This same vulnerability was to cause problems for the Romans' British operations: many parts of the country were forested, while Wales and northern England were mountainous, so both regions took years to be subdued. In fact, the Scottish Highlands were so treacherous that the Romans failed utterly to conquer Scotland.

It is concerning Roman campaigns against the Celts that we have our first written accounts regarding those who were still using the ancient stone circles in Britain (see chapter 9). Between 58 and 50 BCE, Julius Caesar conquered the Celtic territories of Gaul, an area encompassing present-day France, Luxembourg, Belgium, most of Switzerland, and northern Italy, as well as the parts of the Netherlands and Germany on the west bank of the Rhine.[5] But despite this remarkable military achievement, the great general twice failed to invade Britain. In 55 and 54 BCE he fought a series of skirmishes in the southeastern corner of England, but his forces were overstretched, and he was impelled to return to the Continent. The reason he conducted these risky operations—well before he had completed his conquest of Gaul—Caesar explains in his personal account of the Celtic campaigns, *The Gallic Wars*. Writing in the third person, he relates that he was "resolved to proceed into Britain, because he discovered that, in almost all the wars with the Gauls, assistance had been furnished to our enemy from that country."[6] This was not military aid, however, but some kind of detrimental (from the Roman perspective) moral support afforded by a mystical sect that originated in Britain.[7]

The two highest echelons of British society, we are told, were the nobles and a priestly class called the Druids, from the old Celtic *derwijes,* meaning "truth sayers." (Roman writers also refer to them as *prophetas,* meaning "those who see the future or make predictions.") The nobles were the chieftains, their families, and the warrior elite—the aristocracy, if you like—whose influence was pretty much confined to their own tribe (of which there were around fifty in Britain), but the jurisdiction of the Druids exceeded tribal boundaries: they were not only priests, but also acted as teachers, advisors, and judges. They appear to have traveled to Gaul, where they had the influence to unite the chieftains of otherwise quarrelsome tribes to join forces against the Romans. Significantly, these Druids seem to have been the very priesthood referenced by Caesar's contemporary, Diodorus Siculus, as performing ceremonies at Stonehenge (see chapter 9). So problematic was their unifying authority that during the invasion of Britain, a century later, the Romans risked everything to eliminate them.

From Caesar's time, even though Gaul was now fully occupied by the Romans, local insurrections regularly occurred, instigated by British Druids, and it was to eliminate this threat that Emperor Claudius initiated the conquest of Britain. There is a common misconception that the entire country was overrun in 43 CE. In reality, this was merely the year that the invasion began. It occurred in stages, taking the Romans four decades to fully conquer what is now England and Wales, while an attempt to invade Scotland was ultimately abandoned altogether.

The campaign began under the leadership of the general Aulus Plautius, who commanded four legions (the 2nd, 11th, 14th, and 22nd). Together with the auxiliaries, this was around forty thousand men. (Auxiliary units from far and wide were deployed in Britain, including from what are now France, Germany, Spain, and Greece.) By 47 CE the Romans had occupied most of southern and southeastern England and had established the Roman capital at Camulodunum, modern Colchester in the county of Essex. Claudius was in no hurry to complete his conquest of the country, and the next few years were spent consolidating captured territory. Roman towns were established, and a series of fortifications was created, linked by paved roads, making it easy to deploy soldiers where necessary. Large fortresses, known as *castra* (singular *castrum*), were built as permanent barracks for entire legions, while smaller forts housed around five hundred men, usually auxiliaries, whose job it was to patrol an already occupied zone. The border between the Roman-held and native-held areas initially consisted of a road called the Fosse Way, joining a chain of forts that stretched for 170 miles between the fortresses of Isca (modern Exeter in Devon) and Ratae (modern Leicester in east-central Britain). However, there was fierce fighting to the west of this front, in what is now central England. From there, frequent attacks were mounted across the border, led by a British chieftain named Caratacus, who was not defeated until 51 CE.[8]

The Romans then attempted to push farther west but only

succeeded in advancing into a limited part of southeastern Wales and along a narrow corridor of western England, as far as the modern city of Chester, where they established the frontier fortress of Deva. A new fortified road, Watling Street, now ran 160 miles from Deva to the major Roman port of Londinium (modern London) on the River Thames. For the next decade the Romans made repeated attempts to invade South Wales but were consistently repelled, and an entire legion (the 20th) was pushed out of this mountainous region, in which the Romans were ill equipped to fight. It was not only in South Wales that the Romans suffered defeat but also in the northwestern area of England, which they erroneously believed they had already subdued. There they were continually harassed by a tribal coalition led by a renegade chieftain called Venutius. This effective alliance appears to have been cemented by the Druids, whose influence united an otherwise disorganized collection of tribes.[9] Accordingly in 60 CE Claudius's successor, Emperor Nero, decide to gamble everything in an attempt to eradicate them once and for all.

Claudius's cautious policy had been to capture one tribal region at a time, then to secure the area by constructing fortresses, roads, and forts and by building walled towns inhabited by friendly citizens. The Druids had their chief stronghold far from Roman territory on the island of Mona (modern Anglesey), off the northwest coast of Wales. But even though two of the four British legions were widely dispersed—the 20th, based at what is now the town of Caerleon, still fighting the Silures tribe in southeastern Wales and the 2nd engaged against the Dumnonii tribe in the far southwest of England—Nero ordered the 14th legion to open a third front, to march right along the hostile north coast of Wales, deep into enemy country, and cross the Menai Strait to wipe out the Druids on Anglesey. Despite the objections of Suetonius Paulinus, the military governor of Britain, that this would leave only one legion, the 9th, to control the entire southeast, the heartland of Roman Britain, the emperor was adamant. Moreover, Nero insisted that Paulinus himself lead the offensive. The Roman army was completely divided and fighting on three fronts, a rash course of action that very nearly cost the Romans the entire province of Britannia (the Roman name for occupied Britain).[10] But such was the threat the Druids seem to have posed that the emperor and the senate in Rome considered it a gamble worth taking.

Tacitus tells us that once the Britons on Anglesey had been routed, the Romans set about destroying the Druids' sacred places on the island. One of these appears to have been the megalithic complex at Castell Bryn Gwyn, in the district of Llanidan, which archaeology has revealed had been consistently in use from around 2500 BCE (see chapter 9). Pottery and surrounding graves have demonstrated that it had been used by the Neolithic Britons, the Beaker people, the Wessex culture, and throughout the Celtic era. Excavations at the site in 2009 revealed evidence of the Roman military action of 60 CE, such as discarded armor, buckles, arrowheads, and hobnails from Roman boots, and that a contemporary Roman fort was built over the megalithic complex, destroying all but a few monoliths and the henge earthwork. It was only with modern geophysics and aerial photography that the full splendor of the original complex was rediscovered. It had originally consisted of a 180-foot-diameter henge circle linked to a nearby smaller stone circle to the southwest, which survives as the standing stones of Bryn Gwyn (see chapter 5), by an approximately 1,000-foot-long avenue of stones. It must have been a hugely important site, for the surviving stones measure up to 14 feet high.[11]

Archaeology has also shown that other stone circles and their outlying monoliths on the Isle of Anglesey met the same fate at this time, such as Plas Meilw, a mile to the southwest of the modern port of Holyhead, where only two 10-foot-tall stones survive; Plas Bodafon, where only one 4-foot-tall stone survives in woodland near the town of Amlwch on the north coast of the island; a stone circle near the village of Llanfechell, in the north of the island, from which only one 6-foot-tall stone remains; and the so-called Llanfechell Triangle, a megalithic cove arrangement of three similarly sized stones, around a third of a mile to the west.

In Celtic society women seem to have enjoyed equal status to men, something that astonished the misogynistic Romans. The succession of tribal leadership fell to the firstborn, whether male or female, and women even fought alongside men in battle. Tacitus, for instance, tells us that female warriors fought ferociously in defense of Anglesey and that it was a warrior queen, back in the East of England, who took advantage of the Romans' precarious military situation to mount a full-scale rebellion. Queen Boudicca (sometimes referred to as Boadicea) was from the Iceni tribe in what is now the county of Norfolk in eastern England. Her revolt is outlined in the works of both Tacitus and Cassius Dio, who describe how she raised an army, sacked the Roman capital of Camulodunum, and succeeded in all but exterminating the only legion (the 9th) still deployed in eastern Britain. It's likely that the Britons managed to engage them in a forested region, as Tacitus tells us that the infantry was almost completely wiped out; only the commander and some of his cavalry escaped.[12] Boudicca's army continued to grow as tribe after tribe rallied to her side once she sacked the port of Londinium and the Roman city of Verulamium, what is now Saint Albans in the county of Hertfordshire. By the time she began her march north along Watling Street, Cassius Dio tells us that her army had swelled to around 120,000.[13] Strictly speaking, Boudicca's actual fighting force was probably very much less, as most of these people seemed to have been little more than a disorganized rabble of frenzied followers who joined an ever-growing, surging mob as the victorious queen swept through their lands.

Hearing of the disaster, Paulinus withdrew from North Wales and summoned the legions based in the southwest and in South Wales to join him. It seems that the 2nd legion in Devonshire was too embroiled in its own struggle to comply, but some of the 20th retreated from their engagement with the Silures tribe and were able to rendezvous with the governor and part of the 14th legion. With two incomplete legions and various auxiliaries, Paulinus had around ten thousand soldiers, but despite her numerical superiority Boudicca's army was defeated

Fig. 10.1. Early Roman Britain.

somewhere in central England. This is the battle, mentioned earlier, in which eighty thousand Britons perished to the loss of only four hundred Romans. It would seem that the Romans had managed to contrive a favorable location in open countryside to make their stand, and Boudicca, confident in her vastly superior numbers, made the mistake of confronting them head-on.[14]

But this was nowhere near the end of the rebellion. Although Boudicca is said to have died shortly after the battle, her remaining forces continued a guerrilla campaign that went on for two years until Nero finally sent reinforcements from Gaul.[15] Paulinus was eventually replaced by a new governor, Publius Petronius Turpilianus, who was forced to sue for peace, and for the next decade the Romans only remained in charge of the southeast.[16] Britain was almost completely lost to the Romans, and Nero's disastrous policies led in part to his overthrow and suicide in 68 CE, resulting in a series of civil conflicts throughout the Roman Empire. In Britain the situation was so bad that the army there mutinied. Apart from in the southeast, the Britons continued to govern themselves along the old tribal lines, while the diminished region of Roman Britain was in a state of virtual anarchy.[17] During 69 CE a succession of generals seized and lost the imperial throne, until one of them, Vespasian, was strong enough to hold on to power and restore control over the empire. He almost abandoned Britain altogether, but two years later, in a show of determination, he sent new forces to the country and reestablished dominion as far west as the Fosse Way.[18] It was not until 73 CE that the Romans began to extend their territory from what it had been at the time of the Boudicca revolt by conquering the Silures of southeastern Wales. And it was not until 78 CE that they finally retook the Isle of Anglesey.[19] Ultimately the whole of what is now England was conquered, but this took until the mid-80s. The northern tribes mounted fierce resistance, again led by another warrior queen, although this time we are not told her name.[20] The complete conquest of the Roman province of Britannia—what is now England and Wales—was not achieved until four decades after the invasion first began.

Regardless of their own religious notions, successive waves of migrants had continued to use the stone circles once they arrived in Britain, and the Celts were no exception. Roman historical sources, backed up by archaeological evidence, reveal that the Celtic sect still venerating these monuments three millennia after the first of them were built were the Druids. Unfortunately, the early Roman sources concerning life in Britain tell us very little about the specific beliefs of the Druids. We learn that they were a highly revered cult of British priests, that they were a unifying element among the Britons, and that their influence had once stretched into Celtic Gaul. Tacitus describes them during his account of Paulinus's campaign in 60 CE, telling us that their major stronghold had been on the Isle of Anglesey. He describes how they included both men and women and how they stood among the warriors on the shores of the island, where the population fought ferociously to defend their spiritual leaders. And that's about it.

As the classical authors such as Tacitus and Cassius Dio, who wrote about the Roman invasion of Britain, tell us next to nothing about the beliefs of this mysterious sect, if the Druids did preserve some knowledge as to why the stone circles were built, how are we to discover what this might have been? Well, it was not only in the Roman-occupied regions of the British Isles that the Druids existed. Scotland remained free from Roman rule. In the 120s CE, after the Romans had fully conquered what is now England and Wales, Emperor Hadrian built a 70-mile-long wall (known as Hadrian's Wall) across a narrow stretch of northern England to divide occupied Britannia from the hostile Scottish tribes. The Romans referred to these northern Celts as Picts, from the Latin *picti,* meaning "painted" or "tattooed" people.[21] As elsewhere in Britain, some stone circles were certainly still being used by the Picts in the first century CE and continued to be used for some time after. Sadly, though, no written records survive from this early period of Scottish history to directly reveal anything about the Druids. But there was another Celtic area of the British Isles that remained free from Roman rule. And that was Ireland, which the Romans called Hibernia. There, the Druids survived until a time when far more about them could be recorded.

In 476 CE the Roman Empire, which had started life as the city-state of Rome around nine hundred years earlier, finally collapsed throughout Western Europe, when the Germanic chieftain Odoacer deposed Emperor Romulus Augustulus and proclaimed himself king of Italy. By this time Christianity had become the state religion of the

Roman Empire, and the bishop of Rome, later to be called the pope, was its head. Fortunately for the Roman Catholic Church, Odoacer was himself a Christian and allowed what would eventually become the Vatican to remain as a tiny independent state, a status it still enjoys today. (Technically, it is the smallest country in the world, 110 acres in size, with an official population of around one thousand.) Many of the new kingdoms that sprang up throughout what had been the Western Empire retained the Christianity adopted from the Romans and still regarded the pope as their spiritual leader. And it was from missionaries sent by the pope to convert the people of Ireland that we learn much more about the Druids.

The Megalithic culture seems to have stalled in Ireland from about 3000 BCE until it recommenced a thousand years later (see chapter 6). It seems to have primarily been the Beaker people, having immersed themselves in the Megalithic tradition, who first reintroduced the practice of stone circle building to Ireland. Hundreds of their tumuli exist throughout the country, showing that the Beaker people migrated there from around 2000 BCE, possibly due to the Wessex culture's arrival in Britain initiating a westward movement of the population (see chapter 9). However, while the construction of stone circles slowed in mainland Britain around 1200 BCE, Megalithic culture not only continued across the Irish Sea, but the monuments also became even more elaborate, owing to further migrations from the British mainland after the arrival of the Urnfield culture. Ireland, being less populated, did not suffer the same kind of food shortages caused by climate change that were endured by the contemporary inhabitants of Britain; it remained a far more peaceful land and an inviting prospect for British migrants. Many Wessex-style cist mounds have also been found in Ireland dating from this time, while DNA analysis of human remains from the period have revealed that there was a considerable influx by the Britons generally. Some two hundred stone circles survive in Ireland, of which most were built after 2000 BCE, and they continued to be erected and used for almost 2,500 years.[22] The phases during which these sites were erected, modified, or repaired have been established by the radiocarbon dating of organic remains found beneath monoliths, in earthworks, and in pits dug to hold stones, while the periods when they were being used can be ascertained by the radiocarbon dating of charcoal from fires and animal bones (evidence of ceremonial feasting) or by dating pottery fragments found at sites, either by examining their distinctive style or by using scientific techniques such as thermoluminescence and rehydroxylation dating (see chapter 4).

This new period of Irish Megalithic culture that began around 2000 BCE continued for around 2,500 years, well after it ceased to exist in Britain. Examples of stone circles dating throughout this extended period are found all across Ireland. In the South of the Irish Republic, for instance, there's the 30-foot-diameter, nine-stone Templebryan Stone Circle, 1.5 miles north of the town of Clonakilty, and the similarly sized, eleven-stone Canfea Stone Circle at Ardgroom, both in County Cork, as well as the approximately 55-foot-diameter, fifteen-monolith Kenmare Stone Circle in County Kerry. In Northern Ireland, examples include the Drumskinny Stone Circle in County Fermanagh, 40 feet in diameter and originally having thirty-nine monoliths, while in the district of Beaghmore in County Tyrone alone there are no fewer than seven similarly sized stone circles. Throughout the whole of Ireland, new stone circles continued to be built for centuries. To name just a few:

The Beltany Stone Circle near the town of Raphoe in County Donegal, originally consisting of around eighty stones, of which sixty-four survive; radiocarbon dating of organic remains obtained from beneath the stones places the erection of the ring to around 1400 BCE.

The 30-foot diameter, seventeen-monolith Drombeg Stone Circle at Glandore in County Cork, where the dating of a Wessex-style cist tomb just outside the circle places its construction to around 1200 BCE.

The 60-foot-diameter Bocan Stone Circle, near the village of Culdaff in County Donegal, which consisted of about thirty stones. Urnfield graves have been found around and within the ring, dating its construction to about 900 BCE.

And in the district of Auglish, in County Londonderry, there are six stone circles, the earliest dating from around 800 BCE, the last as late as the fifth century CE.

There were also large megalithic complexes just like those found in Britain. At Auglish, for instance, archaeologists have identified the remains of a 100-foot-diameter stone circle originally consisting of forty-one 6-foot-tall monoliths, joined to two smaller rings by stone avenues. The largest megalithic complex in Ireland is the Grange, on the west side of Lough Gur in County Limerick. It is composed of a 150-foot-diameter stone circle of 113 standing stones, up to 13 feet high and weighing as much as 40 tons, and it is surrounded by a ditch and embankment 40 feet wide, with a king stone aligned with sunrise on the midsummer solstice. There are two smaller, satellite stone circles and an earthen avenue on the eastern side leading to a cove of three monoliths. Thousands of Beaker pottery shards have been excavated from beneath these stones, seemingly used to line the pits into which the monoliths were erected, indicating that the complex was built either by or with the help of the Beaker people, just like those in mainland Britain from around 2000 BCE. Organic deposits found beneath some of the stones have revealed that they were re-erected, presumably after toppling, on various occasions right up until 450 CE, meaning that the complex was still in use and being periodically repaired for an astonishing 2.5 millennia.[23]

The Iron Age Celts first arrived in Ireland around 500 BCE, a couple of centuries after they had migrated to Britain, and by the first century CE they had established an almost identical way of life to that of the contemporary Britons. But, unlike Britain, Ireland was never invaded by the Romans and remained a land of individual Celtic tribes until centuries later. So at the time the first Christian missionaries arrived in the fifth century, life in Ireland was still pretty much as it had been in Britain during the Roman invasion four hundred years before. It is not only from archaeological evidence of ceremonial activities or repairs to megaliths at Irish stone circles that we know that many were still being

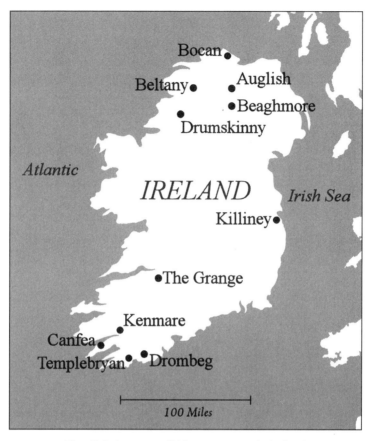

Fig. 10.2. Late megalithic monuments in Ireland.

used for some purpose until this time. There are clear signs of continuous occupation. Many Irish megalithic complexes and stone circles are surrounded by Beaker tumuli, cistvaens, Urnfield graves, and Iron Age burial cairns, indicating that the sites were used by a whole succession of cultures living in harmony, just as they had in Britain, but in Ireland this continued right up until the arrival of Christianity. For example, the Drumskinny Stone Circle has an adjacent Celtic burial cairn dating from around 400 CE; the Beaghmore Stone Circles are interspersed with Celtic burial cairns dating to 450 CE; and just to the north of the Templebryan Stone circle, there are the remains of a number of late Iron Age burial chambers. A further ten-foot-tall standing stone in the direction of the midsummer sunset is marked with a fifth-century CE Ogham inscription (early Irish writing), showing that the site was still in use as late as 450 CE. One of the last megalithic sites known to have been used by the pagan Celts is the Canfea Stone Circle, which had a large Iron Age settlement right next to it; fragments of drinking vessels found there precisely match those unearthed within the ring, indicating that it had seemingly been used during ceremonial feasting dating right up until the mid-fifth century.[24]

In England and Wales the use of megalithic sites was ended by the might of the Roman army, but in Ireland it was the persuasive words of the Roman Catholic Church that led to their demise. However, whereas the Romans reveal little regarding the stone circles, the early Christian missionaries to Ireland tell us far more about these ancient monuments and the people who used them—the enigmatic Druids.

11

The Druids'
Lasting Influence

IN 325 CE EMPEROR CONSTANTINE I oversaw the founding of what would become the Catholic Church, and in 380 CE Emperor Theodosius I made Christianity the state religion of the Roman Empire.[1] By this time the empire was collapsing and being invaded by vast tribes from east of the Rivers Danube and Rhine, such as the Goths, Vandals, and Franks, whom the Romans had long referred to as barbarians. In 410 CE, to help counter this threat, the Roman legions were withdrawn from Britain, and the country rapidly collapsed once again into a state of anarchy. Civilization fell apart, towns were abandoned for more defendable hillforts, and Britain was divided into various feuding kingdoms based around ancient tribal lines. Many people reverted to paganism, but in the western regions, such as Wales, Roman Christianity continued. One British-born Christian was Saint Patrick, who was ordained a bishop in 432 CE and traveled to Ireland to spread the Gospel.[2] Patrick was remarkably successful in converting the Irish Celts, and other missionaries soon followed. Much of Ireland was converted to Christianity over the next few decades, the period from which archaeology has revealed stone circles finally falling into disuse. These missionaries—monks and priests—were educated men who, as well as speaking various Celtic dialects, could read and write Latin, and they and their biographers recorded much concerning the pagan beliefs of those they endeavored to convert. From such works, coupled with the biographies of the early Christian missionaries, usually referred to as Saint's Lives, we learn that the Druids still existed in Celtic Ireland just as they had in Britain many centuries before.

Fig. 11.1. The Western Roman Empire and the surrounding lands.

The various Saints' Lives, or hagiographies, as they are called, were composed by monks writing from the fifth to the seventh centuries CE, and in them the Druids are frequently referred to as a pagan sect that continually challenged the work of the church. For example, in *Vita Sancti Columbae* (Life of Columba), the short biography of the Irish priest Columba, who preached during the mid-500s, written by Adamnán of Iona, the Druids are mentioned eleven times,[3] while *Vita Sancti Patricii* (Life of Saint Patrick) by the seventh-century Irish bishop Muirchu describes how Saint Patrick managed to convert many Celtic chieftains, who then drove the Druids from their lands.[4] Early Christian missionaries in Ireland were later canonized as saints by the Catholic Church (hence the Saint's Lives), and in the fifth century CE alone, dozens of them are recorded as encountering the Druids: Saints Assicus, Banban, Benignus, Dabheog, and Olcán, to name just a few. And what we learn from their hagiographies is that the Druids regarded the stone circles and other megalithic monuments as sacred, having been built by their esteemed forebears.[5]

In Ireland, not only did the Druids meet and perform ceremonies at stone circles, but many of these sites also were, and still are, named after them. For example, the stone circle at Kenmare is known as the Druid Circle, the one at Drombeg is called the Druid's Altar, the Canfea Stone Circle is the Druid's Ring, the Templebryan Stone Circle is called the Druid's Temple (see chapter 10), and a megalithic complex at Killiney near Dublin was called the Druids Sanctuary. The use of stone circles was seemingly of such importance that they were used by culture after culture—the Neolithic people, the Beaker people, the Wessex culture, the Urnfield culture, and the Iron Age Celts—all over the British Isles. It's reasonable to assume, therefore, that the Druids, at the very least, had some notion concerning why these baffling structures were originally built. So can the writings of these early Christian missionaries in Ireland regarding this enigmatic sect help us to finally solve the mystery of stone circles such as Stonehenge?

The early Christian monks in Ireland often documented the beliefs of the pagan people they encountered, much like Victorian missionaries wrote about the tribal religions of Africa. The church at the time was not the kind of authoritarian institution it was to become during the later Middle Ages, and works concerning paganism—at least as a curiosity—were written by clerics throughout the contemporary

Christian world. Monasteries contained just about the only libraries to survive during the post-Roman era in Western Europe—a period commonly referred to as the Dark Ages—and the monks who maintained them were the nearest thing many nations of the period had to historians. In Ireland, in addition to the hagiographies, texts were compiled concerning pre-Christian perceptions, which, until this time, had only been transmitted orally. Although containing various mythological themes, these works, both in poetic and narrative form, also reflected the history of Ireland as it had been envisaged by the earlier Irish Celts. Such documents were originally committed to writing from the fifth to the seventh centuries CE, and they survive today in the form of medieval copies assembled into manuscripts collectively referred to as "early Irish literature." Chief among them are:

- *The Book of Leinster,* kept in Trinity College Dublin, thought to have been originally compiled by a scribe known as Columba of Terryglass on behalf of the chieftain of Leinster, a tribal kingdom in eastern Ireland, during the early 500s CE.
- *Lebor na hUidre* (The Book of the Dun Cow), kept in the Royal Irish Academy, reputedly compiled by Ciarán, the abbot of Clonmacnoise in central Ireland, during the mid-500s CE. (The manuscript was so named as it was written on parchment made from brownish-gray cowhide.)
- *The Annals of the Kingdom of Ireland,* or *Irish Annals* for short, preserved in several manuscripts held at the Royal Irish Academy, Trinity College Dublin, and the National Library of Ireland, a collection of historical chronicles originally compiled during the early Christian era by monks from various monasteries.

Such manuscripts reveal that the pre-Christian Celts believed that when they first came to Ireland, which historically occurred around 500 BCE, the country was occupied by a race called the Tuatha De Danann (pronounced "thoo-a day du-non"): the People of Danu. Who or what Danu was is unclear, and scholars have long debated its meaning: is it the name of a goddess, a ruler, or the place from where these people were thought to have originated? Recent thinking is that the word actually derived from the Celtic term *dán,* meaning "skilled" or "knowledgeable." If so, then the term Tuatha De Danann would mean something like the Wise Ones.

Although these works include clearly mythological themes, such as mythical beings and deities wielding magical powers, the portrayal of the Tuatha De Danann in early Irish literature would appear to have been genuine recollections of the pre-Celtic inhabitants of Ireland handed down through oral accounts embellished over time. The Irish annals tell us that the Tuatha De Danann (Tuatha for short) arrived in Ireland some 2,500 years before the period of the first Christian missionaries—around 2000 BCE by today's dating—which would fit with what archaeology has revealed about the reintroduction of the Megalithic culture by British migrants at this time (see chapter 10).[6] Although in more recent Irish literature the Tuatha are often depicted as tall with light complexions and fair hair, likening them to Vikings (which, incidentally, inspired Tolkien's elves), the earlier accounts differ. They are indeed described as looking different from the Celts, but with red hair, which again tallies with archaeology. Although today red hair is popularly associated with Celtic nations such as Scotland and Ireland, the original Celts, as we shall be examining shortly, generally had brown hair. (The physical features of the various inhabitants of the British Isles have been determined from DNA analysis of ancient human remains and some extraordinarily well-preserved bodies found in peat bogs.) Although various accounts portray the Tuatha as supernatural beings, they are generally depicted as mortal; when they died, we are told, they were interred in the many tumuli that exist all over Ireland (see chapter 10). The Irish annals, for instance, refer to these ancient mounds as *sídhe* (pronounced "shee"), telling us how the Tuatha built them as magic portals and relating that once they were buried beneath them their spirits entered a mystical realm.[7] Once more, this connects the Tuatha with the Megalithic culture. In reality, these tumuli were the burial mounds of the Beaker and Wessex people who existed in Ireland before the arrival of the Celts (see chapter 9).

The most exalted among the Tuatha are said to have been the Clann Lir, the Children of Lir, the offspring of a god called Lir, who were transformed for many years into swans by a jealous stepmother. They were ultimately returned to human form, and from them were descended the Druids, who remained on Earth once the other Tuatha had been buried beneath the mounds. The story of this transformation, as told in a Dark Age Irish tale called *The Fate of the Children of Lir*, preserved in three separate manuscripts at the Royal Irish Academy in Dublin, seems to have been inspired by Druidic attire. The early Christian writers tell us how the Druids, upon initiation, wore a ceremonial cloak called a *tugen*, made entirely from swan feathers. According to the early Irish literature (for example, in Dark Age accounts preserved in the so-called *Speckled Book* in the Royal Irish Academy in Dublin), when the Celts arrived in Ireland they accepted these Druids—those who preserved the spiritual knowledge of the People of Danu —as their priesthood.[8]

Before continuing, it is important to say something about modern-day Druids. During the eighteenth century, the antiquarian John Aubrey made the first modern surveys of megalithic monuments such as Stonehenge and Avebury, and after consulting the works of early Irish missionaries and various Greek and Roman accounts, he associated them with the Druids, initiating a wide interest in this mysterious sect. At that time no proper historical research had been conducted into the beliefs of the ancient Celts, and scholars were left to imagine what Druidism might have entailed. By the early twentieth century various Druid orders had been founded, modeled on Freemasonry and the popular occult societies established during the Gothic revival of the 1800s. Some still exist today, such as those who perform an annual ceremony at Stonehenge at the midsummer solstice. However, these organizations have no direct connection to the Druids of old; their beliefs, rituals, and mode of attire are, for the most part, based on the romantic notions of the Victorian era coupled with modern Wiccan and New Age philosophies. If we really want to know about the Druids who used stone circles in ancient times, we need to examine what the original historical sources reveal.

According to early Irish literature the Druids were endowed with exceptional gifts. In "The Cattle Raid of Cooley" and "The Fate of the Sons of Usnech," two tales found in *The Book of Leinster,* the Druids are portrayed as teachers, healers, herbalists, poets, prophets, diviners, and astrologers.[9] They also wielded political power. We are told that Druids not only acted as advisors to chieftains, such as one Cathbad in "The Fate of the Sons of Usnech," but they also exercised great authority as judges. A work titled "Bricriu's Feast," from *The Book of the Dun Cow,* actually relates that they were more than simply advisors to tribal chieftains but acted as the real power behind the throne: the Druid Sencha, for instance, orders an end to fighting between noblemen when even the king is ignored.[10] "The Cattle Raid of Cooley" also recounts how the Druids' authority exceeded that of royalty: no one could speak before the king, we are told, but even the king could not speak before the Druids.[11] There are several occasions referred to in other stories from *The Book of Leinster* where Druids mediate in feuds between rival tribes, while *Cu Chulainn's Death,* a Dark Age Irish tale preserved in the British Library, refers to a Druid reminding the adversaries that their families will forever be dishonored if they refuse his demands to lay down their arms.[12] Also, throughout early Irish literature there are repeated references to female Druids sharing the same prominent religious and cultural roles as their male counterparts, reflecting Celtic society as a whole, in which women enjoyed equal status to men (see chapter 10). In fact, we learn that Druids lived in mixed-gender communities, set apart from the general population, where they married and had children, and women were often their leaders.[13]

All of this tallies with what we learn from ancient Greek and Roman writers concerning the Druids in earlier Celtic society elsewhere. Writing around 50 BCE, in *The Gallic Wars,* Julius Caesar tells us that "the Druids usually hold aloof from war, and do not pay taxes with the rest; they are excused from military service and exempt from all liabilities."[14] He describes them as "persons of definite account and dignity. . . . It is they who decide in almost all disputes, public and private; and if any crime has been committed, or murder done, or there is any disposes about succession or boundaries, they also decide it, determining rewards and penalties."[15] The Greek philosopher Strabo, in his *Geographica* (Geography), written around 10 BCE, also refers to the Druids as judges: "The Druids are considered the most just of men, and on this account they are entrusted with decisions concerning both private and public disputes."[16] According to Caesar, anyone who disobeys them suffers the "heaviest penalty."[17] Diodorus Siculus, a Greek historian from the island of Sicily, in his *Bibliotheca Historica,* written between 60 and 30 BCE, confirms what the early Irish literature tells us about the Druids acting above and beyond the authority of chieftains, not only as arbitrators but also having the influence to order the cessation of hostilities: "Many times, when two armies approach each other in battle with swords drawn and spears thrust forward, [the Druids] step forth between them and cause them to cease."[18] Strabo relates something similar, saying that the Druids "made the opponents stop when they were about to line up for battle."[19]

The Greek and Roman authors tell us that, as well as being priests, prophets, healers, judges, arbitrators, and advisors, the Druids were believed to commune with the gods. Diodorus Siculus, for example, writes that the Druids were "experienced in the nature of the divine, and speak, as it were, the language of the gods."[20] Pomponius Mela, a Roman geographer writing around 43 CE, in his *Description of the World,* elaborates on this theme by explaining what this "language" entailed: the Druids, he says, claimed to know "the will of the gods from the movement of the heavens and stars."[21] And Hippolytus of Rome, a Christian theologian writing in the early third century, in his *Refutation of All Heresies,* tells us that the Druids made prophesies and pronouncements based on mathematical calculations and equates

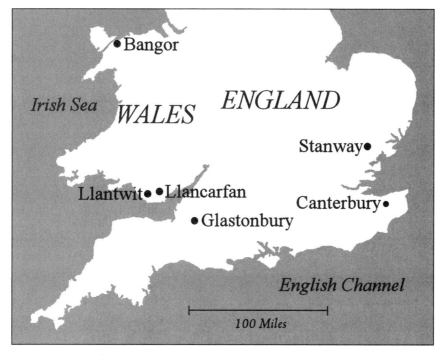

Fig. 11.2. Sites in England and Wales discussed in this chapter.

their ability with that of the ancient astronomer and mathematician Pythagoras.[22] In other words, the will of the gods was revealed through astrology. Julius Caesar explains how such astrological pronouncements were made at specific times of the year and at particular sacred places where individual tribes assembled to hear what the Druids had to disclose.[23] From the evidence we have gathered so far, it would seem that in Britain such places were stone circles and that the specific times of the year were the solstices and equinoxes (see chapter 6).

These classical sources confirm that the Druids included both men and women. Strabo, Pomponius Mela, and the Greek geographer Artemidorus of Ephesus (who wrote around 100 BCE) all refer to female Druids holding the same authority as their male counterparts. And as the early Irish literature suggests, they refer to Druids of both sexes living together in isolated communities. Strabo describes such people living separately from other Celts,[24] as does Pomponius Mela,

who specifically refers to such locations as being in isolated woodland.[25] The first-century Roman poet Marcus Annaeus Lucanus (better known as Lucan), in his work *Concerning the Civil War,* tells us
that they lived in *nemora alta remotis*—"remote woods."[26] Pliny the
Elder, a distinguished Roman author writing about the same time in his
Natural History, tells us that the Druids specifically chose oak woods,
as the tree was sacred to them.[27] And Tacitus, in his *Annals,* relates
how the Romans deliberately targeted such Druid woodlands when
they attacked Anglesey.[28] In fact, the Druids appear to have been a distinct group of people who only procreated among themselves. Caesar[29]
and Pliny the Elder[30] both refer to them as an exclusive class, similar to
an aristocracy. Hippolytus of Rome tells us that the Druids were the
highest caste of Celtic society and likens them to Brahmins of India,
who were known since the time of Alexander the Great in the fourth
century BCE.[31] In ancient Hinduism, society was divided into strict
factions where the Brahmins—the priestly class who protected sacred
learning through generations—were the elite and were forbidden to
procreate outside their caste.

In Ireland the custom of the Druid priestly class living in communities outside normal society would explain an unusual feature of the
first Christian monasteries in the country, which seem to have been
based on the earlier Druidic tradition. The kind of Christianity that
flourished in Ireland during the fifth and sixth centuries CE was very
different from that practiced by the contemporary Roman Catholic
Church. Generally referred to as the Celtic Church, its monasteries were
not the cloistered, single-sex institutions favored elsewhere, but mixed-
gender settlements consisting of families living in a kind of Christian
commune: less like traditional monastic institutions, more like modern
Amish communities. This was a matter of contention when missionaries from the Celtic Church crossed the Irish Sea and began to found
their style of monasteries in Britain during the sixth century CE. One
of the leading figures of the new British branch of the Celtic Church
was a priest called Gildas, who founded such institutions at Bangor in

North Wales and at Glastonbury in the county of Somerset. Not only was he married, but he also sired at least five children, one of whom was to found further such communities at Llantwit and Llancarfan in South Wales.[32] Both Gildas and this son, Neothon, were proclaimed saints by the Celtic Church. According to the eighth-century Anglo-Saxon historian Bede, in 597 CE, in order to reestablish Catholic control over this branch of Christianity, the pope, Gregory the Great, sent a bishop, Augustine, to Britain, where he was ultimately appointed archbishop of Canterbury. However, the Celtic Church refused to submit to his authority, and over the next few decades, further envoys were sent by successive popes until this dissident branch of Christianity was fully integrated within the Roman Catholic Church.[33]

We can glean some idea of how the Roman Catholic Church regarded such institutions from various medieval accounts preserved at St. John's College, Cambridge, and compiled into *Origines Anglicanae* (A History of the English Church) by the historian John Inett in 1704. Such monasteries, we are told, consisted wholly of priests, nuns, and monks who had not taken vows acceptable to the Catholic Church and where no one took an oath of celibacy. Men and women lived together in the same buildings, along with their children, and, perhaps most distasteful of all from the Roman perspective, women were even elevated to the position of abbess in charge of the entire establishment.[34] From what we gather from early Irish literature, the hagiographies, and the classical sources, the Druids had previously lived a very similar lifestyle to the people who dwelt in these Celtic Church communities.

That the Druids were a distinct class who only procreated among themselves actually explains a genetic conundrum: why so many Irish people have red hair. Scientists have determined that a gene known as the melanocortin 1 receptor, MC1R for short, is responsible for red hair, as well as fair skin and a tendency toward freckles. According to genetic research it first appeared in humans around forty-five thousand years ago in central Asia, where it afforded an advantage in weak sunlight and harsh winters: pale skin enabled the production of more vitamin D from sunlight, strengthening bones and increasing the survival rate during pregnancy and childbirth.[35] After the Ice Age ended around 10,000 BCE these people migrated into parts of northern Europe and were the first humans to recolonize the British Isles after the ice retreated by crossing the Doggerland land bridge (see chapter 3). They were the original Neolithic inhabitants of the British Isles, those who built the first megalithic monuments starting around 3100 BCE.[36]

MC1R is what is known as a recessive gene, and a characteristic such as red hair must be inherited from both parents. Although neither parent necessarily has to exhibit this physical trait, MC1R must be present in both. In short, unless the two parents possess this gene there is no chance their children will have red hair. Consequently as a proportion of any population, relatively few individuals have red hair. The British Isles were colonized by wave after wave of migrants in prehistoric times. The Beaker people and the Wessex culture came from what are now Belgium and the Netherlands, and the Urnfield and Hallstatt Celts came from Germany and Austria (see chapter 9). All these groups were already interrelated and had, for the most part, brown hair, and they settled throughout the British Isles. England and Wales had an additional influx of people from throughout the Roman Empire between the first and fifth centuries CE, many of whom were from the Mediterranean region and had dark hair. In addition, England was further invaded by the Anglo-Saxons, from what is now northern Germany and southern Denmark, having light brown hair, and the Vikings from Scandinavia with blond hair, who also settled throughout Scotland and much of Wales. The Normans, from medieval France, who shared a blend of just about every European heritage, invaded England and Wales in the early Middle Ages, and the totally mixed bag of peoples who were the English by the late thirteenth century went on to settle in large numbers in Scotland. Neither the Romans nor the Anglo-Saxons invaded Ireland, although many Vikings settled there, but the Norman invasion of the country in the late twelfth century marked the beginning of a turbulent period of over eight hundred years of English rule and an influx of new people from throughout mainland Britain.[37]

Although today red hair is popularly associated with Celtic nations, such as Scotland and Ireland, that leads to a serious misconception. The original Celts, who spread out from what is now Germany and Austria, had brown hair. The abundance of red hair in what are now considered to be Celtic countries has nothing to do with the genetic makeup of the original Celts. With all the interbreeding that went on for thousands of years in northern Europe, red hair became less and less common, and today is found in around only 2 percent of the general population. Ireland was just as much of an ethnic melting pot, and its inhabitants, we would expect, should have the same low proportion of red-haired people. But it doesn't. An astonishing 10 percent of Ireland's population has red hair. Scotland also has a higher number of red-haired people than usual, around 6 percent, but this is due to Irish migrations during the Dark Ages and the county's abundance of remote islands. For red hair to have persisted for so long requires that certain groups of the original Neolithic people continued to live in isolation through these successive waves of migration. Ireland does have a few remote islands, but nowhere near as many as Scotland, so that cannot account for the high percentage of the Irish population with the MC1R gene.[38] A caste system, which kept specific groups of descendants of the original inhabitants isolated from the general population, could well account for the enigma. Early Irish literature tells us that the Druids were direct descendants of the pre-Celtic people of Ireland—those that had red hair—and that they lived in their own separate communities.

Might something similar have previously been going on for hundreds of years throughout the entire British Isles: a select group of people, the caste that maintained whatever function the stone circles served, living separately from the general population? A social class descended directly from the original Megalithic people? What the Celts called Druids may well have been this same exalted caste. The reintroduction of the stone-circle-building tradition in Ireland, when the Beaker people migrated from Britain around 2000 BCE (see chapter 10), may also have been accompanied by the general acceptance of this ancestral caste who came with them. (Just why such a caste should have been so embraced by a foreign culture is something we shall examine shortly.) If this was indeed the case, as the Megalithic age lasted much longer in Ireland, communities of red-haired people would have been living separately for centuries, years after the practice was abandoned in Britain. Such a practice would indeed account for the higher percentage of red-haired people that Ireland has today.

Accordingly it might not only have been the stone circles that were adopted by culture after culture throughout the British Isles, but also the elite group of people who actually used them. Others helped build the megalithic monuments, venerated them, and presumably attended whatever ceremonies occurred there, but those who oversaw the use of the stone circles—their trustees, guardians, or whatever they were—may always have been the direct descendants of those who first built them. It's a radical theory, but one that could be tested by DNA analysis of Druid remains. The problem is, according to the ancient Greek and Roman writers, that the Druids were cremated and their remains were scattered to the winds. However, there does appear to have been a supreme Druid at any given time whose body was interred in a more lavish and permanent fashion. Julius Caesar, for instance, tells us, "Of all these Druids, one is chief, who has the highest authority among them."[39] Early Irish literature also refers to these chief Druids, saying how they were given a splendid burial. Many of them were women referred to as *bandrui,* found in such accounts as "The Cattle Raid of Cooley" and *The Book of the Taking of Ireland,* a collection of poems and narratives purporting to tell the history of Ireland before the coming of Christianity that is preserved in *The Book of Leinster.* There is indeed archaeological evidence for the leading members of some elevated, perhaps priestly class of the Megalithic period being given elaborate burials.

In Britain there are the cist barrow of Bryn yr Ellyllon near Mold in North Wales, where the occupant's golden shoulder adornment, the

Mold Cape, suggests that the person buried there was a priestess (see chapter 9), and the Rillaton Barrow on Cornwall's Bodmin Moor, in local tradition associated with a Druid, where the stone compartment contained the remains of a man buried with many elaborate items, including a gold cup (see chapter 1). In 2008 archaeologists announced that they had excavated what is thought to be the tomb of a chief Druid dating from just before the Roman invasion. The site, at the village of Stanway in the county of Essex, consisted of a burial chamber beneath a stone cairn. The individual, it is not known whether a man or woman, was interred with his or her belongings, including a cloak decorated with brooches, various gems, and what is thought to have been an ancient medical kit. It consisted of thirteen instruments, including scalpels, forceps, and a surgical saw. There was also a "tea strainer" containing artemisia pollen, commonly associated with herbal remedies such as deworming.[40] Whoever the person was, he or she was a healer, which all the historical sources suggest was the prerogative of the Druids. Moreover, the person was buried with some strange metal poles, identified as diving rods used by Druids, as described in early Irish literature. The problem with these tombs is that nothing remains today to be subjected to DNA testing. The Stanway occupant had been cremated, while the Bryn yr Ellyllon and Rillaton Barrow bones were exhumed and disposed of before modern scientific analysis had been developed.

In Ireland, important Druids do seem to have been buried in a specific fashion, in unusual box cairns (see chapter 9). Although most Celts were either cremated or buried without tombs or markers, during the late Iron Age chieftains were often interred beneath large mounds of stones called cairns. Specifically, they were buried beneath such cairns standing upright, dressed in their armor, facing toward the land of their enemies. In *The Book of the Dun Cow,* for example, we find accounts of these royal burials, and archaeologists have discovered a number of them, such as one in the tumulus called Croghan Erin at Kiltale in County Meath and another in a cairn near Belmullet, County Mayo.[41]

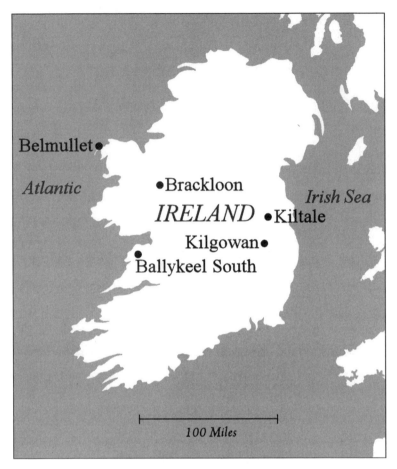

Fig. 11.3. Late Iron Age tombs in Ireland.

But the box cairns seem to have been reserved for important Druids, and they date right up to the period when the Christian missionaries arrived. They are unlike anything else found in Ireland from this period. They consisted of a rectangular structure, averaging about 12 feet long and 6 feet wide, made up of large slabs of rock, some 5 feet high and 6 inches thick, and divided into two parts by a further vertical slab set across the middle (see page 203). The body was buried in one side of the chamber and the grave goods deposited in the other; a series of capstones was then placed over the top, and the entire structure was covered with a large stone cairn. Such box cairns have been excavated at sites throughout Ireland, such as at Ballykeel South in County Clare, Brackloon in County Mayo, and Kilgowan in County Kildare, all of which were constructed adjoining stone circles between 350 and 450 CE.[42] Burial goods similar to those found at the Stanway tomb, such as "medical instruments" and "divining rods," have been unearthed at these tombs, suggesting that, like the Stanway tomb, they too were the graves of leading Druids. Unfortunately even though some still contained human bones, they are too degraded for DNA analysis to render reliable results.

In conclusion, Irish oral tradition, as transcribed by the first Christian missionaries, held that the Druids existed before the Celts arrived and that they were an illustrious class among the previous inhabitants of Ireland. Moreover, it's quite possible that those the Celts referred to as Druids were the actual descendants of the very faction who had overseen the use of stone circles during the earlier Megalithic age. But what could it have been about the Druids that would have made them so indispensible?

12

Astronomy and Medicine in the Stone Circles

PERHAPS BY UNDERSTANDING THE DRUIDS we can finally discover the true purpose of the stone circles. For over three millennia these megalithic monuments continued to be used, despite successive waves of migrants settling throughout the British Isles: the Beaker people, the Wessex culture, and the Urnfield and Hallstatt Celts. Based on the archaeological evidence, such as modes of burial, these groups evidently practiced diverse religions, all quite different from those of the original Megalithic Britons and Irish (see chapter 9). Yet for some reason, stone circles—first built by the Neolithic inhabitants—continued to be erected, maintained, and used by all these foreign cultures, even though they had previously created no such monuments in their homelands. By the time the first written records appeared concerning Britain, and later Ireland, those who officiated at whatever practices took place at stone circles were called Druids, and from the assorted evidence examined in the last two chapters, they appear to have been an elite caste descended from a distinguished class among the Neolithic residents of the British Isles. The word "druid" derives from a Celtic term meaning "truth sayers" (see chapter 10), though what such people were previously called is unknown. So what *do* we know about them?

To start with, it is most unlikely that they were the kind of fanatical savages, up to their necks in bloodletting, portrayed in the works of some Roman writers. They do appear to have uniquely performed sacrifices in Celtic society, but these were mostly animal sacrifices. Strabo does relate how the Druids would sometimes perform the ritual killing of humans, although Caesar implies this mainly involved the execution of criminals. There may actually have been few or no human sacrifices, the notion being disseminated for political propaganda. The Greeks and Romans often accused foreign cultures of such abhorrent rites when there was no archaeological evidence for such practices. In fact, as Hippolytus of Rome, who was a Christian and writing to defame what he regarded as the superstitious beliefs of the Druids, fails to mention their supposed human sacrifices, it seems unlikely that such occurrences were genuine, or at least were rare. Remember, his book was actually titled *The Refutation of All Heresies* (see chapter 11) and was written to deliberately defame all alternatives to Christianity. Hippolytus would certainly have made much of such abhorrent behavior had he been aware of it.

Hippolytus of Rome does, however, reveal something fascinating about the Druids. He likened them to the contemporary Brahmins of India: a priestly caste only permitted to procreate with one another (see chapter 11). Although they lived in isolation, there were many communities of such people scattered throughout India, and marriages were arranged between settlements, preventing inbreeding. It seems to have been the same with the Druids. But there was one big difference between these two sects from opposite sides of the known world. The Brahmins were the Hindu elite among a Hindu population, whereas in the British Isles the Druids seem to have held markedly *different* religious views from the rest of society. According to Julius Caesar, the Celts worshiped a variety of gods, the chief of which he equates with the Roman Mercury, the guider of souls to the underworld. The Druids, on the other hand, venerated a different god, whom Caesar likens to Apollo, a solar deity who was additionally the god of prophecy and healing.[1] Diodorus Siculus also implies that their god was similar to Apollo. When referring to the circular temple that seems to have been Stonehenge (see chapter 9), he tells us that it was sacred to this sun god and that the priesthood who gathered there were devotees of this deity.[2] One thing we do know about stone circles is that they were associated with the sun, as many of them have king stones, avenues, and stone rows aligned with the sunrise or sunset at significant times of the year. The Druids also seem to have held a belief in reincarnation that was not necessarily shared by the Celts in general. Caesar says that "the cardinal doctrine which they [the Druids] seek to teach is that souls do not die, but after death pass from one to another."[3] Strabo and Pomponius Mela relate something similar.[4,5] Conversely the Celts as a whole seem to have believed in an afterlife in an abode of the dead. Tír nAill, pronounced "cheer na awl," or the otherworld of spirits, deities, and fallen heroes, is frequently referred to in early Irish literature.

The Druids, it seems, maintained independent religious concepts to those of the general population of the British Isles, and judging by their funerary customs, they—by whatever name they were originally known—had done so right from the time the first wave of migrants, the Beaker people, had arrived. It went way beyond mere tolerance: they were not only tolerated by newcomers but also respected, venerated, and held in the highest esteem, even accepted as a kind of judiciary (see chapter 11). This all seems a most unlikely scenario—comparable, perhaps, to Catholics, Protestants, and Muslims all revering an autonomous Jewish elite—unless, that is, the Druids served an invaluable function for the wider society that was of a *practical* rather than a religious nature. (In chapter 1 we already considered that stone circles may have served some practical function, accounting for why they continued to be used for so long and throughout such a large area without the infrastructure of civilization.) So were the Druids *really* the priesthood of the Celts? Or were they something else, perhaps more akin to an academic or learned assembly of some kind, with wisdom, knowledge, and skills deemed essential to everyday life?

Although the Druids lived separately from the rest of Celtic society (see chapter 11), they acted as their advisors, arbitrators, and judges. If it was not because of a shared religious heritage, then what was it about the Druids that accorded them such status? One reason seems to be that they were thought able to foresee the future. Early Irish literature is full of accounts of Druids predicting such matters as military defeats and victories, general calamities or achievements, and plentiful or disastrous harvests. The Greek and Roman writers also refer to this role. Diodorus Siculus describes the Druids as diviners and foretellers of impending events,[6] and Hippolytus of Rome tells us, much to his distaste, that "the Celts esteem these [Druids] as prophets and seers."[7] He goes on to explain that their predictions were based on certain mathematical calculations, which the Roman writer Lucan additionally reveals were related to the movement of heavenly bodies.[8] Pomponius Mela says the same, explaining that the Druids were able to determine the future and know "the will of the gods" based on "the movement of the heavens and stars."[9] Julius Caesar describes something similar, in that they gained their knowledge from stellar observations.[10] In other words, the Druids were astrologers. This might account to some extent for why the Celts, and perhaps others before them, sought their advice. So did stone circles serve as ancient celestial observatories?

After establishing that monoliths of stone circles often align with particularly bright stars at certain times of the year, various researchers have suggested that megalithic rings may have been used for astrological calculations (see chapter 1). However, you wouldn't actually need a stone circle to perform astrology. As seen from Earth, the stars are unchanging in relation to each other, forming a fixed background against which the sun, moon, and planets move: the moon as it orbits Earth, the planets as they orbit the sun; the sun also appears to move relative to the stars as Earth orbits it. Ancient astrologers of many cultures assumed that the ever-changing positions of these heavenly bodies were signs of divine communication and that their specific locations within the celestial backdrop, as well as their relative positions to one another, had certain meanings on which proclamations concerning future events and human affairs could be made. This was all based on where the sun, moon, and planets happened to be at a particular time, which would not require any kind of Earth-based grid like a circle of stones. It was where, within the constant background of stellar constellations (specifically, in what today we define as the twelve signs of the zodiac), the bodies of the solar system happened to be that was deemed important. And that could be determined simply by gazing at the sky. A decent view of the heavens was all that was required; no stone circle would have been necessary.

There was, however, another role the Druids performed that must have been of far greater significance than their function as astrologers, one that might indeed have necessitated the use of stone circles as stellar observatories: that of healers. We have already seen how early Irish literature portrays healing as the prerogative of the Druids and how archaeology has indicated that these people were indeed physicians. Discoveries of what were clearly surgical instruments found in tombs that seem to have been reserved for Druids, such as the Stanway site, show an astonishing degree of medical knowledge (see chapter 11). There were saws for amputations, scalpels for surgery, various types of forceps for removing foreign objects from the body and to aid in childbirth, pliers for tooth extractions, slender needles for stitching wounds, and many more items. The kind of tombs in which these Druids were buried and such instruments found were not Iron Age innovations but had been constructed for centuries before the Celts arrived in the British Isles: the unusual box tombs.

So far, we only have discussed the late Iron Age examples of box tombs, but similar monuments had been created long before the arrival of the Celts. The word "cairn" refers to the mound of stones used in this later period to cover the burial chamber, but similar box tombs, covered by earthen tumuli, had been built since the earliest Megalithic times. And these too seem to have been used for the exclusive interment of the Druid predecessors. Whether covered by earth or stone mounds, box tombs date from around 3000 BCE until the end of the Iron Age, in fact right through the entire period that stone circles were being built and used. Found throughout the British Isles, they are unlike other contemporary tombs, consisting of a rectangular structure, averaging about 12 feet long and 4 to 6 feet wide, made up of large slabs of rock, about 5 feet high and 6 inches thick, and divided into two parts by a further vertical slab set widthwise across the middle. The body was buried in one section of the chamber, and grave goods were deposited in the other; a series of capstones was then placed over the top, and the entire structure was covered with a circular mound or a pile of stones. The burial chamber is somewhat similar to a Wessex culture cistvaen, but larger and built above ground level rather than being constructed within a pre-dug pit (see chapter 9).

First appearing around the same time as the first stone circles, box tombs continued to be built long after the general population had abandoned dolmen, long barrow, and passage grave burials. Archaeologists surmise that they must have been reserved for leading figures of a particular group of high-status members of society that existed among the original Megalithic culture, a caste that continued to exist throughout the subsequent periods of Beaker, Wessex, Urnfield, and Iron Age Celtic immigrations; in other words, the Druids and those who appear to have been their predecessors. By way of providing some idea of the extensive period over which these box tombs were constructed and their wide distribution throughout the British Isles, here are a few examples:

- One of the earliest box tombs is the Teergonean Tomb near the village of Doolin in County Clare, Ireland. Dating from around the same time as the first Maeshowe-style tombs (see chapter 4), it consists of two chambers of average size for such structures, one in surprisingly good condition. However, its mound has eroded away, and its capstones are missing.[11]
- Haco's Tomb, erroneously named after a much later Viking king, near the town of Largs in North Ayrshire, Scotland. Dating to

around 3000 BCE, it is some 20 feet long and 4 feet wide. Two chambers survive, one still covered by a capstone. However, its tumulus was removed in 1772.[12]

• A box tomb known as Five Wells, near Taddington in Derbyshire, originally had two adjoining chambers, one of which is well preserved, the other consisting of scattered stones, which were displaced when its covering mound was removed by antiquarians in the nineteenth century. Dating to about 2500 BCE, the surviving chamber is about 7 feet long, 3.5 feet wide, and 3 feet high, but its capstones now lie among the surrounding rubble.[13]

• One of the best preserved box tombs in the British Isles is Bant's Carn on the island of St. Mary's off the coast of Cornwall. It still survives intact beneath a 25-foot-diameter mound. Dating to around 2000 BCE, the chamber is about 15 feet long and 5 feet wide and high, with four large capstones still forming a roof. It was opened and its dividing stone removed during excavations in 1900.[14]

• The remains of a typical box tomb, of average size for such a monument, survive at Curbar Edge in the hilly Peak District of Derbyshire. It dates from around 1500 BCE, and one of its chambers now consists of scattered stones, while the other is partially collapsed. Until the early twentieth century it was covered by a mound, which was removed when the site was excavated in 1913, leaving it in its present dilapidated condition.[15]

• Penywyrlod Cairn, near the village of Llanigon in the county of Powys in Wales, is a mound averaging about 40 feet wide and containing a rectangular chamber in good condition. It is made from sandstone slabs some 6 feet long, 3 feet wide, and 4 feet high. The slightly smaller second chamber is in a ruinous state after its excavation in 1921. Although standing stones in the area have been dated to Neolithic times, the tomb itself dates from about 600 BCE and is one of the earliest examples of a box tomb covered by a stone cairn rather than an earthen mound.[16]

These are all examples of box tombs constructed of stone, but from the middle Iron Age some of them were created from thick wooden boards. Depending on the type of soil, such structures can survive for centuries in remarkably good condition until exposed to the air. Today the timber remains are quickly preserved, but many of these tombs were excavated before the invention of the scientific techniques needed to conserve them, and their wooden chambers have long since decayed. Two such box tombs, thought to date from around 300 BCE, existed near the town of Market Weighton in Yorkshire. Until the nineteenth century they were undisturbed and still covered with stone cairns, each about 30 feet in diameter and over 6 feet high. Between 1815 and 1817, however, the sites were excavated, and the tumuli were found to have covered intact timber box tombs, each measuring about 12 feet long, 4 feet wide, and 4 feet high, and divided across the center into two chambers. Sadly, nothing now remains of either tomb as the area has since been heavily farmed. In both tombs, one chamber held a single female body, while the other was resplendent with grave goods.[17] One was dubbed the Queen's Barrow and the other the Lady Barrow, although neither was a "barrow" in the modern archaeological sense (see chapter 3).

So these box tombs were divided into two equal-sized chambers, the one side holding the body or sometimes cremated remains, the other containing precious possessions, such as jewelry and amulets, plus a selection of items the individual had used in his or her profession. We have seen how these included what can best be described as medical kits, but there is also evidence of substances extracted from plants likely to have been used for pharmaceutical purposes, such as for their analgesic, antiseptic, and curative properties. This has been determined by scientific analysis of the residual contents of pots and other ceramic vessels found in such tombs. Here are just a few examples:

• Dried oil from *Chelidonium majus,* commonly known as greater celandine, and amentoflavone obtained from juniper plants have been extracted from vessels found in a five-thousand-year-old box tomb close to Maeshowe on the Orkney Isles. A mixture made from the root of the former is an effective gargle for toothache and sore throats, and the latter is known for its disinfectant properties and is widely used as an ingredient in modern antiseptic creams.[18]

- At Ashgrove in the district of Fife, Scotland, a box tomb dating from around 2500 BCE held a pottery vessel containing a substance from the flowers of *Tilia cordata,* the small-leaved lime or linden tree, used as an infusion to treat high temperatures and break fevers, somewhat like modern acetaminophen, while another similar tomb nearby contained ceramic fragments coated with a residue made from the leaves of *Tanacetum vulgare,* or common tansy plant, used to treat intestinal parasites and sometimes used in modern deworming veterinary products.[19]

- A cup found in a box tomb at Undy in Aberdeenshire, dating from around 2200 BCE, contained the residue of salicylic acid from the buds of *Filipendula ulmaria,* the meadowsweet herb, an analgesic, which in the nineteenth century was used to produce the first aspirin.[20]

- An urn discovered during excavations at a box tomb at Fernworthy on Dartmoor in Devonshire, dating from around 1500 BCE, held the remains of the seeds of the *Datura stramonium* fruit, also known as the thorn apple. Due to today's cooler climate, it no longer grows naturally in the British Isles. The thorn apple is highly toxic and produces delirium, rapid heartbeat, coma, and death, but if properly prepared, when ingested, it can result in temporary unconsciousness.[21] Certain Native American tribes, in areas where the plant still grows, used it to anesthetize those requiring painful procedures such as amputations, and some archaeologists have suggested that this was what the thorn apple was used for by the ancient people of the British Isles. Astonishingly no effective anesthetic was rediscovered in Europe until the synthesis of ether in the nineteenth century.

- Pottery excavated in 1921 from the Penywyrlod Cairn in Wales, dating from around 600 BCE (see page 204), remained in the vaults of the British Museum for decades before being subjected to scientific testing. The results showed that the ceramic fragments contained the residue of a liquid made from stems of *Scrophularia nodosa,* or figwort herb, used as an effective remedy for treating cuts, sores, and abrasions. Even today, extracts from the plant are used in ointments for the relief of eczema, psoriasis, and hemorrhoids.[22]

During the long period of time over which these tombs were built, the general population of the British Isles was interred in other ways, such as being placed in unmarked graves or simple stone cists, being laid to rest with a single beaker, or having their cremated remains deposited in urns (see chapter 9). Few burials contained the kind of medicinal plant extracts found in box tombs.[23] So were these substances really used for cures?

Box tombs nearly always contain plants that are toxic, foul tasting, or virtually inedible under normal circumstances. You certainly wouldn't eat them for nutritional purposes or as part of your diet. Most of them even lack narcotic effects that might have led to their use as recreational drugs or to induce visions. Their only conceivable uses, it seems, would have been medicinal. And the box tombs that uniquely contained such materials appear to have been those used exclusively for the interment of Druids and their elite caste of predecessors. If the kind of noxious substances found in their graves were, as seems likely, administered as remedies to be ingested or applied to wounds or abrasions, those who prepared them must have been highly skilled herbalists; otherwise they would have been little more than poisoners. Many of the plant extracts found in these box tombs are highly toxic, and for them to perform their curative functions, they not only needed to be prepared according to a precise and careful formula, but also required being harvested at a very specific time and from specific parts of plants, such as the seeds, roots, leaves, stems, flowers, or buds. Moreover, they would often need to be extracted at a very precise time of year. The chemical continuants of live vegetation alter consistently depending on their annual cycle, and sometimes even depending on the time of day or night.[24] You would need to know exactly when to cut or pick the plants and extract the necessary components. It would have taken a great deal of training to become a prehistoric physician, to learn all the plants, their uses, cultivation methods, and times of harvesting. And that's before you got around to adding other ingredients and making sure they corresponded to the correct measures. Creating these herbal remedies would have been an extremely complex and exact procedure.

Let's just consider the substances found in the tombs listed above. Figwort stems and leaves, for instance, need to be harvested in July and dried for later use in liquid extracts, tinctures, and ointments. If picked at the wrong time or not desiccated properly, they are useless as an irritant relief; on the contrary, their application results in excruciatingly painful inflammation. Unless the thorn apple is from an older bush and picked within just a few days each year, it can prove fatal, or at the very least induce severe vomiting, convulsions, and delirium. Tansy flowers bloom in July and August, but unless they are cut about halfway through this period, it would not only be intestinal parasites you will end up killing, but the human host as well. Removing the salicylic acid from the meadowsweet herb for its analgesic properties is an intricate process involving the draining of sap from the herb, not only at specific times of the year but also at a particular time of night. Extract from the root of the greater celandine is extremely poisonous even in moderation, unless obtained at a specific time of the winter when the perennial plant is dormant and just before it begins to return to life. If you gargled with an infusion made from the stuff picked even a day or two from the correct time, it would be like rinsing your mouth with cyanide.

The Romans, themselves expert physicians of the time, were impressed by the medicinal skills of the Druids. Julius Caesar, for example, was amazed by how they could cure even "those smit-

Fig. 12.1. Sites discussed in this chapter.

ten with the most grievous maladies."[25] Pliny the Elder tells us that the Druids knew the secrets of countless plants and believed that all things that grew were endowed with divine, curative properties that they alone claimed to understand. He mentions mistletoe, for instance, saying how a preparation made from the plant was considered an antidote for many poisons.[26] The young twigs, collected just before the berries form and then slowly dried, were then ground into a powder. Modern medicine has used viscin, a sap produced by mistletoe branches, as an anticonvulsive drug to control seizures—often the most life-threatening aspect of poisoning—keeping the patient stable until the toxin is naturally expelled from the body. The physiological effect of the substance is to suppress impulses to the brain that would otherwise trigger convulsions.[27] (Mistletoe residue, adhering to pottery fragments, has been found in many box tombs, including the sites at Fernworthy, Penywyrlod, and Ashgrove.) The Druids who acted as physicians were educated for many years and from an early age. Caesar tells us that "some persons remain twenty years under training."[28] Pomponius Mela, who also relates that instruction could take as much as two decades, says they were taught in strict isolation in the Druids' woodland sanctuaries.[29] Without the ancient physicians knowing precisely what they were doing, patients could end up far worse off than they were already and very probably dead. So for goodness sake, do not try preparing such concoctions at home.

It seems, then, that the elite caste among the ancient inhabitants of the British Isles, known as the Druids by the Celts, would have been indispensable. Most people died as children from maladies that today, in the First World at least, have either been eliminated by vaccines or rendered little more than a nuisance by a whole variety of drugs. The likelihood of the death of a baby or mother during childbirth was high. A chill or common cold could kill anyone of any age, as it frequently developed into pneumonia under the conditions in which these people lived. And even for the able-bodied, life would often have been painful: stomach bugs, intestinal worms, headaches, tooth rot, and arthritis at an early age, to name just a few such ailments. Even something as simple as backache or a sprain could render you unable to work and support your family. Food poisoning must have been a regular occurrence, and a simple cut could result in infection or septicemia. And you could bleed to death from the kind of wounds that the ancients risked every day, let alone if you fought in a battle.

From the archaeological discoveries and from what the classical sources tell us, the Druids appear to have had preparations for pain relief, cures for parasites, decongestants, remedies for the control of fever, antiseptics, disinfectants, antidotes for various poisons, and much more besides. And judging by both the plant extracts and medical instruments found in their tombs, they could render aid with difficult childbirth, stitch wounds, extract foreign bodies, and perform amputations with the patient under anesthesia. Their role as physicians would have been one very good reason for the general population to more than tolerate a caste whose religious beliefs differed from their own—especially as the Druids seem to have kept their medical knowledge to themselves (see chapter 13).

Remarkably the cultivation and harvesting of vegetation for medicinal purposes may actually explain why stone circles were built. As discussed, there was no need to build monolithic rings for astrological reasons relating to the bodies of the solar system. Nevertheless, some researchers have noted that the megaliths at stone circles do seem to have been placed to deliberately align with the rising and setting of particularly bright *stars* at specific times of the year.[30] When first proposed in the 1960s, such theories involved complex mathematical calculations, because in the distant past stars would appear to be in slightly different locations relative to Earth compared with where they are today. Although stars, as opposed to the bodies of the solar system, remain in a set position compared with one another, over the course of many centuries this stellar background appears to move very slowly. Due to something called axial precession—a gradual shift in the Earth's axis of rotation, or a slow wobble—the North and South Poles appear to move in circles against the fixed backdrop of stars, taking approximately twenty-six thousand years to complete each circuit. Accordingly where each star rises or sets today is somewhat different from the past. The proposed alignments were determined on this basis. These days anyone can see where the stars were in relation to the Earth at any period of history by downloading a common app to a cell phone.

Of course, as there are so many stars, such apparent alignments may be down to pure chance. Even so, stone circles do very much seem to have been deliberately sited at locations where the heavens could best be observed. One of the many riddles concerning stone circles is that nearly all of them were built some distance from the communities where their creators actually lived. A culture's monuments or places of worship are usually built at the heart of the civilization's settlements: shrines in villages, temples in towns, and more elaborate complexes or sanctuaries in cities. As discussed, during the long Megalithic era, apart from the foundations of small clusters of huts where it is thought the priesthood or custodians of the monuments may have dwelt, the nearest settlements were often miles from the stone circles. Villages were usually built in fertile valleys, offering such amenities as natural shelter, waterways, and good farming land, whereas the monolithic rings were invariably situated in locations such as open plains, barren moorlands, and exposed hills. These were settings that provided a panoramic view of the sky, which would plausibly explain why the circles were erected there: so that the firmament could be best observed.

Put simply, in the Northern Hemisphere, southerly stars rise and set above the horizon in gradually differing locations as the year progresses. Standing in the center of a stone circle, you could use the monoliths as fixed points to determine where such celestial objects were with accuracy. Stars in question appearing at a specific location above or between the stones would give you a precise moment of the year, a very exact calendar that would not again be available until the invention of the mechanical clock. Remember how the preparation of the ancient medicinal substances often required precision harvesting, sometimes down to the hour of night on a certain day, as the chemical properties of many plants gradually alter during the hours of darkness. You would not need such an accurate calendar for general horticultural purposes such as planting and reaping. These could be determined by the progression of the sun. The sun, however, would not enable such accurate timing, as it is large and bright. Working out the precise moment when the edge of the sun first moved around a stone, for example, would require looking through the kind of darkened glass now used by welders and solar astronomers. Without such a glass you would go blind trying to work it out and still not have a clear enough view of the sun's disk; besides which, many such observations would need to be made at night. (The moon could not stand in for the sun as its orbit around the Earth, coupled with the solar orbit of both gravitationally linked bodies, makes its movements appear far too erratic.) By using certain stars as guides—when they were in a particular position with relation to the stones—you could accurately determine a very specific moment of any day of the year. The stone circle would serve as an accurate clock to reveal the precise times for the various processes involved in the preparation of medications. (A ring of wooden posts could serve the same purpose, and archaeologists have found indications of such structures, but they would be prone to movement due to weather, not to mention rot; besides which, circles of stone would be more permanent and more impressive status symbols for those who used them.)

As we have seen, stone circles were not constructed to the same design: their size and number of stones varied. This might be an argument against their being purely religious monuments, but it wouldn't matter for an astronomical calculator. All you needed to do was remember where each star was meant to be in relation to your own stone circle when a particular plant needed to be harvested, or its leaves, stem, bud, flower, seeds, fruit, or sap needed to be picked, cut, or extracted.

Stone circles would remain as accurate timepieces for years, but after a while axial precession would begin to throw them out of sync. However, the Druids and their forebears might have made the necessary adjustments: the classical writers suggest that they had been quite capable of performing such mathematical calculations. Julius Caesar and Pomponius Mela both say that the Druids had expert knowledge of the stars and their apparent movements,[31,32] while Hippolytus relates that the Druids were accomplished mathematicians, likening their wisdom to that of Pythagoras, one of the greatest mathematicians of ancient Greece.[33]

Often, though, it seems that new stones were erected or old ones moved to compensate for the precession. We have already seen how, over the long period during which megalithic monuments were used, many stone circles had additional rings of monoliths added periodically in the immediate vicinity, often within a few hundred feet of the original (see chapter 6). For example, further stone circles were added to either side of the Hurlers in Cornwall; at Knowlton in Dorset three further circles were built within a stone's throw of Church Henge, one to the south, the others to the northwest; on Moor Divock in Cumbria at least four further stone circles were built within half a mile of an original over a period of around 2,000 years; and at Machrie Moor on the Isle of Arran no fewer than six stone circles were added in the vicinity over a period of more than 2,500 years until the first century BCE. The grander stones circles often had additional rings built inside them, such as at Stonehenge and Avebury.

Undoubtedly, stone circles became highly prestigious sites in their own right, serving as locations for various ceremonial activities, as evidenced by archaeology (see chapter 9). We know from the classical sources that the Druids venerated a sun deity and that outlying king stones marked important days in the annual solar cycle, such as the solstices and equinoxes: times when ritual or social events must have occurred. However, when even the inner rings of the most impressive stone circles no longer aligned correctly with the right stars, the circles still were such spectacular monuments that they probably continued to be used for mass gatherings. This might account for why satellite stone circles were erected at the end of avenues linked to the main ring, such as the West Amesbury Henge at Stonehenge (see chapter 7) and the Overton Hill Sanctuary at Avebury (see chapter 6). Interestingly, geophysics surveys conducted at both of these sites have revealed that the stones were periodically adjusted over time. It was perhaps at these new circles that the calculations were made, while the original, grander monuments continued to be employed primarily for ceremonial purposes.

Stone circles were clearly ceremonial meeting places of the Druids and their forebears, but judging by the medical skills of this elite caste, for the general population who did not necessarily share the Druids' religious beliefs, the megalithic rings may have served as healing sanctuaries where diagnoses were made, surgical procedures performed, and cures dispensed; in effect, stone circles may have been the ERs or casualty units of the time.

13

Secret of the Stones and the Red-Haired Druids

THE CLASSICAL AUTHORS TELL US that it took years of instruction for Druids to become the accomplished physicians and apothecaries they evidentially were (see chapter 11). But there's a mystery here. The Greeks and Romans also had a surprising amount of medical knowledge for the time, and they too had physicians who spent years in education. Their schooling, however, involved the study of centuries of acquired knowledge conserved on scrolls and parchments housed in libraries. The peoples of the British Isles—the Neolithic, Beaker, Wessex, and Celtic cultures—had no form of writing until the Romans arrived. In a wet climate such as that of the British Isles, even during warmer times, with no permanent buildings to preserve them, written documents would not have survived long: even if someone had gotten around to inventing writing, it would have been of little use. So how was their shared wisdom, gradually acquired over millennia, actually preserved? The answer to this question leads us to what was perhaps the crucial and most extraordinary role the Druids performed. It seems that they themselves—their minds—were the living libraries of the ancient cultures of Britain and Ireland.

Early Irish literature and the biographies of the first Christian missionaries to Ireland frequently refer to the Druids as poets, their verse considered a "sacred art" in which the collective knowledge of the Celts was preserved. Reference is made to a distinctive class of Druids who acted as the guardians of wisdom.[1] Called the Filid (singular Fili), they were charged with memorizing society's acquired learning in the form of poetry, as its rhyming, rhythmic scheme was easier to recall than prose.[2] The classical writers Strabo and Diodorus refer to a druidic sect called the Bardoi, seemingly the same as the Irish Filid.[3,4] (It is from them that the medieval word "bard" was derived to mean a Gaelic or Welsh poet and later used as an epithet for Shakespeare.) It seems that the Filid or Bardoi were divided into groups, like the sections of a library, each group collectively committing to memory a particular subject area, such as history, agriculture, or medicine, while some composed new poems to record current events or fresh ideas. Caesar, whose writings reveal more about the Druids than any other ancient works, says that these people spent years acquiring their knowledge in the form of vast numbers of verses they were required to learn by heart. Evidently they employed what today we would call mnemonic techniques—such as visual imagery, acronyms, rhymes, and other cognitive strategies—to efficiently store and retrieve information. They were selected as children, he tells us, probably from those already demonstrating a natural aptitude for memory.[5]

The Druids had inherited a remarkable way to preserve collective knowledge in a world without writing. They occupied a unique position among the varied ethnic groups of the British Isles, ensuring them a privileged place in society. So how did it all begin? As we have surmised, the stone circles were erected primarily to calculate the meticulous timings involved in the preparation of a whole range of medicines (see chapter 12). It would seem that, having no form of writing, the ancient herbalists who initiated the building of the first stone circles were impelled to conceive a sophisticated system of memorizing their medical expertise gained by trial and error over generations. The knowledge that they committed to collective memory, however, came to incorporate more than just medicinal matters. These people became living archives of the laws, codes, and history of their culture. There evolved a learned elite who lived apart from other members of society: the priestly caste of the late Neolithic age. When others migrated to the British Isles, they too appreciated the value of this exceptional sect. The Druids' exclusive role to preserve knowledge, along with their healing skills, made them impossible to live without. The price to pay, so to speak, was to accept them as overseers. It would appear that by acting as advisors, judges, and arbitrators, this remarkable order of men and women cemented the diverse tribal cultures of the British Isles into what was effectively a single society for over three thousand years.

The Celts called them Truth Sayers— *druids* in their vernacular— but what previous inhabitants of the British Isles had called them is unknown, perhaps an equivalent term in their now forgotten tongues. We started our investigation by addressing the central mystery of the Megalithic culture: how it survived for so long, over such a wide area, without the usual trappings of civilization (see chapter 1). It seems it was the Druids and their predecessors who held it together. And how did it end? Ultimately it may not only have been the Romans' military might and later their religious influence that brought about their demise, but also the introduction of writing that came with them. The Druids, as living libraries, eventually became superfluous. And with their extinction the stone circles were finally abandoned.

What we have pieced together concerning this extraordinary sect has facilitated a new perspective on the megalithic monuments of the British Isles. One of the enduring puzzles concerning the stone circles is why they varied so much from one another in their size and number of monoliths (see chapter 6). If they were used for the reasons postulated—as a means to determine the precise timings essential for the cultivation and preparation of medicinal plants—then their exact size or number of stones wouldn't matter. A specific time of the year could be determined by the position of a particular star—any star—in relation to a particular stone—any stone—so long as you remembered the juxtaposition and what it related to: the time to pick a certain berry, fruit, or flower; extract sap from a tree or shrub; take a cutting from a root; harvest a plant; or whatever was necessary for the medicinal ingredient. There must have been a myriad of such star-stone relationships to memorize for the manufacture of countless concoctions, but memory was something the stone circle builders seem to have developed to a fine art. Some stone circles do appear to have been unnecessarily large, but this was probably a matter of prestige. Remember that those who used them were also regarded as mystics and prophets. As in most societies, such people would likely be acclaimed with elaborate symbols of their status. Stone circles were probably as big as the local population and geography allowed. The richest and most populated area of the British Isles was the mid-south of England, and it was there that Avebury, the largest stone circle, and Stonehenge, the most elaborate stone circle, were built.

There are still many enigmas concerning these ancient monuments. The satellite stone circles at megalithic complexes may be explained by the need for new rings due to axial precession (see chapter 12), but what about the henges, avenues, and artificial hills? They may have been inspired by some purely religious motive. If alien beings were to visit a postapocalyptic Earth where all records had been destroyed, would they ever figure out the reasoning behind the design of churches, synagogues, and mosques? Or perhaps there was some other purpose. Without records, who would guess the reasoning behind the construction of the Egyptian pyramids, the Taj Mahal, or the Roman Coliseum? And there are other mysteries too. What were the petrospheres? Why were spirals carved onto the monoliths of early megalithic sites (see chapter 4)? Perhaps we'll never know. However, we *are* now in a position to explain what purpose Stonehenge actually served. Everything we have examined suggests that it was primarily an essential aid to preparing medicines, modified over the centuries to compensate for the apparent and gradual shifts in the positions of stars. There were clearly embellishments, such as its unique lintel stones, perhaps to afford it greater prestige, or maybe they held some sacred significance. The real secret of Stonehenge, however, lies not with its stones, but with the remarkable people who built and maintained it: the physicians and living libraries of the prehistoric British Isles. It clearly served as the meeting place for successive cultures where others could interact with these enigmatic people. What was Stonehenge? To those who officiated there it may have embodied many beliefs, but to the population at large it would have been a place of healing—a hospital.

The full extent of whatever medical knowledge the Druids possessed has been lost to history. Modern pharmacology may have surpassed their ancient medicinal know-how, but have we rediscovered it all? Astonishingly the Druids might even have found a cure for cancer. In his *Natural History,* Pliny the Elder tells us that the Druids "held nothing more sacred than the mistletoe." He describes how they cut the plant at a specific time of the year as determined by the position of the heavenly bodies and prepared it in a secret way to create a cure for "the most grievous maladies."[6] Today, scientists have extracted a compound called lectin ML1 from mistletoe for use in chemotherapy. The substance adheres to natural antibodies, enabling them to recognize and attack cancer cells.[7] We can only guess what cures the Druids possessed. Sadly their secrets seem to have died with them. The last Druids were recorded in fifth-century Ireland (see chapter 10). So is this when and where the final vestige of the Megalithic age ultimately came to an end?

The Megalithic era—it all began with the Stones of Stenness around 3100 BCE, Stonehenge was its finest achievement, and it persisted for 3,500 years. But where was the last stone circle to be used by Druids? And where were the last of these people laid to rest? Stone circles were still being used by the Celts in Ireland until the mid-fifth century, when the country was rapidly converted to Christianity (see chapter 11). Significantly the last stone circles in Ireland, where archaeology has uncovered evidence of the most recent ceremonial activity, all have an unusual feature: one or two freestanding monoliths erected close to the center of the ring. Examples include the Uragh Stone Circle near Tuosist in County Kerry, the Robinstown Great Stones in County Wexford, and Kenmare in County Kerry. Although less impressive than their predecessors, new megalithic complexes were also still being built at this time. Carrigagulla is a late megalithic complex near Ballinagree in County Cork that includes a 25-foot-diameter stone circle of fifteen monoliths (originally seventeen) and an accompanying avenue, 800 feet long, leading to a cove of five standing stones. Inside the stone circle there originally stood two further monoliths; one now lies fallen, and the other was removed in the nineteenth century.[8]

The very last of the stone circles known to have been used by the pre-Christian Irish were on the east side of Ireland, in an area now encompassed by County Kildare and the district of Dublin. This is the most urbanized part of the country, so most of these monuments were destroyed long ago, only recently having been identified by geophysics surveys. However, one of these, at Killiney, just south of Dublin, still survived intact to be surveyed in the nineteenth century. Called the Killiney Ring, it was 30 feet in diameter and consisted of ten 8-foot-tall stones and two 10-foot-tall central monoliths. Unfortunately much of the site was destroyed in the late 1800s when the stones were moved by the local landowner to create a scenic garden. Like many of these late stone circles, the Killiney Ring was adjoined by a box cairn, which *does* survive.

The chief megalithic complex in this area, however, seems to have been in what is now the town of Kildare, but all traces of it were destroyed when a cathedral was built on the site in the thirteenth century. From what can be gathered from early Irish literature, the complex was centered on a large henge monument associated with Brigid, the Celtic goddess of healing, where a sacred flame was kept burning in her honor and the sick came in the hope of cures. Also known as Brig or Bride, this goddess was principally venerated at the festival of Imbolc around February 1, midway between the winter solstice and the spring equinox. She appears in various accounts in *The Book of Leinster*,[9] and according to *Sanas Cormaic* (Cormac's Narrative), compiled by

Cormac mac Cuilennáin, the bishop of Munster in the late 800s, she had been the principal deity of the district where the last Druids resided, on the east side of central Ireland.[10] Interestingly this goddess provides a vital clue to reveal what may have been the very last stone circle used by the ancient Druids.

During the fifth century, when the Kildare region was converted to Christianity, a monastery is said to have been founded on the site of the healing sanctuary by a woman "coincidentally" called Brigid. This Brigid, referred to by the modern church as Saint Brigit, appears in a number of Dark Age writings, the oldest to survive being *Vita Sanctae Brigidae* (Life of Saint Brigid) by Cogitosus, a monk from Kildare who wrote around 675 CE. According to these various accounts, all written two centuries or more after the events described, Brigid is said to have been a Druid captive born in 451 CE. She was freed when her tribe was converted to Christianity, became a nun, and rose to be an abbess, founding the monastery at Kildare in 480 on the site of the pagan shrine. Curiously she is said to have continued the custom of the eternal flame, with she and a number of nuns tending to the sacred beacon, from that time thought to represent the perpetual light of Christianity. As we have seen, the Celtic Church in Ireland, with its mixed-gender monastic institutions where both men and women acted as priests, became something quite different from the Roman Catholic Church (see chapter 11). Brigid herself, we are told, actually became head of the Irish Church. Known as the "superior general," she had the power to appoint bishops throughout the country. After her death, Brigid was proclaimed a saint, and on her annual feast day—February 1—people from all over Ireland flocked to the site of her monastery in the hope of miraculous cures.[11]

Many historians consider Saint Brigid to have been a legendary figure, invented by the Christians to supplant the pagan Brigid. The saint and the goddess share the same name, they are linked with the same site and the sacred flame, both are associated with healing, and their principal day of adulation is what had once been the festival of

Imbolc. Just as early churches were built on the sites of previous pagan shrines (see chapter 8), ancient deities were often reinvented as saints. It was all part of a deliberate strategy adopted by the early church. Called Interpretatio Christiana (Christian Reinterpretation), it was part of the policy of adapting non-Christian elements into the faith. Pagan gods had performed specific roles: appeals were made to individual deities in the hope of eliciting particular results. There were gods of the harvest and weather, childbirth and fertility, health and well-being—just about everything. But Christianity taught that there was only one God. That a single divinity could fulfill all these commitments was a difficult concept for the newly converted pagans to grasp. Accordingly if it was to succeed in its intended mission to convert the world, the church was impelled to adopt the notion that multiple heavenly beings could intervene in mortal affairs; that is, so long as they were regarded as saints.

As in today's Catholicism, Christian figures considered to have lived particularly pious lives and to have exhibited an exceptional degree of holiness, such as having miracles attributed to them, were canonized. They were declared "saints," from the Latin *sanctus,* meaning "sanctified." These deceased individuals were said to hold an esteemed position in heaven and to have been granted the power by God to intercede in earthly matters. Many became "patron saints." Just like the old gods, they were regarded as heavenly advocates of specific nations, locations, and activities—all manner of things. There had once been individual gods of crafts, fertility, health, farming, healing, and a myriad of other affairs, so the converted Christians were given equivalent saints. They were usually real, historical figures, although their lives may have been embellished by their biographers, but during the late Roman and post-Roman era many saints were the reinventions of ancient deities.

To give just a few examples: Mars, the Roman god of war, became linked with Saint Martin, the patron saint of warriors, supposedly a Roman soldier who was ordained a bishop in the fourth century. Bacchus, the Roman god of wine, feasting, and theater, became Saint Bacchus, supposedly a flamboyant Roman citizen martyred in the early 300s CE. The Egyptian Osiris, the god of the dead, became Saint Onuphrius, the patron saint of the sick and dying, purportedly a Christian mystic who lived as a hermit in the desert of southern Egypt during the fourth century. The goddess Venus became associated with Saint Venera, allegedly a second-century CE Christian martyr: she was the patron saint of a Maltese town where a great temple to Venus had once stood. Saint Brigid was most likely such a contrived historical figure accredited with attributes of the earlier pagan goddess, although some scholars believe she was a real person. It has been suggested that Brigid may have been the chief Druid of the Kildare shrine, a woman bearing the honorary name of the goddess who converted to Christianity but retained some of the old customs in her mode of worship.[12]

Whether or not Saint Brigid was a historical figure, the goddess of that name was the principal deity of the County Kildare/Dublin region when it appears to have been the last stronghold of Druidism in Ireland. And the supposed time of her conversion to Christianity, in the mid-fifth century CE, tallies with the final demise of the Irish Druids. Surprisingly, however, this might not actually have been the last enclave of Megalithic culture in the British Isles. There is a megalithic site associated with the goddess Brigid in western England that seems to have been completely overlooked by archaeologists and historians alike. The work of an eighteenth-century antiquarian reveals that it may have been the last stone circle to be used by the Druids in all the British Isles: the place where the 3,500-year-old Megalithic culture finally came to an end.

The last of the Irish Druids may have fled to mainland Britain. Although church tradition holds that a few holy men such as Saint Patrick converted Ireland to Christianity, the reality was somewhat different. The Roman Empire was collapsing, and the departure of the Roman army in 410 CE left many parts of Britain to fall into a state of anarchy. Because of the civil conflicts that ensued, with various warlords vying for power along old tribal lines, a wave of wealthy Roman citizens fled Britain for Ireland, and along with them came the hierarchy of the British Catholic Church. It was a mass migration of educated Christians. Along with these migrants came the full-scale introduction of writing to Ireland as well as the technology to create paper and books and to build monasteries to preserve them—rapidly making the Druids obsolete. The Irish chieftains, long under the sway of the Druids, quickly broke free from their authority, and the appeal of being endorsed by a new, almighty Roman deity was a powerful incentive for them to convert. In Britain the opposite was happening: the internecine strife brought about the virtual collapse of the organized church and a return to paganism. By the mid-fifth century CE, Irish pagans, now in the minority, were fleeing to Britain. Records are few from this period, but the British monk Gildas, writing around the year 545 CE, tells us that the Irish occupied much of the west of the country. (Gildas actually refers to the Irish as the Scoti, an old Roman term for the Celts. The Scots at this time, i.e., the Scottish, he refers to as the Picts.) Archaeology bears him out. Not only have Irish settlements been found in western Britain from this time, but their graves also have been unearthed. It is possible, then, that there may have been a brief reintroduction of Druidism to parts of Britain before the country became, according to Gildas, temporarily reunited and nominally re-Christianized around 470 CE.[13] And there is one megalithic site that may actually have been reoccupied by the Druids at this time.

Just north of the village of Biddulph Moor in the county of Cheshire, about 25 miles inland from the Mersey Estuary, which joins the Irish Sea, is a megalithic monument called the Bridestones. As noted, Bride was one of the names for the Irish goddess Brigid. The site is thought to have been of particular importance in Megalithic times as the hill that overlooks it, called the Cloud, is so shaped that the mid-summer sun, as seen from the southeast, appears to set twice. The profile of the hill means that the sun sets behind one ridge to reemerge and set again behind a second. Remember how important the midsummer solstice appears to have been to those who built the stone circles. The Bridestones consists of the remains of a box tomb, composed from stones averaging about 1 foot wide and 5 feet high, creating a chamber with inner dimensions of about 6 by 14 feet and divided into two equal parts by a further, broken slab. For years the monument has been mistaken for a pre-Megalithic long barrow due to two 10-foot-tall monoliths that now stand at one end, like the portal stones at monuments such as Wayland's Smithy (see chapter 3). However, these two stones originally lay fallen nearby, until the 1930s when members of the Department of Geography at Manchester University re-erected the monoliths in their present positions, wrongly believing they were restoring the site to its original condition.[14]

Luckily a survey of the Bridestones was made by the Welsh antiquarian Henry Rowlands in the early eighteenth century and published in his work *Mona Antiqua Restaurata* (Ancient Anglesey Restored) of 1723.[15] The two monoliths were originally part of a stone circle that stood next to the tomb, all but these two having been removed in the nineteenth century to be used in the construction of an ornamental garden in the area. The circle consisted of ten approximately 10-foot-tall stones in a ring about 27 feet in diameter. What Rowlands reveals about the tomb is that it must have been over three thousand years younger than the era of long barrows (see chapter 3)—the period from which many modern guidebooks and websites date the Bridestones. In his day, the box tomb still had a roof made from horizontal stone slabs and was covered by a large mound of rocks, which had fallen away at one end, exposing the chamber and giving it the appearance of an "artificial cave." These rocks were removed in the mid-eighteenth century to be used in the construction of a nearby road.[16] In other words, it was a box tomb covered by a rock cairn, dating it to the late Celtic period (see chapter 12).

Astonishingly the Bridestones box cairn may actually have been built well after the period when the Romans invaded Britain. Rowlands's book includes a diagram showing the stone circle with the tomb adjoining it on the western side. This is exactly the same arrangement we have seen so many times before with late Celtic cairns in Ireland, such Ballykeel South,

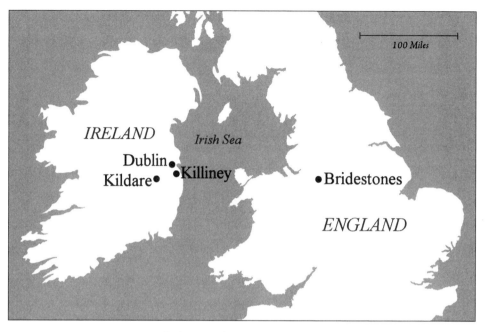

Fig. 13.1. Locations of what may be the very last megalithic stone circles.

Brackloon, and Kilgowan, dating from the fifth century CE (see chapter 11). Moreover, the stone circle is shown to have two further monoliths close to the center of the ring. As discussed, this unusual feature has been found exclusively at the late stone circles of pre-Christian Ireland. In fact, the original Bridestones is almost identical to the Killiney site (see page 221), which consisted of a ring of ten similarly sized stones with two monoliths at its center and a box cairn built right next to it. This arrangement of box cairn and stone circle with double standing stones at its center has been considered unique to fifth-century CE Ireland— nearly four hundred years *after* the Druids were thought to have been eradicated in Britain. The county of Cheshire is an area that archaeology has determined to have been settled by Irish migrants during the mid to late fifth century CE. Could the Bridestones—which actually bears the name of the principal goddess of east-central Ireland—have been built by the pagan Celts who had fled to Britain in the fifth century CE? And was the tomb the final resting place of the last Druids?

No modern archaeological work has been undertaken at the Bridestones, but it cries out to be properly excavated. There has been a great deal of disturbance to the site over the years, but it may still be possible to date material from beneath the stones of the box tomb, even if it proves difficult to scientifically date the stone circle. However, there is a strange anomaly in the area that may well indicate that late members of the Druid caste did settle there and that their descendants survived until recent times. The hilly district around the Bridestones seems to have remained socially isolated for generations. The village of Biddulph Moor, a couple of miles to the south of the stones, has been inhabited from around the fifth century CE. Remarkably as late as the nineteenth century, the people of Biddulph Moor held two annual gatherings at the site: one on midsummer evening, when the village elders made predictions concerning the coming year, and one on February 1, when it was believed the sick could be cured. The Druids were considered prophets, and many stone circles have midsummer alignments, while Brigid's sacred day had been around February 1, a time when appeals were made to the goddess to facilitate healing. Linked together, these traditions relate specifically to the pagan practices of east-central Ireland during the mid-fifth century CE. Not only might the villagers have been continuing customs that date back to a time when Irish Druids settled there in the mid-400s CE, they also may well have been their direct descendants.

The village of Biddulph Moor was a remote, hillside farming community until the sprawling industrial region to the south finally encroached on it in the late 1900s. Today it is composed of modern houses, a suburb of the city of Stoke-on-Trent, created from the adjoined towns of this ceramic-manufacturing area in 1910. Before this time it was a reclusive village of just a few hundred people who seem to have lived in virtual isolation for centuries.

In chapter 11 we examined how the Druids appear to have had red hair, a characteristic inherited from their Neolithic ancestors. As discussed, red hair is due to a recessive gene; both parents need to have it for the trait to be passed to their children, meaning that since the multiple waves of migration to the British Isles over the last 4.5 millennia, only insular communities have retained it as a predominant feature. The Druids and their predecessors were an exclusive class who appear to have procreated only among their own caste, resulting in a greater number of redheaded people in the place where the sect survived the longest—Ireland. Red hair occurs in around 10 percent of the modern Irish population, but only 2 percent of the English. Accordingly there are a few remote villages in Ireland with a redheaded majority, but none in England, except for one curious exception that existed until the nineteenth century: Biddulph Moor.

Before the age of the motorcar and the influx of modern commuters, various writers referred to the inhabitants of Biddulph Moor as all having red hair and said that they spoke a different dialect from the rest of the area. Their unusual appearance was noted by the Staffordshire historian John Sleigh in his *A History of the Ancient Parish of Leek* in 1862; he says that the townspeople of nearby Leek believed that their neighbors were descended from Arabs captured and returned to England during the crusades.[17] Arab people of the Middle Ages, however, had dark hair, perhaps something unknown to these country folk during a period before modern communications. In 1909 Charlotte Burne, the president of the British Folklore Society, in an article for the organization's *Quarterly Review,* suggested that their ancestors were Gypsies who once settled on Biddulph Moor. The people she referred to as Gypsies were actually those today known as Irish Travelers. The problem with this theory is that although they are a distinctive ethnic group originating in Ireland, few of them have red hair; no more, in fact, than the general population.

Those who settled at Biddulph Moor during the fifth century CE may well have been those who built the Bridestones box cairn and used its adjoining stone circle. Perhaps they had all been members of the insular Druid caste who fled Ireland at this time, their offspring remaining genetically isolated in this hilly district until the encroachment of the wider society during the Industrial Revolution. Biddulph Moor is now a commuter neighborhood for the city of Stoke-on-Trent, the indigenous population having left or been assimilated with others. During the 1970s, as part of a blood-screening study, the Stoke-on-Trent coroner, Fred Hails, reported that there was indeed a significant difference in the blood types of the older inhabitants of Biddulph Moor compared with others in the local area.[18] However, this was before the advent of genetic testing, so it was impossible to determine from what part of the world this trait originated. In 2003, as part of a BBC radio show called *Meet the Descendants,* genetic tests were carried out on the few remaining families whose ancestors had lived in Biddulph Moor for generations. Unfortunately the program specifically intended to test the crusader captive legend, and the tests were searching for genetic markers of Middle Eastern ancestry, of which no evidence was found. No one thought to test for Irish or Neolithic DNA.

For the time being the origin of the red-haired inhabitants of Biddulph Moor remains a mystery. But regardless of their heritage the Bridestones seems to have been the site of one of the last—perhaps *the* last—megalithic stone circle anywhere in Britain or Ireland. And its tomb may have been the final resting place of the last remnant of the enigmatic sect the Celts called Druids, an extraordinary people whose monuments once spanned the entire British Isles and were erected for well over three thousand years and whose most famous accomplishment was Stonehenge.

Notes

CHAPTER 1.
AN ENIGMA IN STONE

1. Prior, *BC: Life in Britain and Ireland.*
2. Hawkins, *Stonehenge Decoded.*
3. Geoffrey of Monmouth, *History of the Kings of Britain.*
4. Darvill and Wainwright, "Beyond Stonehenge."
5. Holland, *Haunted Wales.*
6. Underwood, *Where the Ghosts Walk.*
7. Oliver, *Journal of Samuel Curwen, Loyalist.*
8. Conroy, *Breton-English, English-Breton Dictionary.*
9. Aubrey and Fowles, *Monumenta Britannica.*
10. Burl and Mortimer, *Stukeley's Stonehenge.*
11. Burl, *Stone Circles of Britain, Ireland and Brittany.*
12. Burl, *Prehistoric Avebury.*

CHAPTER 2.
THE BIRTH OF CIVILIZATION

1. Peregrine, *World Prehistory.*
2. Guthrie, *Nature of Paleolithic Art.*
3. Reid, *Prehistoric Houses in Britain.*
4. Thomas, *Understanding the Neolithic.*
5. Langmaid, *Prehistoric Pottery.*
6. Tylecote, *History of Metallurgy.*

7. Barber, Martyn. *Bronze and the Bronze Age.*

8. James and Thorpe, *Ancient Inventions.*

9. Landau, *Sumerians: Cradle of Civilization.*

10. Crawford, *Sumer and the Sumerians.*

11. Crawford, *Sumer and the Sumerians.*

12. Kramer, *Sumerian Mythology.*

13. Charvát, *Birth of the State.*

14. Smith and Masson, *Ancient Civilizations of Mesoamerica.*

15. Plato, *Timaeus and Critias.*

16. Plato, *Timaeus and Critias.*

17. Phillips, *Act of God.*

18. de Camp, *Lost Continents.*

19. Cox and Hart, *Plate Tectonics: How It Works.*

20. Ramaswamy, *The Lost Land of Lemuria.*

21. Cunliffe, *Extraordinary Voyage of Pytheas the Greek.*

CHAPTER 3.
PRELUDE: THE EMERGING CULTURES
OF THE LATE STONE AGE

1. Trump, *Malta: Prehistory and Temples.*

2. Moore, *Prehistory of South America.*

3. Dyson and Rowland, *Archaeology and History in Sardinia.*

4. Hodder, *Leopard's Tale.*

5. Hodder, *Leopard's Tale.*

6. Collins, *Göbekli Tepe.*

7. Burl, *From Carnac to Callanish.*

8. Le Roux and Lecerf, *Le Grand Cairn de Barnenez.*

9. Thom, *Megalithic Remains in Britain and Brittany.*

10. Pettitt, *Palaeolithic Origins of Human Burial.*

11. Ehlers, Hughes, and Gibbard, *Ice Age.*

12. Thomas, *Understanding the Neolithic.*

13. Gaffney, Fitch, and Smith, *Europe's Lost World.*

14. Bradley, Raymond, *Paleoclimatology.*

15. Smith and Brickley, *People of the Long Barrows.*

16. Smith and Brickley, *People of the Long Barrows.*

17. Smith and Brickley, *People of the Long Barrows.*

18. Malone, *Neolithic Britain and Ireland.*

CHAPTER 4. THE BEGINNING:
THE STONES OF STENNESS

1. Ritchie, Graham, *Stones of Stenness, Orkney.*
2. Hunt, *Oxford Handbook of Archaeological Ceramic Analysis.*
3. Bradley, Richard, *Prehistory of Britain and Ireland.*
4. Cleal and MacSween, *Grooved Ware.*
5. Tilley, *Ethnography of the Neolithic.*
6. Clarke, *Skara Brae.*
7. Smith and Brickley, *People of the Long Barrows.*
8. Ritchie, Anna, *Prehistoric Orkney.*
9. Ritchie, Anna, *Prehistoric Orkney.*
10. Wickham-Jones, *Orkney: A Historical Guide.*
11. Clarke, *Skara Brae.*
12. Ritchie, Anna, *Prehistoric Orkney.*
13. Clarke, *Skara Brae.*
14. Wickham-Jones, *Monuments of Orkney.*
15. Richards, *Building the Great Stone Circles.*
16. Renfrew, *Prehistory of Orkney.*
17. Foster, *Maeshowe and the Heart of Neolithic Orkney.*
18. *Orcadian,* July 20, 1861.
19. Marshall, "Carved Stone Balls," 108.
20. Sharples, *Excavations at Pierowall Quarry.*

CHAPTER 5. PROGRESSION: THE DISCOVERY OF STONE
CIRCLES THROUGHOUT THE BRITISH ISLES

1. Ashmore, *Calanais: The Standing Stones.*
2. Armit, *Archaeology of Skye and the Western Isles.*
3. Armit, *Archaeology of Skye and the Western Isles.*
4. Brophy, MacGregor, and Ralston, *Neolithic of Mainland Scotland.*
5. Clare, *Prehistoric Monuments of the Lake District.*
6. Barrowclough, *Prehistoric Cumbria.*
7. Ó Nuallain, *Stone Circles in Ireland.*
8. Stout and Stout, *Newgrange.*
9. Armit et al., *Neolithic Settlement in Ireland and Western Britain.*
10. Mount, "Aspects of Ritual Deposition."
11. Lynch, *Prehistoric Anglesey.*

12. "Stonehenge May Have Been First Erected in Wales, Evidence Suggests," *Guardian,* December 7, 2015.

13. "Stonehenge 'Bluestone' Quarries Confirmed 140 Miles Away in Wales," *UCL News,* December 7, 2015.

14. "Stonehenge, Older than Believed," *BBC News,* October 9, 2008.

15. Parker Pearson, *Stonehenge: Exploring the Greatest Stone Age Mystery.*

16. Gibson, *Prehistoric Pottery.*

17. McGrail, *Ancient Boats and Ships.*

CHAPTER 6. THE PHASES OF MEGALITHIC COMPLEXES

1. Peterson, *Neolithic Pottery from Wales.*

2. Malone, *Neolithic Britain and Ireland.*

3. Gibson, *Prehistoric Pottery.*

4. Wickham-Jones, *Monuments of Orkney.*

5. Bradley, Richard, *Prehistory of Britain and Ireland.*

6. Lynch, *Prehistoric Anglesey.*

7. Burl, *Stone Circles of Britain, Ireland and Brittany.*

8. Reid, *Prehistoric Houses in Britain.*

9. Barber, Elizabeth, *Prehistoric Textiles.*

10. Burl, *Stone Circles of Britain, Ireland and Brittany.*

11. Pollard, *Neolithic Britain.*

12. Burl, *Prehistoric Avebury.*

13. Wickham-Jones, *Monuments of Orkney.*

14. Strong, *Stanton Drew.*

15. Harding, Jan, *Henge Monuments of the British Isles.*

16. Burl, *Prehistoric Avebury.*

17. Burl, *Prehistoric Avebury.*

18. Gillings et al., *Landscape of the Megaliths.*

19. Strong, *Stanton Drew.*

20. Leary, *Silbury Hill.*

21. Wickham-Jones, *Monuments of Orkney.*

CHAPTER 7. RIVALRY AMONG THE MEGALITHIC COMPLEXES

1. Welfare, *Great Crowns of Stone.*

2. Burl, *Stone Circles of Britain, Ireland and Brittany.*

3. Harding, Dennis, *Iron Age Hillforts.*
4. Bayliss, Bronk-Ramsey, and MacCormac, "Dating Stonehenge."
5. Wainwright and Renfrew, *Henge Monuments.*
6. Parker Pearson et al., "Age of Stonehenge."
7. Parker Pearson et al. "Bluehenge."
8. Gaffney, Chris, et al. "The Stonehenge Hidden Landscapes Project."
9. Burl, *Stone Circles of Britain, Ireland and Brittany.*
10. Burl, *Prehistoric Avebury.*
11. Davies, "New Avenues of Research."
12. Bayliss, Bronk-Ramsey, and MacCormac, "Dating Stonehenge."
13. Pitts and Whittle, "Development and Date of Avebury."
14. Bayliss, Bronk-Ramsey, and MacCormac, "Dating Stonehenge."
15. "Avebury Stone Circle Contains Hidden Square, Archaeologists Find," *Guardian,* July 29, 2017.

CHAPTER 8.
LONG STONES AND LEY LINES

1. Byng, *Dartmoor's Mysterious Megaliths.*
2. Ray, *Archaeology of Herefordshire.*
3. Barber and Williams, *Ancient Stones of Wales.*
4. Ross, *Ancient Scotland.*
5. Scarre, *Megalithic Monuments of Britain and Ireland.*
6. Watkins, *Old Straight Track.*
7. Michell, *View over Atlantis.*
8. Watkins, *Old Straight Track.*
9. Devereux and Thomson, *Ley Hunter's Companion.*
10. Devereux and Thomson, *Ley Hunter's Companion.*
11. Devereux and Thomson, *Ley Hunter's Companion.*
12. Mills, *Dictionary of British Place Names.*
13. Devereux and Thomson, *Ley Hunter's Companion.*
14. Devereux and Thomson, *Ley Hunter's Companion.*
15. Giot, *Prehistory in Brittany.*

CHAPTER 9. THE MIGRATION OF
THE BEAKER PEOPLE AND OTHER CULTURES

1. Martínez and Salanova, *Bell Beaker Transition in Europe.*
2. Martínez and Salanova, *Bell Beaker Transition in Europe.*

3. Wainwright, *Durrington Walls.*

4. Parker Pearson, *Stonehenge: Exploring the Greatest Stone Age Mystery.*

5. Garwood, *Beaker Burials in Britain and North-West Europe.*

6. Scarre, *Megalithic Monuments of Britain and Ireland.*

7. Martínez and Salanova, *Bell Beaker Transition in Europe.*

8. Parker Pearson, *Bronze Age Britain.*

9. Powell, "Gold Ornament from Mold."

10. Taylor, *Bronze Age Goldwork.*

11. Burl, *From Carnac to Callanish.*

12. Darvill, *Prehistoric Britain.*

13. Bruck, *Bronze Age Landscapes.*

14. Barber, Martyn, *Bronze and the Bronze Age.*

15. Bruck, *Bronze Age Landscapes.*

16. Henderson, *Atlantic Iron Age.*

17. Cunliffe, *Ancient Celts.*

18. Koch, *Celtic Culture: A Historical Encyclopedia.*

19. Cunliffe, *Iron Age Britain.*

20. Harding, Dennis, *Iron Age Hillforts.*

21. Armit, *Iron Age Lives.*

22. Harding, Dennis, *Death and Burial.*

23. Diodorus Siculus, *Bibliotheca Historica,* bk. 2, ch. 47.

24. Darvill and Wainwright, "Stonehenge Excavations 2008."

CHAPTER 10. CELTIC INHERITANCE AND THE ROMAN INVASION

1. Southern, *Roman Army.*

2. Southern, *Roman Army.*

3. Tacitus, *Annals,* bk. 14, ch. 37.

4. Velleius, *Compendium of Roman History,* bk. 2.

5. Caesar, *Gallic Wars.*

6. Caesar, *Gallic Wars,* bk. 4, ch. 20.

7. Caesar, *Gallic Wars,* bk. 4, ch. 13.

8. Tacitus, *Annals,* bk. 12.

9. Tacitus, *Annals,* bk. 12.

10. Tacitus, *Annals,* bk. 14.

11. Smith, George, *Rediscovered Stone Circle.*

12. Tacitus, *Annals,* bk. 14, ch. 32.

13. Cassius Dio, *Roman History,* bk. 62, ch. 2.

14. Tacitus, *Annals,* bk. 14.

15. Tacitus, *Annals,* bk. 14, ch. 38.

16. Tacitus, *Annals,* bk. 14, ch. 39.

17. Tacitus, *Life of Julius Agricola,* bk. 1.

18. Tacitus, *Life of Julius Agricola,* bk. 1.

19. Tacitus, *Life of Julius Agricola,* bk. 1.

20. Tacitus, *Life of Julius Agricola,* bk. 1.

21. Clarkson, *Picts: A History.*

22. Burl, *Stone Circles of the British Isles.*

23. Weir, *Early Ireland: A Field Guide.*

24. Weir, *Early Ireland: A Field Guide.*

CHAPTER 11.
THE DRUID'S LASTING INFLUENCE

1. Novak, *Christianity and the Roman Empire.*

2. Freeman, *St. Patrick of Ireland.*

3. Adamnán, *Vita Sancti Columbae.*

4. Howlett, *Muirchú Moccu Macthéni's "Vita Sancti Patricii."*

5. Plummer, *Bethada Naem Nerenn.*

6. O'Donovan, *Annals of the Kingdom of Ireland.*

7. O'Donovan, *Annals of the Kingdom of Ireland.*

8. Ó Cuindlis, *Leabhar Breac.*

9. Best and Bergin, *Book of Leinster.*

10. Best and Bergin, *Lebor Na Huidre.*

11. Best and Bergin, *Book of Leinster.*

12. Kimpton, *Cu Chulainn's Death.*

13. Best and Bergin, *Book of Leinster.*

14. Caesar, *Gallic Wars,* bk. 6, ch. 14.

15. Caesar, *Gallic Wars,* bk. 6.

16. Jones, *Strabo: Geography,* bk. 4.

17. Caesar, *Gallic Wars,* bk. 6.

18. Welles, *Diodorus Siculus,* bk. 4.

19. Jones, *Strabo: Geography,* bk. 4.

20. Welles, *Diodorus Siculus,* bk. 4.

21. Romer, *Pomponius Mela's Description of the World,* bk. 2, ch. 3.

22. Hippolytus, *Refutation of All Heresies,* bk. 1, ch. 2.

23. Caesar, *Gallic Wars,* bk. 6.

24. Jones, *Strabo: Geography,* bk. 4.

25. Romer, *Pomponius Mela's Description of the World,* bk. 2, ch. 3.

26. Duff, *Lucan: The Civil War,* bk. 1.

27. Healey, *Pliny the Elder,* bk. 16.

28. Tacitus, *Annals,* bk. 14.

29. Caesar, *Gallic Wars,* bk. 6.

30. Healey, *Pliny the Elder,* bk. 30.

31. Hippolytus, *Refutation of All Heresies,* bk. 1, ch. 2.

32. Williams, *Two Lives of Gildas.*

33. Sherley-Price, *Bede,* bk. 1.

34. Inett, *Origines Anglicanae,* vol. 1.

35. Harding et al. "Evidence for Variable Selective Pressures."

36. Pala et al., "Mitochondrial DNA Signals."

37. Balaresque et al., "Predominantly Neolithic Origin."

38. O'Dushlaine et al., "Population Structure and Genome-Wide Patterns."

39. Caesar, *Gallic Wars,* bk. 6.

40. Crummy, *Stanway.*

41. Joyce, *Smaller Social History of Ancient Ireland.*

42. Joyce, *Smaller Social History of Ancient Ireland.*

CHAPTER 12. ASTRONOMY AND MEDICINE IN THE STONE CIRCLES

1. Caesar, *Gallic Wars,* bk. 6, ch. 17.

2. Diodorus Siculus, *Bibliotheca Historica,* bk. 2, ch. 47.

3. Caesar, *Gallic Wars,* bk. 6, ch. 14.

4. Jones, *Strabo: Geography,* bk. 5, ch. 4.

5. Romer, *Pomponius Mela's Description of the World,* bk. 2, ch. 3.

6. Diodorus Siculus, *Bibliotheca Historica,* bk. 5, ch. 31.

7. Hippolytus, *Refutation of All Heresies,* bk. 1, ch. 22.

8. Duff, *Lucan: The Civil War,* bk. 1.

9. Romer, *Pomponius Mela's Description of the World,* bk. 2, ch. 3.

10. Caesar, *Gallic Wars,* bk. 6, ch. 14.

11. Walkowitz, *Megalithic Syndrome.*

12. Shore-Henshall, *Chambered Tombs of Scotland,* vol. 2.

13. Radley and Plant, "Two Neolithic Sites at Taddington."

14. Ashbee, "Excavations at Halangy Down."

15. Barnett, *Barrows in the Peak District.*

16. Britnell and Savoury, *Gwernvale and Penywyrlod.*

17. Greenwell and Rolleston, *British Barrows.*

18. Renfrew, *Prehistory of Orkney.*

19. Chiasson et al., "Acaricidal Properties of *Artemisia absinthium.*"

20. Darvill, *Prehistoric Britain.*

21. Soni et al., "Pharmacological Properties of *Datura stramonium.*"

22. Bown, *Royal Horticultural Society New Encyclopedia of Herbs and Their Uses.*

23. Livarda, Madgwick, and Riera Mora, *Bioarchaeology of Ritual and Religion.*

24. Sequin, *Chemistry of Plants.*

25. Caesar, *Gallic Wars,* bk. 6, ch. 16.

26. Healey, *Pliny the Elder: Natural History,* bk. 16, ch. 95.

27. Kowalchik and Hylton, *William H. Rodale's Illustrated Encyclopedia of Herbs.*

28. Caesar, *Gallic Wars,* bk. 6, ch. 14.

29. Romer, *Pomponius Mela's Description of the World,* bk. 2, ch. 3.

30. Magli, *Archaeoastronomy.*

31. Caesar, *Gallic Wars,* bk. 6, ch. 14.

32. Romer, *Pomponius Mela's Description of the World,* bk. 2, ch. 3.

33. Hippolytus, *Refutation of All Heresies,* bk. 1, ch. 2.

CHAPTER 13. SECRET OF THE STONES AND THE RED-HAIRED DRUIDS

1. Hull, *Text Book of Irish Literature.*

2. *Encyclopædia Britannica.*

3. Jones, *Strabo: Geography,* bk. 4, ch. 4.

4. Diodorus Siculus, *Bibliotheca Historica,* bk. 5, chapter 31.

5. Caesar, *Gallic Wars,* bk. 6, ch. 14.

6. Healey, *Pliny the Elder: Natural History,* bk. 16, ch. 95.

7. Lean, "Druids Offer Up Cancer Cure."

8. Weir, *Early Ireland: A Field Guide.*

9. Best and Bergin, *Book of Leinster.*

10. Meyer, *Sanas Cormaic: Cormac's Glossary.*

11. Connolly, *Vita Prima Sanctae Brigitae.*

12. Ó hÓgáin, *Myth, Legend and Romance.*

13. Gildas, *De excidio Britanniae.* Vol. 7.

14. Morgan and Morgan, *Prehistoric Cheshire*.

15. Rowlands, *Mona Antiqua Restaurata*.

16. Dunlop, *Transactions of the Lancashire and Cheshire Antiquarian Society*.

17. Sleigh, *History of the Ancient Parish of Leek*.

18. Biddulph & District Genealogy & Historical Society, "Meeting Report: Greenway Moor."

Bibliography

Adamnán. *Vita Sancti Columbae.* New York: AMS Press, 1979.

Armit, Ian. *The Archaeology of Skye and the Western Isles.* Edinburgh: Edinburgh University Press, 1996.

———. *Iron Age Lives: The Archaeology of Britain and Ireland 800 BC–AD 400.* Abingdon, UK: Routledge, 2016.

Armit, Ian, Eileen Murphy, Eimear Nelis, and Derek Simpson. *Neolithic Settlement in Ireland and Western Britain.* Oxford: Oxbow Books, 2015.

Ashbee, Paul. "Excavations at Halangy Down, St Mary's, Scilly." *Cornish Archaeology* 9 (1970).

Ashmore, Patrick. *Calanais: The Standing Stones.* Edinburgh: Historic Scotland, 2002.

Aubrey, John, and John Fowles, eds. *Monumenta Britannica.* London: Little Brown, 1982.

"Avebury Stone Circle Contains Hidden Square, Archaeologists Find." *The Guardian,* July 29, 2017.

Balaresque, Patricia, Georgina R. Bowden, Susan M. Adams, Ho-Yee Leung, Turi E. King, Zoë H. Rosser, Jane Goodwin, et al. "A Predominantly Neolithic Origin for European Paternal Lineages." *PLOS Biology* 8.1 (2010).

Barber, Chris, and John Godfrey Williams. *The Ancient Stones of Wales.* Llanfoist, UK: Blorenge Books, 1989.

Barber, Elizabeth Wayland. *Prehistoric Textiles.* Princeton, N.J.: Princeton University Press, 1993.

Barber, Martyn. *Bronze and the Bronze Age.* Stroud, UK: The History Press, 2002.

Barnett, J. *Barrows in the Peak District*. Sheffield, UK: J. R. Collis Publications, 1996.

Barrowclough, David. *Prehistoric Cumbria*. Stroud, UK: The History Press, 2010.

Bayliss, A., C. Bronk-Ramsey, and F. G. MacCormac. "Dating Stonehenge." *Proceedings of the British Academy* 92 (2016).

Best, Richard Irvine, and Osborn Bergin, eds. *The Book of Leinster: Formerly Lebar na Nuachongbala*. Dublin: Dublin Institute for Advanced Studies, 1954.

———. *Lebor Na Huidre: Book of the Dun Cow*. Dublin: Dublin Institute for Advanced Studies, 1970.

Biddulph & District Genealogy & Historical Society. "Meeting Report: Greenway Moor (Biddulph Moor) and the Saracens–21st November 2005." Biddulph, UK: Biddulph Public Library Publications, 2005.

Bown, Deni. *The Royal Horticultural Society New Encyclopedia of Herbs and Their Uses*. London: Dorling Kindersley, 1995.

Bradley, Raymond. *Paleoclimatology: Reconstructing Climates of the Quaternary*. Cambridge, Mass.: Academic Press, 2014.

Bradley, Richard. *The Prehistory of Britain and Ireland*. Cambridge: Cambridge University Press, 2007.

Britnell, W. J., and H. N. Savoury. *Gwernvale and Penywyrlod*. Carmarthen, UK: Cambrian Archaeological Association, 1984.

Brophy, Kenneth, Gavin MacGregor, and Ian Ralston, eds. *The Neolithic of Mainland Scotland*. Edinburgh: Edinburgh University Press, 2016.

Bruck, Joanna. *Bronze Age Landscapes: Tradition and Transformation*. Oxford: Oxbow Books, 2002.

Burl, Aubrey. *From Carnac to Callanish: The Prehistoric Stone Rows of Britain, Ireland, and Brittany*. New Haven, Conn.: Yale University Press, 1993.

———. *Prehistoric Avebury*. New Haven, Conn.: Yale University Press, 2002.

———. *The Stone Circles of Britain, Ireland and Brittany*. New Haven, Conn.: Yale University Press, 2000.

———. *The Stone Circles of the British Isles*. New Haven, Conn.: Yale University Press, 1979.

Burl, Aubrey, and Neil Mortimer, eds. *Stukeley's Stonehenge: An Unpublished Manuscript, 1721–1724*. New Haven, Conn.: Yale University Press, 2005.

Byng, Brian. *Dartmoor's Mysterious Megaliths*. Los Angeles: Barron Jay, 1979.

Caesar, Julius. *The Gallic Wars*. St. Petersburg, Fla.: Red and Black Publishers, 2008.

Cassius Dio. *Roman History*. Cambridge, Mass.: Loeb, 1989.

Charvát, Petr. *The Birth of the State: Ancient Egypt, Mesopotamia, India, and China*. Chicago: University of Chicago Press, 2014.

Chiasson, Hélène, André Bélanger, Noubar Bostanian, Charles Vincent, and André Poliquin. "Acaricidal Properties of *Artemisia absinthium* and *Tanacetum vulgare* (Asteraceae) Essential Oils Obtained by Three Methods of Extraction." *Journal of Economic Entomology* 94 (2001).

Clare, Tom. *Prehistoric Monuments of the Lake District*. Stroud, UK: The History Press, 2007.

Clarke, D. V. *Skara Brae: Northern Europe's Best Preserved Neolithic Village*. Edinburgh: Historic Scotland, 2003.

Clarkson, Tim. *The Picts: A History*. Edinburgh: Birlinn, 2013.

Cleal, Rosamund, and Ann MacSween, eds. *Grooved Ware in Great Britain and Ireland*. Oxford: Oxbow Books, 1999.

Collins, Andrew. *Göbekli Tepe: Genesis of the Gods*. Rochester, Vt.: Bear & Company, 2014.

Connolly, S. *Vita Prima Sanctae Brigitae: A Critical Edition*. Dublin: University College Dublin, 1970.

Conroy, Joseph. *Breton-English, English-Breton Dictionary and Phrasebook*. New York: Hippocrene Books, 1997.

Cox, Allan, and Robert Brian Hart. *Plate Tectonics: How It Works*. Hoboken, N.J.: Wiley-Blackwell, 1986.

Crawford, Harriet. *Sumer and the Sumerians*. Cambridge: Cambridge University Press, 2004.

Crummy, Philip. *Stanway: An Elite Burial Site at Camulodunum*. Cambridge: Cambridge University Press, 2007.

Cunliffe, Barry. *The Ancient Celts*. Oxford: Oxford University Press, 1997.

———. *The Extraordinary Voyage of Pytheas the Greek*. London: Penguin Books, 2003.

———. *Iron Age Britain*. London: Batsford, 2014.

Darvill, Timothy. *Prehistoric Britain*. Abingdon, UK: Routledge, 2010.

Darvill, Timothy, and Geoff Wainwright. "Beyond Stonehenge: Carn Menyn Quarry and the Origin and Date of Bluestone Extraction in the Preseli Hills of South-West Wales." *Antiquity* 88, no. 342 (2014).

———. "Stonehenge Excavations 2008." *Antiquaries Journal* 89 (2015).

Davies, Simon R. "New Avenues of Research." *Internet Archaeology* 27 (2009).

de Camp, Lyon Sprague. *Lost Continents: Atlantis Theme in History, Science and Literature.* Mineola, N.Y.: Dover Publications, 1970.

Devereux, Paul, and Ian Thomson. *The Ley Hunter's Companion.* London: Thames & Hudson, 1979.

Diodorus Siculus. *Bibliotheca Historica.* Charleston, S.C.: Nabu Press, 2011.

Duff, J. D., trans. *Lucan: The Civil War.* Cambridge, Mass.: Loeb, 1989.

Dunlop, M. *Transactions of the Lancashire and Cheshire Antiquarian Society.* Vol. 53. Manchester, UK: Lancashire and Cheshire Antiquarian Society, 1939.

Dyson, Stephen, and Robert Rowland. *Archaeology and History in Sardinia from the Stone Age to the Middle Ages.* Philadelphia: University of Pennsylvania Press, 2007.

Ehlers, Jürgen, Philip Hughes, and Philip Gibbard. *The Ice Age.* Hoboken, N.J.: Wiley-Blackwell, 2015.

Encyclopædia Britannica. Hoiberg, Dale, editor-in-chief. Chicago: Encyclopædia Britannica, Inc. 2010.

Foster, Sally. *Maeshowe and the Heart of Neolithic Orkney.* Edinburgh: Historic Scotland, 2006.

Freeman, Philip. *St. Patrick of Ireland: A Biography.* London: Simon & Schuster, 2004.

Gaffney, Chris, Vince Gaffney, Wolfgang Neubauer, and Michael Doneus. "The Stonehenge Hidden Landscapes Project." *Archaeological Prospection* 19, no. 2 (2012).

Gaffney, Vincent, Simon Fitch, and David Smith. *Europe's Lost World: The Rediscovery of Doggerland.* York, UK: Council for British Archaeology Publishers, 2009.

Garwood, Paul. *Beaker Burials in Britain and North-West Europe 2600–1800 BC.* Abingdon, UK: Routledge, 2012.

Geoffrey of Monmouth. *History of the Kings of Britain.* Translated by Lewis Thorpe. London: Penguin, 1977.

Gibson, Paul. *Prehistoric Pottery in Britain & Ireland.* Stroud, UK: The History Press, 2002.

Gildas. *De excidio Britanniae: History from the Sources.* Vol. 7. Translated by Michael Winterbottom. Chichester, UK: Phillimore, 1978.

Gillings, Mark, Joshua Pollard, Rick Peterson, and David Wheatley. *Landscape of the Megaliths: Excavation and Fieldwork on the Avebury Monuments, 1997–2003.* Oxford: Oxbow Books, 2010.

Giot, Pierre-Roland. *Prehistory in Brittany: Menhirs and Dolmens.* Chateaulin, France: Jos le Doare, 1995.

Greenwell, William, and George Rolleston. *British Barrows: A Record of the Examination of Sepulchral Mounds in Various Parts of England.* Charleston, S.C.: Nabu Press, 2010.

Guthrie, R. Dale. *The Nature of Paleolithic Art.* Chicago: University of Chicago Press, 2006.

Harding, Dennis. *Death and Burial in Iron Age Britain.* Oxford: Oxford University Press, 2015.

———. *Iron Age Hillforts in Britain and Beyond.* Oxford: Oxford University Press, 2012.

Harding, Jan. *Henge Monuments of the British Isles.* Stroud, UK: The History Press, 2003.

Harding, Rosalind M., Eugene Healy, Amanda J. Ray, Nichola S. Ellis, Niamh Flanagan, Carol Todd, Craig Dixon, et al. "Evidence for Variable Selective Pressures at MC1R." *American Journal of Human Genetics* 66, no. 4 (2000).

Hawkins, Gerald. *Stonehenge Decoded.* London: Doubleday, 1965.

Healey, John, trans. *Pliny the Elder: Natural History.* London: Penguin, 2004.

Henderson, Jon. *The Atlantic Iron Age: Settlement and Identity in the First Millennium BC.* Abingdon, UK: Routledge, 2007.

Hippolytus. *The Refutation of All Heresies.* Pickerington, Ohio: Beloved Publishing, 2016.

Hodder, Ian. *The Leopard's Tale: Revealing the Mysteries of Çatalhöyük.* London: Thames & Hudson, 2011.

Holland, Richard. *Haunted Wales: A Guide to Welsh Ghostlore.* Stroud, UK: The History Press, 2011.

Howlett, David. *Muirchú Moccu Mactheni's "Vita Sancti Patricii": Life of Saint Patrick.* Dublin: Four Courts Press, 2006.

Hull, Eleanor. *A Text Book of Irish Literature.* Charleston, S.C.: Nabu Press, 2010.

Hunt, Alice, ed. *The Oxford Handbook of Archaeological Ceramic Analysis.* Oxford: Oxford University Press, 2016.

Inett, John. *Origines Anglicanae, or a History of the English Church from the Conversion of the English Saxons till the Death of King John.* Vol. 1. Charleston, S.C.: Nabu Press, 2010.

James, Peter, and Nick Thorpe. *Ancient Inventions.* New York: Ballantine Books, 1995.

Jones, Horace L., trans. *Strabo: Geography.* Book 4. Cambridge, Mass.: Loeb, 1989.

Joyce, Patrick W. *A Smaller Social History of Ancient Ireland.* Wokingham, UK: Dodo Press, 2008.

Kimpton, Bettina. *Cu Chulainn's Death: A Critical Edition of Brislech Mor Maige Muirthemne with Introduction, Translation, Textual Notes and Vocabulary.* Maynooth, Ireland: National University of Ireland, Faculty of Philosophy, 2009.

Koch, John, ed. *Celtic Culture: A Historical Encyclopedia.* Santa Barbara, Calif.: ABC-CLIO, 2006.

Kowalchik, Claire, and William H. Hylton. *William H. Rodale's Illustrated Encyclopedia of Herbs.* Emmaus, Pa.: Rodale Press, 1998.

Kramer, Samuel Noah. *Sumerian Mythology.* Philadelphia: University of Pennsylvania Press, 1998.

Landau, Elaine. *The Sumerians: Cradle of Civilization.* Minneapolis, Minn.: Millbrook Press, 1997.

Langmaid, Nancy. *Prehistoric Pottery.* London: Shire Books, 1978.

Lean, Geoffrey. "Druids Offer Up Cancer Cure as Mistletoe Bestows Kiss of Life." *Independent* (London), December 24, 1995.

Leary, Jim. *Silbury Hill: The Largest Prehistoric Mound in Europe.* London: English Heritage, 2014.

Le Roux, Charles-Tanguy, and Yannick Lecerf. *Le Grand Cairn de Barnenez.* Paris: Monum, 2003.

Livarda, Alexandra, Richard Madgwick, and Santiago Riera Mora, eds. *The Bioarchaeology of Ritual and Religion.* Oxford: Oxbow Books, 2017.

Lynch, Frances. *Prehistoric Anglesey: The Archaeology of the Island to the Roman Conquest.* Llangefni, UK: Anglesey Antiquarian Society, 1991.

Magli, Giulio. *Archaeoastronomy: Introduction to the Science of Stars and Stones.* New York: Springer, 2015.

Malone, Caroline. *Neolithic Britain and Ireland.* Stroud, UK: The History Press, 2001.

Marshall, D. N. "Carved Stone Balls." *Proceedings of the Society of Antiquaries of Scotland,* 108, 1979.

Martínez, Maria, and Laure Salanova, eds. *The Bell Beaker Transition in Europe.* Oxford: Oxbow Books, 2015.

McGrail, Sean. *Ancient Boats and Ships*. London: Shire Books, 2006.

Meyer, Kuno, ed. *Sanas Cormaic: Cormac's Glossary*. Burnham-on-Sea, UK: Llanerch Press, 1994.

Michell, John. *The View over Atlantis*. New York: Ballantine Books, 1977.

Mills, Anthony David. *A Dictionary of British Place Names*. Oxford: Oxford University Press, 2011.

Moore, Jerry. *A Prehistory of South America*. Boulder: University Press of Colorado, 2014.

Morgan, Victoria, and Paul Morgan. *Prehistoric Cheshire*. London: Landmark Publishing, 2004.

Mount, Charles. "Aspects of Ritual Deposition in the Late Neolithic and Beaker Periods at Newgrange, Co. Meath." Proceedings of the Prehistoric Society 60 (1994).

Novak, Ralph, M. *Christianity and the Roman Empire: Background Texts*. Manchester, UK: Trinity Press, 2001.

Ó Cuindlis, Murchadh. *Leabhar Breac: Celtic Language & Literature Series*. New York: AMS Press, 1978.

O'Donovan, John, ed. *Annals of the Kingdom of Ireland by the Four Masters*. Whitefish, Mont.: Kessinger, 2004.

O'Dushlaine, Colm T., Derek Morris, Valentina Moskvina, George Kirov, International Schizophrenia Consortium, Michael Gill, Aiden Corvin, James F. Wilson, and Gianpiero L. Cavalleri. "Population Structure and Genome-Wide Patterns of Variation in Ireland and Britain," *European Journal of Human Genetics* 8, no. 11 (2010).

Ó hÓgáin, Dáithí. *Myth, Legend and Romance: An Encyclopaedia of the Irish Folk Tradition*. Upper Saddle River, N.J.: Prentice Hall, 1991.

Oliver, Andrew, ed. The *Journal of Samuel Curwen, Loyalist*. Cambridge, Mass.: Harvard University Press, 1972.

Ó Nuallain, Sean. *Stone Circles in Ireland*. Dublin: Town House, 1995.

Orcadian, The. Kirkwall, UK: Orkney Media, July 20, 1861.

Pala, Maria, Anna Olivieri, Alessandro Achilli, Matteo Accetturo, Ene Metspalu, Maere Reidla, Erika Tamm, et al. "Mitochondrial DNA Signals of Late Glacial Recolonization of Europe from Near Eastern Refugia." *American Journal of Human Genetics* 90, no. 5 (2012).

Parker Pearson, Mike. *Bronze Age Britain*. London: Batsford, 2005.

———. *Stonehenge: Exploring the Greatest Stone Age Mystery*. London: Simon & Schuster, 2012.

Parker Pearson, Mike, Ros Cleal, Josh Pollard, Colin Richards, Julian Thomas, Chris Tilley, Kate Welham, et al. "The Age of Stonehenge." *Antiquity* 81, no. 313 (2007).

Parker Pearson, Mike, Josh Pollard, Julian Thomas, and Kate Welham. "Bluehenge." *British Archaeology,* no. 110 (2010).

Peregrine, Peter. *World Prehistory: Two Million Years of Human Life.* Upper Saddle River, N.J.: Prentice Hall, 2002.

Peterson, Rick. *Neolithic Pottery from Wales: Traditions of Construction and Use.* Oxford: BAR Publishing, 2003.

Pettitt, Paul. *The Palaeolithic Origins of Human Burial.* Abingdon, UK: Routledge, 2010.

Phillips, Graham. *Act of God.* London: Pan, 1998.

Pitts, M., and A. Whittle. "The Development and Date of Avebury." *Proceedings of the Prehistoric Society* 58 (1992).

Plato. *Timaeus and Critias.* Translated by R. Waterfield. Oxford: Oxford University Press, 2009.

Plummer, Charles. *Bethada Naem Nerenn: Lives of Irish Saints.* Ithaca, N.Y.: Cornell University Press, 2009.

Pollard. Joshua. *Neolithic Britain.* London: Shire Books, 2002.

Powell, T. G. E. "The Gold Ornament from Mold, Flintshire, North Wales." *Proceedings of the Prehistoric Society* 19 (1953).

Prior, Francis. *BC: Life in Britain and Ireland before the Romans.* London: Harper Perennial, 2011.

Radley, J., and M. Plant. "Two Neolithic Sites at Taddington." *Derbyshire Archaeological Journal* 87 (1967).

Ramaswamy, Sumathi. *The Lost Land of Lemuria: Fabulous Geographies, Catastrophic Histories.* Berkeley: University of California Press, 2004.

Ray, Keith. *The Archaeology of Herefordshire: An Exploration.* Little Logaston, UK: Logaston Press, 2015.

Reid, M. L. *Prehistoric Houses in Britain.* London: Shire Books, 1993.

Renfrew, Colin, ed. *The Prehistory of Orkney: 4000 BC–1000 AD.* Edinburgh: Edinburgh University Press, 1987.

Richards, Colin. *Building the Great Stone Circles of the North.* Barnsley, UK: Windgather Press, 2013.

Ritchie, Anna. *Prehistoric Orkney.* London: Batsford, 1995.

Ritchie, Graham. *The Stones of Stenness, Orkney.* Edinburgh: NMS Enterprises, 1997.

Romer, Frank E., trans. *Pomponius Mela's Description of the World*. Ann Arbor: University of Michigan Press, 1998.

Ross, Stewart. *Ancient Scotland*. New York: Barnes & Noble, 1991.

Rowlands, Henry. *Mona Antiqua Restaurata*. Whitefish, Mont.: Kessinger Publishing, 2010.

Scarre, Chris. *The Megalithic Monuments of Britain and Ireland*. London: Thames & Hudson, 2007.

Sequin, Margareta. *The Chemistry of Plants: Perfumes, Pigments and Poisons*. London: Royal Society of Chemistry, 2015.

Sharples, Niall. *Excavations at Pierowall Quarry, Westray, Orkney*. Cardiff: Cardiff University, 1985.

Sherley-Price, Leo, trans. *Bede: A History of the English Church and People*. London: Penguin, 1955.

Shore-Henshall, Audrey. *The Chambered Tombs of Scotland*. Vol. 2. Edinburgh: Edinburgh University Press, 1972.

Sleigh, John. *A History of the Ancient Parish of Leek*. London: British Library Historical Print Editions, 2011.

Smith, George. *A Rediscovered Stone Circle, Bryn Gwyn, Anglesey*. Bangor, UK: Gwynedd Archaeological Trust, 2011.

Smith, Martin, and Megan Brickley. *People of the Long Barrows: Life, Death and Burial in the Earlier Neolithic*. Stroud, UK: The History Press, 2009.

Smith, Michael, and Marilyn Masson, eds. *The Ancient Civilizations of Mesoamerica*. Hoboken, N.J.: Wiley-Blackwell, 2000.

Soni, Priyanka, Anees Ahmad Siddique, Jaya Dwivedi, and Vishal Soni. "Pharmacological Properties of *Datura stramonium* L. as a Potential Medicinal Tree: An Overview." *Asian Pacific Journal of Tropical Biomedicine* 2 (2012).

Southern, Patricia. *The Roman Army: A History 753 BC–AD 476*. Stroud, UK: Amberley Publishing, 2014.

"Stonehenge, Older than Believed." *BBC News*, October 9, 2008.

"Stonehenge 'Bluestone' Quarries Confirmed 140 Miles Away in Wales." *UCL News*, December 7, 2015.

"Stonehenge May Have Been First Erected in Wales, Evidence Suggests." *The Guardian*, December 7, 2015.

Stout, Geraldine, and Matthew Stout. *Newgrange*. Cork, Ireland: Cork University Press, 2008.

Strong, Gordon. *Stanton Drew and Its Ancient Stone Circles*. London: Bloomsbury, 2009.

Tacitus. *Annals*. Translated by Cynthia Damon. London: Penguin, 2012.

———. *The Life of Julius Agricola*. Cambridge: Cambridge University Press, 2014.

Taylor, Joan J. *Bronze Age Goldwork of the British Isles*. Cambridge: Cambridge University Press, 1981.

Thom, Alexander. *Megalithic Remains in Britain and Brittany*. Oxford: Oxford University Press, 1978.

Thomas, Julian. *Understanding the Neolithic*. Abingdon, UK: Routledge, 2002.

Tilley, Christopher. *An Ethnography of the Neolithic: Early Prehistoric Societies in Southern Scandinavia*. Cambridge: Cambridge University Press, 2008.

Trump, David. *Malta: Prehistory and Temples*. Santa Venera, Malta: Midsea Books, 2002.

Tylecote, Ronald F. *A History of Metallurgy*. Leeds, UK: Maney Publishing, 2013.

Underwood, Peter. *Where the Ghosts Walk: The Gazetteer of Haunted Britain*. London: Souvenir Press, 2013.

Velleius. *Compendium of Roman History*. Book 2. Translated by Fredrick W. Shipley. Cambridge, Mass.: Loeb, 1989.

Wainwright, Geoffrey J. *Durrington Walls: Excavations 1966–1968*. London: The Society of Antiquaries, 1971.

Wainwright, Geoffrey, and Colin Renfrew. *The Henge Monuments: Ceremony and Society in Prehistoric Britain*. London: Thames & Hudson, 1990.

Walkowitz, Jürgen, E. *The Megalithic Syndrome: European Cult Sites of the Stone Age*. Langenweissbach, Germany: Beier & Beran, 2003.

Watkins, Alfred. *The Old Straight Track*. London: Sphere, 1974.

Weir, Anthony. *Early Ireland: A Field Guide*. Belfast, UK: Blackstaff Press, 1980.

Welfare, Adam. *Great Crowns of Stone: The Recumbent Stone Circles of Scotland*. Edinburgh: Royal Commission on the Ancient and Historical Monuments of Scotland, 2011.

Welles, C. Bradford, trans. *Diodorus Siculus: Library of History*. Book 4. Cambridge, Mass.: Loeb, 1989.

Wickham-Jones, Caroline. *Monuments of Orkney*. Edinburgh: Historic Scotland, 2015.

———. *Orkney: A Historical Guide*. Edinburgh: Birlinn, 2015.

Williams, Hugh, trans. *Two Lives of Gildas*. Burnham-on-Sea, UK: Llanerch Press, 1990.

Index

Numbers in *italics* preceded by *pl.* indicate color insert plate numbers.

BOOKS OF RELATED INTEREST

Lost Knowledge of the Ancients
A Graham Hancock Reader
Edited by Glenn Kreisberg

Secrets of Ancient America
Archaeoastronomy and the Legacy of the Phoenicians,
Celts, and Other Forgotten Explorers
by Carl Lehrburger

The Mystery of Skara Brae
Neolithic Scotland and the Origins of Ancient Egypt
by Laird Scranton

Point of Origin
Göbekli Tepe and the Spiritual Matrix for the World's Cosmologies
by Laird Scranton

Göbekli Tepe: Genesis of the Gods
The Temple of the Watchers and the Discovery of Eden
by Andrew Collins
Introduction by Graham Hancock

Black Genesis
The Prehistoric Origins of Ancient Egypt
by Robert Bauval and Thomas Brophy, Ph.D.

Forgotten Civilization
The Role of Solar Outbursts in Our Past and Future
by Robert M. Schoch, Ph.D.

Sacred Geometry of the Earth
The Ancient Matrix of Monuments and Mountains
by Mark Vidler and Catherine Young

INNER TRADITIONS • BEAR & COMPANY
P.O. Box 388 • Rochester, VT 05767
1-800-246-8648 • www.InnerTraditions.com

Or contact your local bookseller